Lessons for Life

Lessons for Life

The Schooling of Girls and Women, 1850–1950

Edited by Felicity Hunt

Basil Blackwell

Copyright © Basil Blackwell Ltd 1987

First published 1987

Basil Blackwell Ltd
108 Cowley Road, Oxford, OX4 1JF, UK

Basil Blackwell Inc.
432 Park Avenue South, Suite 1503
New York, NY 10016, USA

British Library Cataloguing in Publication Data

Lessons for life: the schooling of girls and
  women, 1850–1950.
  1. Education of women—Great Britain
  —History
  I. Hunt, Felicity
  376'.941   LC2042
  ISBN 0–631–14974–0
  ISBN 0–631–14975–9 Pbk

Library of Congress Cataloging in Publication Data

Lessons for life.
  Bibliography: p.
  Includes index.
  1. Women—Education—Great Britain—History—19th
century. 2. Women—Education—Great Britain—History—
20th century. 3. Educational equalization—Great Britain
—History—19th century. 4. Educational equalization—
Great Britain—History—20th century. I. Hunt,
Felicity, 1951–
LC2042.L47   1987   376'.941   87–10307
ISBN 0–631–14974–0
ISBN 0–631–14975–9 (pbk.)

Typeset in 10 on 11½ Plantin
by Cambrian Typesetters, Frimley, Surrey
Printed in Great Britain by Billing & Sons Ltd, Worcester

Contents

Editor's Acknowledgements   vii

Illustrations   viii

List of Contributors   ix

Introduction
Felicity Hunt   xi

Part I Ideologies in Education   1

1   Divided Aims: the Educational Implications of
    Opposing Ideologies in Girls' Secondary Schooling,
    1850–1940   *Felicity Hunt*   3

2   Miss Buss and Miss Beale: Gender and Authority in the
    History of Education   *Carol Dyhouse*   22

3   The Ideology of Femininity and Reading for Girls,
    1850–1914   *Deborah Gorham*   39

4   Learning Through Leisure: Feminine Ideology in
    Girls' Magazines 1920–50   *Penny Tinkler*   60

Part II Inequalities in Education   81

5   Learning Her Womanly Work: the Elementary
    School Curriculum, 1870–1914   *Annmarie Turnbull*   83

6   Inequalities in the Teaching Profession: the Effect
    on Teachers and Pupils, 1910–39   *Alison Oram*   101

7   Better a Teacher Than a Hairdresser? 'A Mad Passion for Equality' or, Keeping Molly and Betty down *Deborah Thom*   124

Part III   Experiences in Education   147

8   Cultural Reproduction in the Education of Girls: a Study of Girls' Secondary Schooling in Two Lancashire Towns, 1900–50   *Penny Summerfield*   149

9   Pioneer Women Students at Cambridge, 1869–81 *Perry Williams*   171

Notes   192

Index   218

Editor's Acknowledgements

My thanks and appreciation are due to Sue Corbett and Virginia Murphy at Basil Blackwell for support and advice, to Jenny Rudge and to Angela John for help, encouragement and valuable critical comments on the Introduction. This book would not have been possible without the contributors and them I thank not only for their chapters but their friendly encouragement and co-operation along the way. Finally, more than thanks to Charles Hunt whose patient and unfailing confidence in all my enterprises is both essential support and inspiration, while his technical assistance in providing some of the illustrations is practical expression of the same support.

Illustrations

A science laboratory and cookery class at the Bedford Modern School for Girls (now the Dame Alice Harpur School) in the 1930s (p. 14). Reproduced by kind permission of the Dame Alice Harpur School, Bedford.

Frances Mary Buss, aged 33 (p. 30) and Dorothea Beale as a young woman (p. 31), from *How Different from Us* by Josephine Kamm, Bodley Head, 1958. Reproduced by permission.

'The Student', illustration from *The Quiver*, May–Oct. 1911 (p. 42). Reproduced by kind permission of Cassell Publishers Ltd.

The cover of *The Girls' Favourite* magazine, 20 June 1925 (p. 63). Reproduced by permission of Syndication International/IPC.

Teaching the teachers – a cookery demonstration (p. 93). 'Practical Cookery' from *Our Mothers*, edited by Alan Bott and Irene Clephane, 1932. Reproduced by kind permission of Victor Gollancz Ltd.

A male teacher with a mixed class at Bentworth Road School, Hammersmith, 1930 (p. 107). Reproduced by kind permission of the Greater London Photograph Library.

A page of the Ryburn Group Intelligence Tests, H. V. Clark, 1926, Glasgow (p. 127).

The arts' sixth form at the Park School, Preston, in 1920 (p. 159) (courtesy of Oral History of Girlhood Project, University of Lancaster).

Punch satirizes the new generation of female undergraduates: 'St Valentine's Day at Girton' from *Punch*, 26 February 1876 (p. 186) (Mansell Collection).

List of Contributors

Carol Dyhouse teaches history and education at the University of Sussex. Her research interests are in the social history of women in nineteenth- and twentieth-century England and in women's education. Her published work includes *Girls Growing Up in Late Victorian and Edwardian England* (Routledge & Kegan Paul, 1981) and various articles on women's history and the history of educational provision for girls.

Deborah Gorham is an Associate Professor in the Department of History, Carleton University, Ottowa, Ontario. She is the author of *The Victorian Girl and the Feminine Ideal* (Croom Helm and Indiana University Press, 1982). She is now writing a book about Vera Brittain's life and work, to 1939, to be published by Basil Blackwell.

Felicity Hunt is a Research Associate in the Department of Education, University of Cambridge. She is currently working on the development of a policy for girls' schooling between 1902 and 1944. Her published work includes 'Opportunities lost and gained: mechanization and women's work in the London bookbinding and printing trades' in Angela V. John (ed.), *Unequal Opportunities: Women's Employment in England 1800–1918* (Basil Blackwell, 1986) and articles on women's labour and education history.

Alison Oram job-shares a Tutor–Organizer post for the Workers Educational Association London District, and also teaches women's studies for London University's Extra-Mural Department. She has been involved in the London Feminist History Group for several years and is currently researching the history of the National Union of Women Teachers.

Penny Summerfield is Lecturer in the Social History of Education at Lancaster University. She is the author of *Women Workers in the Second World War* (Croom Helm, 1984) and various articles on women, war and popular culture. She is currently directing a project on the oral history of childhood in Lancashire.

Deborah Thom is currently working on an ESRC research project on 'Maladjustment in context: child guidance clinics and school psychological services, 1920–1970' at the Child Care and Development Group, Social and Political Sciences, at the University of Cambridge and teaches history at Robinson College, Cambridge. Her recent published work includes articles on the 1944 Education Act, women's trade unionism and intelligence testing.

Penny Tinkler studied for a history degree at Sussex University and this led to an interest in the social history of girlhood. She is currently living in Lancaster and researching girls' magazines 1920–50 for a PhD thesis. She is an active member of the Women's Research Centre at Lancaster University.

Annmarie Turnbull trained initially as a teacher of English and Drama; later she studied for an MSc and PhD in sociology. She currently works as a research officer in the social services department of a London borough and teaches with the Open University.

Perry Williams is a member of the Wellcome Unit for the History of Medicine at the University of Cambridge. He has mainly worked on the Victorian period, his interests including the women's movement and men's responses to it, and various aspects of the history of science and medicine. Currently he is looking at the changing role of nurses and the admission of women to medical training and practice.

Introduction

Felicity Hunt

One of the most exciting developments in history in the last 15 years has been the growing influence of feminist analysis. The exploration of women's experience, especially in our recent industrial past, goes back much earlier than this. Ivy Pinchbeck's *Women Workers and the Industrial Revolution*, first published in 1930, showed the discerning reader that knowledge of the lives and experiences of working women necessarily altered our perspective on the industrial revolution. Yet it has taken another four decades for this message to come home and even now there is by no means universal acceptance that 'women's history',[1] or what in this context is more accurately called feminist history, has an important part to play in our understanding of the past.

It would be misleading to suggest that all feminist scholars agree in every detail about the means, methods and ends of feminist analysis.[2] What is becoming more and more inescapable is the realization that the incorporation of women's experiences into the historical record changes the nature of the record. Sheila Rowbotham's classic text showed us where to look.[3] The Marxist tradition showed us a necessary, though not sufficient, theoretical explanation in patriarchy.[4] American scholarship in particular demonstrated that a key to understanding was to be found in the study of the social relations of the sexes.[5] Yet ultimately, as Leonore Davidoff has graphically described, the concept which has been lacking is that of gender.[6]

Gender is a complex category, including the feminine and the masculine. Gender can describe the subjects of social history, it refers to women and to men. But it is also much more than this, for gender is also a category of social analysis, just as class (to which we are so accustomed in British social history) and race (so familiar a concept to American social historians) are categories of social analysis. What is different about gender is that neither its reality nor its utility are universally accepted.

Nevertheless its importance cannot be underestimated, as is clear from the earlier companion volumes in this series, *Unequal Opportunities* edited by Angela V. John and *Labour and Love* edited by Jane Lewis. Whether in the area of women's employment or the home and family life, women's experience cannot be properly understood without a full recognition of the masculine and the feminine in society and social relations.[7] But waged work and full domestic responsibilities take their place in women's lives after the most formative childhood years are over or, should class and economic status allow it, not until young adulthood. Before this stage is reached come the years of socialization, of schooling into particular roles; the period of inculcation of societal values and cultural *mores* which help to shape the rest of women's lives.

In the past the approach to the gender dimension in the history of education has been, at best, conservative. Either it has been assumed that all schooling was much the same for boys and girls (and the word 'boys' is frequently used synonymously with 'pupils') or, where distinctions clearly have to be made, girls' education has been considered in comparison to that of boys, where boys' education is the norm, the bottom line.[8]

Where the education of women is concerned, the historiography has tended to fall into two categories, general histories of education and separate accounts of girls' schooling, especially middle-class schooling, for it was in the middle classes that girls and women were placed in separate institutions.[9] Generally speaking these accounts have been relatively straightforward, premised in a progressive, whiggish framework.[10] Yet in spite of the dual problem feminist historians faced of finding that female experience in education was either subsumed in the male or treated entirely separately, in some respects the possession of separate histories has been advantageous. Using these works as a foundation, feminist historians over the last decade or so have brought an entirely new perspective to education history.

In their studies of girls' education they have introduced the gender dimension, exploring the relationship between class and gender;[11] recognizing the pervasive influence of femininity and high ideals of womanliness;[12] pointing up the neglect of distinctive class differences in the gender context and distinguishing the inherent tension in girls' education where 'schooling for role' necessitated a debate over that role.[13] Indeed we find that much of our investigation into women's educational experience must be understood in terms of the conflict between waged work and domestic responsibilities for women.

Recent work in the history of women's education has been seated in the fundamental concerns of feminist scholarship and has developed in tandem with it. Work in education by feminist historians has clear implications for investigations in other areas of social and feminist history. Within the educational process and inside educational institutions, whether schools or colleges, we discover the nurturance of gender divisions in society. The reflection of particular values in our schooling is one half of the equation where education $\equiv$ society. The other half demonstrates the reinforcement of these societal values through our educational system. It is through the history of education that we can begin to understand some of the ways in which we are as we are. Historically it is only quite recently that the implications of education for women's employment, marital and political status has been properly recognized.[14] Thus the history of women's education sheds important light upon other areas of feminist history as part of the explanation of the ways in which women experience their lives; ways already documented in the companion volumes in this series.

This collection focuses, therefore, on the history of girls' and women's education in the period 1850 to 1950. In considering education and growing up, both inside and outside the school, the chapters explore the various ways in which girls received their schooling and help delineate the structure of the educational system. All of the chapters explore ideologies in education and the ways in which prevailing values and social judgements were brought to bear on growing girls at home and at school. Collectively they consider the gender inequalities only lately revealed in our recent educational past and something of the actual educational experience of women at all levels.

As they grew into young women the girls discussed in these chapters learnt many lessons about the lives they were expected to lead. Annmarie Turnbull and I found evidence that both middle-class and working-class girls performed domestic tasks at home which impinged on their school time and clearly conveyed messages about their life's work. Deborah Gorham and Penny Tinkler show how, in their spare time, whether after school or after work, girls and young women found their leisure reading full of messages about desirable feminine behaviour and aspirations.

Within the formal education system lessons and study were of course the order of the day. The curriculum designed for Victorian elementary school girls, described by Annmarie Turnbull, stands in stark contrast to the privileged experience of young women students at Cambridge in the 1870s revealed by Perry Williams. As all the chapters show, the details of the learning experience could be very different according to the social class of the pupil and the time at which she went to school. Yet, as we see from the work of Carol Dyhouse, Alison Oram and Penny Summerfield, working-class and middle-class girls alike received the same mixed messages from teachers and teaching as the pioneer women students in the 1870s.

To some extent at least this is due to the inheritance of the past which has remained integral to every stage of educational organization, right up to the present. Indeed, despite educational and legislative initiatives in the 1960s and 1970s towards a more egalitarian approach, the educational structure of England and Wales (Scotland is administratively and historically separate and is not dealt with in this volume) still retains something of the character of the pre-1944 system, which in turn rested upon its Victorian predecessor.

During the Victorian period the school system grew in two separate entities, deliberately organized on a basis of social class. There was also a gender dimension to this structure which was class dependent. The vast mass of children – some 80 to 85 per cent – were gradually and more effectively directed into elementary schools, where girls and boys were taught together, although that did not mean they necessarily learnt the same things or received the same treatment, as Annmarie Turnbull shows in her examination of the elementary school curriculum. At first these elementary schools were organized voluntarily, mostly by churches, with two voluntary societies (the non-conformist British and Foreign Schools Society and the Anglican National Society) taking the largest part.[15] There were also private enterprises, dame schools for example, which provided an alternative to the sectarian teaching in the voluntary schools.[16]

All these schools charged fees of at least a few pence each week, but from 1830 the voluntary schools were eligible for grants administered by a committee of the Privy Council – the Committee of Council on Education. In 1862, in an attempt to reduce rapidly increasing expenditure, the government of the day introduced a grant control system, which came to be known as 'payment by results'.[17] Schools earned grants according to attendance and performance by the children in examinations conducted by Her Majesty's Inspectorate (HMI), and the government thus kept an iron hand on the curriculum, although expenditure soon rose again to pre-1862 levels.[18]

The 1870 Elementary Education Act marked a staging point in English and Welsh education history when, for the first time, local authorities were enabled to open schools funded by a specially raised school rate.[19] No suitable authority existed (county councils for example were not set up until 1888) but individual parishes could elect school boards to raise and administer the rate. Both compulsory attendance and free schooling were yet to come, but each arrived in due course (in 1876–80 and 1891 respectively) and by the 1890s the much hated payment by results system had relinquished its stranglehold.

But, as the 1862 measure suggested, then as now education was always an object of political, religious and financial wrangling. The education of the working classes in particular was subjected to disputes over power and control. Voluntary societies competed with one another and, after 1870, with the school boards for local ascendancy. Successive governments sought to control expenditure, to mediate between (or sometimes to play off) religious factions and the school boards.[20] Increasingly, too, the elementary teachers were becoming more confident about expanding their professional role. By 1900 the time was ripe for a major reorganization of the elementary education system and the 1902 Education Act was to prove the occasion for innovation in both the elementary and the non-working-class sectors.

Victorian middle class education was organized quite separately from working class and was regarded by both parents and government as something entirely different. Whereas even the most *laissez-faire* administrations conceded some necessity for public funding for schooling for the working classes (though free education came reluctantly and late) it was assumed that middle- and upper-class parents not only ought to pay for their children's schooling, but would not wish to lose the control and independence implicit in doing so. Nevertheless, and ironically, middle-class education was subsidized.

There was a long history of educational endowment in England and Wales and by the 1840s there were some 400 endowed grammar and public schools in various states of liveliness or decay. These were largely (and public schools exclusively) attended by middle and upper class boys. The boys' public school sector was to expand over the Victorian period.[21] Schools for middle-class girls were much more restricted, with far fewer charitable resources. Most middle- and upper-class girls were taught at home; some went to private day and boarding schools.[22] For almost all, their education was superficial and non-academic, with much time and effort spent on 'accomplishments'.

All middle-class schools were as much concerned with turning out gentlemen (and ladies) as with training the intellect (although, as I show in the next chapter, these two functions could be regarded as identical). Endowed schools offered scholarships, sometimes even free education for local boys, but generally middle-class schools charged fees ranging from a few pounds to many guineas a year. Boarding schools were, of course, more expensive than day schools.

But middle-class status was dependent on occupation and gentility rather than income and many middle-class families found it difficult to afford a suitable education for their sons, leave alone their daughters. Attendance at an elementary school was, of course, out of the question. By the 1860s there was concern that middle-class parents were being excluded from a suitable education for their sons because they could not afford to pay school fees. As a result of this concern the Liberal administration of 1864 appointed a Royal Commission on middle-class education, the Schools' Inquiry Commission (SIC, or Taunton Commission). The intention was to explore the possibilities of streamlining the many local charities and endowments in England and Wales. In every locality 'schemes' would reorganize these resources (not all of which had specifically been intended for education) to fund subsidized and therefore cheap schools for the middle classes. A rapid and successful campaign mounted by Emily Davies, who was later to found Girton College, Cambridge, ensured the inclusion of girls in the investigation and in 1868 the SIC reported its conclusions.[23] The result was the 1869 Endowed Schools Act which, much to the chagrin of many local townspeople, ensured that endowed grammar schools, and new endowed schools set up under the act, were almost exclusively middle class and regarded as unsuitable for working-class children. Only a few exceptionally bright, privileged elementary school children entered the middle-class schools by winning scholarships.[24]

The seeds of a parallel system of education in England and Wales were planted before the industrial revolution but after the acts of 1869 and 1870 the young growths of middle- and working-class schools developed vigorously but entirely separately. The scholarship 'ladder' was almost impossible for the bright working-class child to climb. It was the initial struggle across the elementary and middle class divide which was so difficult – and even more for a girl than for a boy. In spite of this distinction middle-class education increasingly came to be described as 'secondary', implying an end-on relationship with elementary schooling which really did not exist.[25] In 1895 another Royal Commission investigated what was called 'Secondary Education' and referred generally to the education of the older child, over about the age of 12.[25] But in spite of its recommendations for a more universal 'higher' education for all classes of children, elementary and secondary education were destined to remain very separate for 40 years after the passing of the 1902 Education Act.

Under the 1902 act there were radical changes in the organization and administration of both elementary and secondary schools. The school boards were abolished and existing local authorities were empowered to become education authorities and administer the elementary schools – now to be known as public elementary schools instead of board schools.[27] Furthermore, the local education authorities (LEAs) were permitted to set up secondary schools, funded partly by the rates and partly by central government grants. The central authority itself had been rationalized in 1899 when the Education Department joined forces with other departments with an education function and became the Board of Education.[28] Now it was to expand its administrative and inspecting function from the elementary schools to include the new municipal secondary schools and all those existing secondary schools which chose either to become 'recognized' (for grant purposes) or 'efficient' (i.e. remaining financially autonomous but fulfilling certain criteria laid down by the Board). The Code of Regulations for Public Elementary Schools and the Regulations for Secondary Schools laid down administrative, financial and curricular ground rules for all schools, the Inspectorate was expanded and for the first time there was state education in the way we understand it today.

Over the Victorian period children's 'school lives' had gradually been extended. Real headway was not made in elementary schools until after the arrival first of compulsory and then free education. In 1899 the school-leaving age was raised to 12, then again, though permissively, in 1900 to 14 and finally compulsorily to 14 in 1918. The length of school life was one of the points of difference between elementary and secondary school for secondary school children, after early years spent at home, or in a preparatory or junior department

xviii

or school, embarked on secondary school at about the age of 12. Increasingly they were then encouraged to stay at school for a minimum four-year course until the age of 15 or 16, and 18 or 19 if they (the tiny minority only) were to go on to university. The idea of an educational staging point at about the age of 11 had taken root in the elementary schools in the 1890s and certain school boards developed higher grade schools with special courses for 12–14 year olds. The higher grade schools were sacrificed in the 1902 reorganization, but only in their administration not their concept. From the 1900s increasing numbers of LEAs sought to develop special courses for 12–14 year olds in elementary schools and in the elementary sector types of school proliferated. There were central schools, selective and non-selective (these, especially the latter, increasingly sought a more academic curriculum). There were technical and trade schools and, in areas with few resources or lacking the will, there were 'senior classes' with more advanced curricula than for pupils under 11.

But what remained was the divide between the elementary sector and the secondary sector. Opportunity for crossing the divide was to increase, beginning with the introduction of the free place scheme in 1907.[29] But secondary schools all charged fees and it was possible for fee-paying children to take up places in schools even when places had not been found for all children qualified by scholarships.[30] The curriculum in secondary schools was avowedly more academic, though by no means all children in these schools were of an academic bent. Secondary schools had, since 1853 (1865 for girls) used the university local examinations (especially formulated first by Cambridge, then Oxford and the other universities) to test performance. In 1917 the local examinations were rationalized and streamlined and the new school certificate examination became the sole means of matriculation and ultimately of entry to the universities and many of the professions. Elementary school children were not allowed to take school certificate. Not surprisingly the middle class dominated the secondary sector and the concept of schooling in the elementary and secondary schools remained very different.[31]

In one respect a similar policy was pursued in both sectors. Many of the new municipal secondary schools were mixed (or 'schools for boys and girls', as the Board of Education preferred to call them) but where resources allowed most administrators and educationists preferred single sex schools. Similarly, as elementary schools diversified and reorganized their post-11 education, authorities aimed to provide separate schools or departments for boys and girls, which had repercussions for both teachers and pupils as Alison Oram shows. The differences in the underlying premise for the education of girls and that of boys, in both sectors, is explored in the following chapters. But, as Deborah Thom concludes, the whole issue of gender was perceived very differently from that of class by contemporaries in the inter-war period.

The 1944 Education Act wrote the largest changes yet on the education system – but still achieved little real equality of opportunity. Crucially, the act introduced free secondary education and made real the division of schools into primary and secondary sectors which had been called for since the 1920s.[32] The parallel systems of elementary and secondary schools were replaced by primary schools which took pupils until the age of 11, when they passed into 'secondary' schools – 'secondary grammar', 'secondary technical' and 'secondary modern'. In 1947 the leaving age was raised to 15. Yet the post-1944 system retained many characteristics of its precursor. Technical schools were few and far between. The grammar school sector incorporated a number of the old central schools but essentially remained the old secondary sector, writ egalitarian. The secondary modern schools, which housed 65 to 70 per cent of the post-11 school population were, inevitably at first, old senior schools renamed.

Programmes of school building and curricular development gradually encouraged the secondary modern schools to feel less under-privileged, but the principle of 'parity of esteem', which was supposed to premise the tripartite system, did not really exist.[33] Whereas ever since 1902 secondary schools had aimed to achieve a four-year school course, culminating in school certificate and a leaving age of 16, secondary modern pupils were not permitted to take the school certificate until it was replaced by the general certificate of education (GCE) in 1951, and not until 1972 was the school leaving age raised to 16.[34]

This was the education system experienced by the girls discussed in this volume. The nine chapters which follow each look in some detail at a particular aspect of education and growing up and all of them are concerned with the influence of the feminine ideology on girls' lives. But this influence carries on beyond school into the university sector, and outside school into the leisure time of girls and women, and this collection considers those dimensions of their lives too. The book is divided into three parts. In Part I each of the chapters considers ways in which femininity is integrated into the substance of girls' growing up, both at home and at school. In Part II three chapters explore some of the inequalities contained within elementary and secondary schools throughout the period. Finally, in Part III, two chapters explore two very different sets of experience in education, in a privileged Victorian university and the inter-war secondary school.

In the first chapter in Part I, I explore the relationship between two ideologies which fought for dominance in girls' schooling in the period from 1850 to 1950. The Victorian concept of femininity or womanliness underwrote the intentions and practices of the early pioneers in the new schools for middle-class girls in the mid-Victorian period. Yet the schools were developed in the context of the concept of liberal education, the training of the intellect and the emotions which produced the gentleman and scholar. The women educationists could see no real contradiction between these two concepts. In their opinion what was suitable for a gentleman was equally suitable for a lady, especially when femininity was redefined to embrace not just the domestic or maternal role, but one of social and civic service too. But while middle-class society might have been prepared to accept the necessity of employment as an unavoidable *alternative* for women (if, for example, no suitable husband was to be found) there was little sympathy for a *combination* of roles and increasingly the function of school was defined as role preparation. Thus what Victorian headmistresses had conceived of as a dual aim in their schools came to be perceived as a divided aim – preparation for employment and for home seemed to be incompatible functions in the school. By the Edwardian period middle-class girls' schools were faced with serious logistical and educational problems in accommodating an expanded curriculum. They were problems which were never resolved and which left girls' schools with the alternatives of either somehow failing to live up to the full demands of the domestic ideology or sacrificing academic standards or educational ends to those demands. Ultimately the dilemma was that of the perceived incompatibility of paid work and the domestic role and how that social perception was visited upon the schools.

In chapter 2 Carol Dyhouse explores another perceived incompatibility – that of true femininity with the real display of authority. She argues that education history is a valuable arena for investigating sexual politics because it is one of the few contexts in which women have, and do, achieve positions of relative power in appreciable numbers. Concentrating on two key figures in Victorian education, Frances Buss and Dorothea Beale, Carol Dyhouse considers how two very different women, both of them equally wedded to the idea of womanliness and feminine behaviour, yet both equally determined to improve the education of girls, negotiated the gender constraints which required them to behave in a ladylike way. Both had to operate in the 'public sphere' and tangle with such unladylike enterprises as fund-raising, campaigning and public negotiation. She discusses the different strategies each adopted and the ways in which both their biographers and, later, feminist historians have attempted to tackle the seeming contradictions of their lives.

The last two chapters in Part I each examine leisure reading for girls during the periods from 1850 to 1914 and from 1920 to 1950. Both examine the messages which were conveyed to readers about appropriate feminine behaviour and life styles. Each also gives us some idea of the contradictions felt by readers when they discuss the correspondence and advice columns in girls' magazines which reveal how problematic life could be for girls who attempted to live up to those messages in the real world. In chapter 3 which covers the earlier period Deborah Gorham looks at the way in which leisure reading material for girls (and indeed young women) went through a process of transition from the mid-Victorian period to the years preceding the 1914–18 war. The importance of femininity and womanliness, and of ladylike behaviour was a consistent message. But, just as Victorian schools were suggesting to pupils that their role of duty and service could be played in a broader context than that of the family, their leisure reading also came to suggest that the 'daughter at home' could step into a 'widening sphere'. Yet that role was carefully restricted and ultimately the characteristic Victorian seriousness of purpose was replaced by commercial ventures, concentrating upon idealized school-girl adventures, which failed to explore the tensions and ambiguities in girls' lives.

Deborah Gorham notes the modifications in the messages of femininity conveyed to working-class, as opposed to middle-class, girls but she finds that there is an equal lack of realism in magazines whatever the class of readership. Nevertheless, the move into school-girl fiction in the Edwardian period hardened the class lines of such literature, a pattern which was to be repeated in subsequent periodical literature.

In her study of such publications in the years from 1920 to 1950 (chapter 4) Penny Tinkler notes that the magazines and periodicals were frequently aimed at particular readerships which were demarcated very much on class lines. She discusses an expanded genre where magazines proliferated for all ages and classes. The sub-divisions which tended to follow class lines also, of course, followed different patterns of experience. The working-class elementary school girl who left school at 14 and went into a full-time job had different interests and resources from the middle-class girl whose life was more closely defined by home and who would remain at school for several more years. School-girl magazines for the middle classes paid little attention to marriage but enthusiastically promoted certain sorts of career, that is those considered suitably 'feminine'. 'Working girl' and 'mother and daughter' magazines contained romantic fiction and 'job', rather than 'career' advice. But work was seen as a prelude to marriage or, latterly, as a suitable substitute for marriage – though marriage was always more desirable. All the magazines regarded sexuality as a taboo or suspect subject and once again it is the advice columns which reveal the tensions readers experienced in attempting to accommodate their femaleness in a world which prescribed an asexual femininity, confined to a restricted sphere.

The three chapters in Part II all examine some aspect of inequality in the school system. In a study of the elementary school curriculum from 1870 to 1914 (chapter 5) Annmarie Turnbull examines how the domestic ideology came to have more and more influence on curricular prescriptions for working-class girls. She shows how, even in apparently neutral subjects, girls and boys received different messages about behaviour and role. As practical training in domesticity became increasingly dominant, especially for older girls, discrepancies between the school curriculum and girls' home experience became clear. Proponents of a domestic curriculum were undeterred by this, and by both child and parental objections. Indeed opposition was very muted and she points out how enthusiasts were often women who saw in teaching domestic subjects a very real opportunity for an expanded professional role for women. Noting the renewed emphasis on educating for the home which accompanied Edwardian imperial and eugenic ideals Annmarie Turnbull concludes that the 'separate spheres doctrine' was ultimately 'educationally legitimated and institutionalized' in the public elementary schools.

In a change of focus in chapter 6 Alison Oram considers the role of women and men teachers in the elementary schools between the wars. There was every reason for gender-based professional rivalry in the teaching profession. Women teachers earned less than men for the same work, although women increasingly dominated the profession in numbers, men held far more headships and senior positions. Yet it was the men teachers who really went on the offensive in the 'sex antagonism' which arose. The National Union of Schoolmasters (NAS) attacked women teachers both as destructive to the masculinity of boys and as being unfeminine. Those of the women who responded, mainly as members of the National Union of Women Teachers (NUWT), did so as avowed feminists. They argued for equality of opportunity in schools for pupils and for teachers, for ungendered teaching and less insistence on domesticity for girls and finally, faced with an increasingly gender-differentiated school organization, for the importance of ensuring that women teachers achieved senior posts in mixed, as well as single sex, schools. The resistance of the NUWT to gender stereotyping in schools was premised on a rejection of gender roles which were accepted as 'common sense' by most teachers and administrators in education. Indeed the women teachers, representing as they did the unusual vision of professional women in command of their own incomes and in positions of authority, offered an obvious challenge to the traditional feminine role. Alison Oram finds that the phenomenon of women in authority examined by Carol Dyhouse in the nineteenth century continued into the twentieth and it was perhaps the very success of the women teachers which ensured the opposition and antagonism they aroused among some men teachers when they made that challenge explicit and public.

In the final chapter in Part II Deborah Thom considers why it was that, while social class was considered so much of a problem in achieving educational equality between the wars and after the 1944 act, gender inequality was barely noticed or discussed. Focusing on intelligence testing she explores the difference in performance of boys and girls. The fact that girls frequently scored better marks than boys in such tests proved to be the occasion for differentials in required performances to qualify for entrance to secondary school and, even more intriguingly, the perception of this phenomenon as a problem of disadvantage for boys. Just as this situation was not regarded as a major problem of educational inequality so too it seems to have been largely overlooked by psychologists in England. Deborah Thom too finds evidence that, in the minds of education 'experts', the educational needs of girls were perceived as different from those of boys and were seen to be connected to particular social, i.e. 'domestic', functions. The expanding role of women in industry and commerce was either unremarked by the experts or set aside as a short-term experience, out of character with the rest of their lives. As a consequence of all these perceptions there was to be no real administrative, educational or psychological challenge to the gender inequalities inherent in the school system.

In the two chapters in Part III the writers are once again juxtaposing ideologies of femininity and education, this time through the words and reactions of girls and women in schools and college. In chapter 8, Penny Summerfield has used both archival and oral history sources for a facinating exploration of six single-sex secondary schools in two Lancashire towns between the wars. Seeking to define intentions rather than outcomes, she asks whether such schools were really aiming to prepare suitable wives for the bourgeoisie? Her answer is necessarily complex. She finds that schools were engaged in the transmission of femininity – but a feminity redefined along the lines which had begun to develop in the Victorian period. Thus pupils were encouraged to aim for certain professions, notably teaching, in a direct challenge to dominant forms of gender relations. Yet, while domesticity was not under-written by the schools in any real practical way, and marriage was rarely overtly presented as a desirable aim (though in the convent schools it was certainly presented as a *legitimate* aim), the standards of behaviour, dress and demeanour demanded of the pupils all conveyed powerful messages about women's role. And while the goal of university or teaching dominated the school curriculum and in several of the schools clerical and secretarial jobs were regarded as very much second rate, few of the girls were actually able to go to university. Both rules of behaviour and academic goals suggested that the schools conflated academic and social status, as did the direction of the pupils towards particular careers. Practical training in domesticity, that is the teaching of domestic science, was regarded as incompatible with a 'liberal education'. Thus femininity as transmitted in these schools, while it certainly incorporated womanly and ladylike behaviour, did not suggest approval for the domestic role. That few of the pupils could have succeeded in living up to this redefined ideal must have meant that the ambiguity over 'the mission to create a new breed of middle-class women' for which Penny Summerfield finds evidence in the ideas of those running the schools, may well have been reflected in the attitudes of the pupils.

Finally we turn to a small group, privileged among women, the early students at Newnham and Girton colleges at Cambridge during the 1870s. Using their own words Perry Williams explores in chapter 9 the impact of this novel experience on the lives of young women who stepped beyond the bounds of convention in entering the academic life of one of the ancient universities. He explores their motivation and the various sorts of opposition they faced – and the encouragement which was sometimes expressed so dubiously as to undermine their purpose. He too finds evidence of the diversification of femininity and of justification for higher education 'in the service of marriage'. For the students themselves there were rewards of a new sense of identity and individuality, the possibility of female friendships, of fulfilling work and possibly even a more equal marital relationship. But whatever the changes in individual experience there is no evidence of radical change in either expectations or experience. The forces of femininity, diversified or redefined, remained the greatest power in the students' lives.

That comment usefully serves as a conclusion for all the chapters. Education and growing up were very different experiences for boys and for girls. There were powerful influences in girls' lives which suggested that their role was a very limited and particular one and it is clear that gender was a category of overwhelming importance in the structure and organization of education, as well as in defining the educational experience of pupils. The redefinition of femininity was complex, both moving towards a new emphasis on domesticity and towards an expanded 'caring' role. Ultimately there were mixed messages and ambiguities in girls' lives at every stage of growing up and every level of education. Deborah Gorham and Penny Tinkler found very potent evidence of this in the correspondence columns of magazines. And throughout, the complications of social class in an education system rooted in a solid class structure helped to dictate the educating and socializing experience of girls. The messages about femininity came across differently for girls of different social classes and, as Penny Summerfield and Deborah Thom demonstrate, while the impact of the message was socially differentiated the nature of the message was (and had been) obscured by social class considerations.

Part I

Ideologies in Education

1

Divided Aims: the Educational Implications of Opposing Ideologies in Girls' Secondary Schooling, 1850–1940

Felicity Hunt

In the 1920s and 1930s it was fashionable to accuse girls' secondary schools of neglecting the 'feminine' side of their pupils' development. The Victorian pioneers (and Miss Buss and Miss Beale were frequently cited on these occasions) were supposed to have adopted a model of 'liberal education' and in doing so had 'assimilated' the 'boys' curriculum' and ignored the needs of femininity in their schools.[1] The result, said the accusers, was that girls' education was a 'slavish imitation' of boys' and by definition, therefore, inappropriate for girls.[2]

There were a number of assumptions implicit in this accusation. The most fundamental of these was held by those who believed that girls and boys experienced an identical education, but that it was in fact wholly inappropriate for girls to share either the curriculum or the ethos of boys' schools because each sex had special needs in education which were associated with their gender. At the heart of the matter was the assumption that while there seemed to be no incompatibility for boys between an economic and a parental role, precisely the opposite was true for girls. Some even went so far as to say that girls who did not become mothers, for whatever reason, were failures as women. 'What they really need,' said the *Journal of Education* in a comment on spinster teachers and office workers, 'is marriage, a home and family.'[3]

Whether or not the Victorian pioneers would have agreed with this sentiment is a moot point. What they *did* recognize was that not all girls would fulfil this ideal female role. Their successors shared this recognition and this chapter is an account of how succeeding generations of headmistresses tried to cope with the conflicting educational demands of a society which defined women's primary social role as motherhood and regarded this function as incompatible with anything else.

The Victorians were much exercised by the problem of 'redundant women' and how to ensure a livelihood for these 'surplus' women who failed to marry. Appropriate occupations seemed hard to find but many indigent middle-class women turned to teaching. It was an over-crowded, under-trained profession and during the late 1840s the founders of the Governesses' Benevolent Institution recognized that the real key to helping these women was to give them both education and pedagogical training. It was for this reason that they founded Queen's College, Harley Street. Work at the College marked a limited recognition at least of the link between women's lack of marketable skills and their education. During the 1850s and 1860s middle-class women campaigned to extend employment opportunities and improve those skills, and pioneers in women's education were frequently involved in this work.

By the 1870s, education was seen as the essential key for opening the door to productive and useful lives for middle-class girls. Central to this strategy was the knowledge that the ideal of family life was simply not available to a significant number of women. In 1874 Isabella Tod summed up prevailing attitudes. Middle-class parents, she wrote, looked forward to '*all* their daughters marrying, to all these marriages being satisfactory, and to the husbands being *always* able and willing to take the active management of everything . . . We shall not stop to discuss whether such a state of things is even desirable. It is sufficient to point out that it does not and cannot exist.'[4]

It was not enough, however, to recognize education as a crucial strategy. A formula for that education had to be devised and naturally the pioneers looked first to existing canons, and in particular to that known as 'liberal education'. The Victorian idea of a liberal education and the Victorian practice were, inevitably, two rather different things. The idea was formulated in its purest and most refined form by J. H. Newman in 1862 in *The Idea of a University*. For Newman 'liberal knowledge' was that 'which stands on its own pretensions, which is independent of sequel, expects no complement, refuses to be *informed* (as it is called) by any end, or absorbed into any act, in order duly to present itself to our contemplation.' Once given this knowledge the true scholar would find all disciplines opened to him, whether the doctrines of law or medicine or the realms of natural science or philosophy. Yet there was more to it still. Dr Johnson defined liberal education as 'becoming a gentleman'. What had been the exclusive training of the sons of the aristocracy became a means for the new middle classes to acquire both gentility and learning.

Women educationists shared a belief in the excellence and effectiveness of a liberal education. Maria Grey, founder of the Women's Education Union and the Girls' Public Day School Company, and possibly one of the most prolific writers on education in the Victorian period, defined education as 'moral and intellectual training' which was as necessary to girls as to boys, for whom it 'must be conducted on the same principles and by the same methods'. Few headmasters would have disagreed with what she went on to tell the Social Science Congress in 1871 when she described education as 'the drawing out and cultivation of all the faculties with which it has pleased God to endow his human creatures, – intelligence, affections, will, conscience, the training of each individual to guide himself [sic] aright through the circumstances of life, to know his duty and to do it.'[5]

The discussion at the Congress was part of a wider debate about the direction that middle-class education ought to take. New public schools for boys like Cheltenham and Wellington Colleges had found that a 'modern side', encompassing modern languages and science, was popular with parents whose sons faced army and civil service examinations. With the evidence of scientists like Michael Faraday before them, the Clarendon Commissioners recommended the inclusion of mathematics, French, history, geography and English in the curricula of the great public schools. School, as opposed to university education, was diversifying in the face of rapidly changing social and economic conditions.

The movement for curricular reform was taken many stages further when the Schools Inquiry Commission (SIC) reported in 1868. Their recommendations for three grades of school to give three variations of 'secondary' education to the upper, middle and lower middle classes set a pattern for future school development.[6] Classics, which were held to be the true heart of a liberal education, retained their supremacy, but a new dimension was entering educational thinking, for the three grades of school were intended to prepare, very directly, for work in adult life. The subsequent strivings by boys' schools for upward social/academic mobility underlined the importance attached to the idea of a classical education as the most desirable form of schooling, but their aspirations are another story.[7] What is of relevance is that in practice the middle-class grammar, or 'secondary' schools incorporated a 'vocational' element into their curricula, as did many of the public schools. Classical and modern 'sides' in virtually all the boys' public schools were a practical acknowledgement of this principle. It was a dimension of middle-class schooling which made some uncomfortable for it seemed, indeed was, antithetical to Newman's definition of liberal education. Nevertheless, the principles of a liberal education bore a variety of interpretations, while the practice was overtly linked to adult occupation.

The women pioneers engaged in the search for an educational formula for middle-class girls were acutely aware that liberal education was in the process of change. In their evidence to the SIC Emily Davies, Frances Buss and Dorothea Beale, all key figures in nineteenth-century girls' education, emphasized that the question of whether girls and boys should receive the same education was complicated by the fact that the whole content of boys' schooling was a matter for debate.[8] What they wanted to do was take those elements of a male liberal education which seemed most effective and worthwhile and discard the rest. Yet they knew that too marked a divergence in curriculum practice would lead to accusations of inferiority.[9]

In practice this meant that Victorian headmistresses adopted a broadly based curriculum which, by the 1870s, included English subjects (scripture, history, literature and geography), languages (French, German and Latin), sciences (mathematics and natural science) and the aesthetic subjects (music, singing and drawing).[10] Within another decade the growing numbers of middle-class girls' schools had achieved a broad consensus on curricular practice. The headmistresses only took what they saw to be of proven worth from the 'boys' curriculum. They attempted to strike a balance between the 'English' subjects, languages and science, though like many boys' schools their science teaching was limited and lacked resources.[11] The aesthetic subjects, which were derived from the old accomplishments, were taught systematically but often relegated to non-compulsory afternoon school. They were not considered of first importance, though few of the new schools dreamt of omitting them entirely.[12]

At the same time Victorian headmistresses emphasized the need for ladylike behaviour and feminine qualities. Rules were strict (which helped discipline) and were avowedly intended to promote a favourable public image. At one of their earliest meetings, in 1876, the Association of Head Mistresses (AHM) resolved 'That it is desirable that a high standard of public opinion be aimed at in Girls' Schools.'[13] Schools encouraged charitable works and the 'Dorcas' meetings at the North London Collegiate School, which allowed practice in sewing while making garments for the poor, were copied at many other schools. But often the greatest energy was directed at preaching high standards of service and duty to the girls. Frances Buss combined a powerful desire 'to lighten ever so little the misery of women brought up "to be married and taken care of" and left destitute', with a firm belief in the complementary roles of women and men.[14] It was her conviction that for women this was exemplified in 'a refined and cultivated mind . . . the gentle self-forgetful, sympathising, innocent heart'. Yet by playing a part in the life of the school she believed that every young woman would acquire 'the wider public-spiritedness of the citizen and the Englishman [sic]'.[15]

Many Victorian headmistresses shared Frances Buss's ideas. Whether, like her, they believed in complementary roles for women and men or 'that subordinate part in the world' to which Dorothea Beale believed women were called they were at one in teaching generations of girls that as women their goals in life were duty and service.[16] This was true whether they were destined for life at home or life at work, and in neither sphere could they ignore the need to be feminine and ladylike. And for the headmistresses there was only one way of achieving this ideal, through the practice of their interpretation of a liberal education, both in the formal sense and through its moral dimension, referred to by Maria Grey in 1871.

There was, however, one notable exception from the debate about curriculum and schooling for the womanly role. The headmistresses' educational strategy embraced a general (though not universal) disdain for any training in practical domestic duties. Maria Grey summed up most of her listeners' feelings when she told the AHM that a girl's 'professional training as a woman' was appropriate only after her school education.[17]

The headmistresses could see no reason for making fundamental distinctions between schooling for girls and boys. As Dorothea Beale put it: 'The old rubbish about masculine and feminine studies is beginning to be treated as it deserves. It cannot be seriously maintained that those studies which tend to make a man nobler or better, have the opposite effect on a woman.'[18] This was the premise for Victorian middle-class girls' schooling and the headmistresses' adoption of the principles of a liberal education was based on a genuine belief in its excellence and the conviction that what helped make a man 'nobler and better' would fit a woman for a feminine role of duty and service, whether in the home or in the outside world. The dual aim of preparing for both home and work was an integral element in the new schooling for middle-class girls.

By the 1890s the exclusive emphasis on Latin and classical studies in boys' schools seemed to be dying away. Secondary or middle-class school curricula had diversified. Classical study remained the highest goal, but it was to be achieved at university, not at school. This diversification reflected wider aims in the secondary school. By the turn of the century these largely middle-class schools were not divided neatly into first, second and third grades but fell, roughly speaking, into two types with differential fees and leaving ages of about 16 and 18. Those with the higher leaving age, often called first grade schools, prepared boys, and indeed girls, for university and upheld a classical tradition, though there were differences between boys' and girls' schools. Boys' schools were usually divided into 'sides', modern and classical. Girls' schools had a more flexible arrangement perhaps not least because fewer girls would go to university and once there were more likely to read other subjects than classics.[19] For boys the classical sides prepared them to enter the whole spectrum of middle-class occupations, but especially law, the church and the civil service, all of which were closed to women. For girls the most favoured profession was teaching.

But careers like this only concerned a minority of the pupils at secondary schools and the more overtly vocational dimensions in middle-class curricula so clearly specified in the plans of the SIC seemed to have become a reality. This was so much the case that the 1895 Report of the Bryce Commission, while defining secondary education as 'a process of intellectual training and personal discipline', readily recognized the need for a technical (or practical) element. Secondary education should be 'conducted in view of the special life that has to be lived with the express purpose of forming a person fit to live it.' In the Commissioners' view 'a girl, like a boy, may be fitted by education to earn a livelihood' (though they added 'or at any rate to be a more useful member of society').[20]

The 1890s saw a great upsurge of interest in technical education which the Bryce Commission reflected in its report. The AHM welcomed this in principle but resisted any suggestion that for girls it was to be restricted to training in the 'Domestic Arts and Sciences'.[21] There were, however, developments in the next decade which ensured that practical training for girls *would* be seen in these terms, and almost exclusively.

Throughout the 1870s and 1880s opposition to women's education had gone through all the permutations of current medico- and socio-biological debates.[22] The fears of doctors focused on the effect of intellectual development upon maturation and puberty. Counter evidence that study did not result in sterility for women caused opposition to be reasserted in the shape of fears that highly educated women would be disinclined for motherhood and their 'natural' role.[23] But much of this opposition had been directed at higher, not secondary education. In contrast the middle-class girls' secondary schools had been remarkably successful in achieving 'a high standard of public opinion' and in deflecting criticism.

The headmistresses' insistence on adequate health care was one ingredient in this success. All of them concentrated heavily on health and medical care and this included rules about dress, holding medical inspections and encouraging gymnastics and games.[24] The remainder was owed to a recipe of careful curriculum planning, attention to good behaviour and nurture of the qualities of duty, service and charity. All this was made easier because the balance of power in the control of school activities and policy had swung from parents to headmistresses.[25] This was a sign of the schools' success and of their power to direct the lives of their pupils. Criticism had not disappeared and had indeed helped to mould the schools into their present shape, but it was held at bay.

In one sense it was the schools' achievements which opened the door to the new problems they were to face in the twentieth century, as they showed how effectively they trained useful members of society. For in the closing decades of the century a new concern gathered force over the quality of racial fitness and the health of the nation. This debate over 'national efficiency' targeted women and their domestic role in nurturing good health. Because greater efficiency in the home demanded training in the work of wife and mother the schools were an obvious focus. This was particularly true of middle-class schools for one important faction, the eugenists, believed the middle class had an important role to play in improving national efficiency because of their 'natural' hereditary superiority.[26]

In 1894 Karl Pearson, leading light of the eugenics movement, argued that women's only valid function was maternity and that if only the middle-class leaders of the women's movement would understand this then they could redirect their energies into encouraging marriage and motherhood. He considered himself a 'feminist' and argued for women's 'rights', but always in the context of 'social efficiency', which confined women's individual development to the maternal sphere.[27] Other eugenists agreed. Elizabeth Sloan Chesser defined the 'function' of women. 'Not only to bear children, but by their work and influence to evolve, purify and beautify the higher nature of the race.'[28] The eugenist message was that women were biologically determined for motherhood, instinctively fitted for it, and destined for the social as well as the biological role. Yet, strangely enough, instinct was not in itself sufficient to make a good mother. In Pearson's words, instinct 'without training or knowledge . . . is apt to be blind to facts.'[29] Generally eugenists thought of education as treatment, or even amelioration, while the more appropriate means to a eugenic society (which was of course dependent on heredity) were prophylactics such as birth control and sterilization. But in this context education and training *were* seen to be appropriate.

Eugenists shared a concern over women's role with other groups who were considering the problem of 'national efficiency' at the turn of the century. The eugenist thinking of the late 1890s and early 1900s both influenced and received considerable encouragement from the *Report of the Inter-Departmental Committee on Physical Deterioration* which had been set up in the wake of serious concern generated by the low standards of physical health in Boer War recruits.[30] Both this and Dr (later Sir) George Newman's 1906 book, *Infant Mortality: A Social Problem*, blamed high rates of infant mortality and general ill-health upon neglect and ignorance by working-class mothers.[31] The immediate response of the Board of Education was to make hygiene a compulsory subject in both training college and elementary school curricula.[32]

Many of those concerned with 'national efficiency' were not eugenist and some who were in a position to influence educational policy were anti-eugenist. Nevertheless they shared the idea that women's duty lay in the domestic sphere. Medical Officers of Health, as a group, were largely anti-eugenist, because the eugenic thesis that ameliorating environmental conditions interfered with the process of natural selection, undermined their whole raison d'être.[33] Arthur Newsholme, Chief Medical Officer at the Local Government Board (1907–18), was a former MOH who firmly held the view that working mothers were responsible, through neglect, for high rates of infant mortality.[34] He was also a convinced environmentalist and anti-eugenist.[35] It was for *environmental* reasons that Newsholme advocated both a traditional domestic role for women and the need for education for motherhood. In his series of reports on infant mortality for the Local Government Board Newsholme took the opportunity to preach these ideas.[36]

Regardless of their other disagreements the common concern of both the nature and nurture schools was to advocate a primarily domestic role for women. By now it was an accepted part of *elementary* school practice that girls should learn domestic skills at school.[37] It was but an extension of this to add lessons in infant care, which were started in elementary schools in the 1900s.[38]

Thus, at the turn of the century, the interest in technical or practical education at secondary level coincided with a belief that girls needed training in domestic and mothering skills: a belief already translated into practice in elementary schools. These events also coincided with the 1899 Board of Education Act, reorganizing the central state educational departments into the Board of Education, and with the 1902 Education Act. Under this latter Act for the first time the state was directly involved in the planning and control of secondary education.

At first sight it seemed unlikely that the combined effect of the strongly vocational dimension in elementary schooling and the newly awakened interest in technical education would have any impact on secondary practice for girls. For just at this point Robert Morant, newly appointed Permanent Secretary at the Board, set out a formula for secondary education which expressly excluded any vocational element and pressed hard for the purest form of 'liberal education'.[39] However Morant himself was a proponent of 'national efficiency' and his interest in the secondary school curriculum led him to examine details of girls' and boys' curricula. As a result he suggested, for the first time, that curricular differentiation was needed to match 'the differences inherent in the nature of the two sexes'.[40] It was a conclusion which was to have an impact on the secondary curriculum for girls.

Until 1902 the headmistresses had been safe with their own interpretations of a liberal education. Now they were being brought, sometimes directly, sometimes indirectly, under the aegis of a state controlled education authority.[41] The Permanent Secretary and the new Secondary Branch of the Inspectorate at the Board concentrated in these early years on structuring the details of the secondary curriculum via the Regulations for Secondary Schools. The co-incidence of events and ideas combined to ensure new prescriptions for middle-class girls' schooling which came into direct conflict with the practice of a liberal education, both in the reformed Victorian mode and in the post-1902 Morant mode.[42]

Practical training in the female role was formally imposed on the schools by the Board through the Regulations in 1905 when 'housewifery' was made a compulsory subject for girls.[43] This innovation received a mixed reception. Not all the headmistresses regarded it unfavourably. The AHM had been discussing the general issue of practical or technical subjects for at least ten years. Furthermore some of the second and third generation headmistresses were beginning to consider whether there was in fact room in their schools for a more practical approach to inculcating femininity, through direct training in domestic skills. Some considered it appropriate for duller girls, some for those who did not anticipate taking a job on leaving school.[44] There was no consensus to be found, but once the Board itself began to incorporate the idea into the Regulations the debate became a live and difficult one.

The whole issue of the inclusion of training in domestic skills and the domestic role was part of a wider curriculum debate. In these early years of experiment and dictate, officials at the Board became aware that the interpretation of a liberal education varied between grades of school and schools for the two sexes. Where girls' schools were concerned there seemed to be clear areas of strength and weakness. The female accomplishments tradition which had ensured a place for the aesthetic subjects in the curriculum now meant that girls' schools had built up both expertise and reputation in music and art. Similarly the emphasis which the pioneers had placed upon literary subjects, especially English, gave girls' schools an advantage in these disciplines.

Ironically, however, the schools' high reputation in these subjects reinforced the idea that they were areas particularly important for girls. In the official mind the natural corollary of this seemed to be that such 'feminine' subjects lacked academic status. For example, J. W. Headlam, one of the first Inspectors appointed in the Secondary branch at the Board, wrote to his Chief Inspector in 1908 about promoting the teaching of history. Anxious because history lacked academic status in schools he wanted an experiment in history teaching similar to the 'educational experiment' in Latin teaching at the (boys') Perse School in Cambridge.[45] But Headlam's strategy only became clear when he said, 'I could easily get a good girls [sic] school to take up the work, but I want a boys [sic] school – and one of the first grade.'[46]

Similarly the Board was keen to promote music in school as 'an important part of the foundation of true culture' and regretted the neglect of the subject in boys' schools, compared with girls'.[47] Yet, against the advice of the newly appointed Inspector of Music, Arthur Somervell, there was reluctance to make its presence compulsory in any sense. One senior civil servant in the Secondary branch, suggested to his superior, W. N. Bruce, that headmasters in particular should be persuaded to promote it.[48] But timetabling was a problem and neither the Chief Inspector nor Morant himself thought it should be made obligatory.[49] The decision is an interesting contrast to their attitude on adding another compulsory subject or set of subjects (for 'housewifery' including cookery, needlework and laundrywork) to the girls' curriculum, especially when it is remembered that the emphasis on music in girls' schools was to continue.

Conversely weaknesses in girls' schools were seen to lie in the areas of science and mathematics. This had to do with both ability and relevance. The Board recognized that there was debate between 'those who hold that there is an actual difference of capacity for the subject between boys and girls and those who hold that there is not.' There was also recognition of the argument that 'on the whole girls have not had as good a chance as boys.' In spite of this recognition the Board was prepared to argue that girls did in fact lack the same capacity for mathematics as boys.[50] This attitude was exemplified in the Regulations for 1907 when certain girls were permitted to replace science with domestic science.[51] By 1909 mathematics, except for arithmetic, could be dropped too.[52] Meanwhile the substitute subject – domestic science – although apparently a primary desideratum of girls' schooling, had a dubious reputation in educative terms. As the Board's *Annual Report* of 1906–7 put it: 'the subject of Domestic Work needs further and increased attention before it can be considered as having an educational value comparable with such practical subjects as are dealt with in boys' [secondary] schools.'[53]

After experimenting with domestic science the headmistresses were sharply divided on how much was either desirable or necessary, though one group believed it to be useful not just as a preparation for 'home life' but for the female professions.[54] They were agreed that elementary science in schools was a necessary preparation for domestic science (an argument which helped reinforce the need for

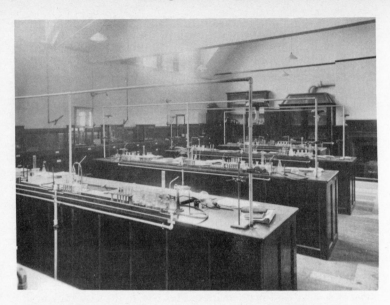

A science laboratory (top) and cookery class (bottom) at the Bedford Modern School for Girls (now the Dame Alice Harpur School) in the 1930s.

science in girls' schools) and were anxious to control the quantity of domestic subjects in the curriculum. There was also agreement that it had a different part to play in different types of schools.[55]

They decided in 1907 that, whatever its desirability, there were problems in teaching domestic science to girls who left school at 16, because of pressure of work in preparing for competitive examinations for intending clerks and teachers. They thought that the answer was to omit domestic subjects, justifying their decision on the grounds that this class of girl already gained practical experience by helping out at home, that parents of poorer students begrudged time spent on such subjects and that if girls were to be expected to pass their examinations at the same time as boys compulsory domestic subjects 'would be an ill-advised step and certainly prejudicial to health'.[56]

The answer seemed to be to provide any domestic training at the end of a general school course. But this created problems too. Girls leaving at 16 would have no chance of learning any domestic science; 18 and 19 year-old leavers going on to higher education would have no time after they were 16 because of the demands of academic examinations. Only girls who could afford to stay at school but were not going to college would have any opportunity at all. One way out of the problem might be, they thought, to combine domestic and elementary science but this solution raised many insuperable difficulties too, both practical and intellectual, and most educationists rejected it.[57]

In spite of the many doubts and problems domestic science did gain a place in the curriculum, though the extent and nature of its teaching varied widely from school to school.[58] But on one point the AHM remained immovable. As a body they were adamant that what was important was a *general* education. In their own words: 'Training in Domestic Arts should supplement and not replace the general subjects of a liberal education as given in public secondary schools for girls.'[59]

Prevailing attitudes within the Board of Education at this period were exemplified in the comment of the Assistant Secretary of the Secondary branch, J. W. Mackail. He wrote to the Chief Woman Inspector, Maude Lawrence, that the 'heart of the matter' was 'the necessity of a girl's education being such as will help her to fit herself for the common duties of life such as all women have to a greater or lesser degree to undertake.'[60] This view was officially endorsed by the issue in 1911 of an *Interim Memorandum on the Teaching of Housecraft in Girls' Secondary Schools*, followed in 1913 by the *Report*

of the Consultative Committee on Practical Work in Secondary Schools
which devoted a good deal of discussion to the desirability and
practice of teaching domestic subjects.[61]

Whether or not the headmistresses approved (and they remained
divided over the issue) domestic subjects had come to stay.
Furthermore the curriculum itself now seemed to be reflecting the
desired characteristics of the feminine woman. The aesthetic and
literary subjects were apparently those best suited to promoting
feminine virtues and were also areas where girls and women had
attained both expertise and efficiency. Domestic science, though an
object of suspicion for many educationists, was nevertheless a
necessary element in a girl's schooling. It was argued that science
and mathematics might well be less appropriate for girls because
they lacked innate capacity for their study; in any case for some girls
they could be sacrificed to domestic training.

The difficulty now facing the girls' secondary schools was two-
fold. Extra subjects meant pressure on the timetable and including
practical subjects meant compromising a liberal curriculum. At the
turn of the century Michael Sadler had described what he called the
'divided aim' of girls' education and spoke of the 'unsettlement of
thought' surrounding it, because preparation for home life was at
odds with preparation for paid employment.[62] By the time of the
1914–18 war the new emphasis which had emerged suggested that
practical training in domesticity should, in principle at least, take
priority over a more general approach. It was a principle which
assumed the necessity for a gender-differentiated curriculum.

The 1920s and 1930s were notable for the arguments over the
practical difficulties which followed from the two-fold dilemma of
timetable pressure and compulsory practical subjects. For the girls'
schools the eventual focus of debate was the School Certificate which
all secondary school pupils were supposed to take at the age of 16.
But before the controversy over School Certificate reached its full
height there was to be an investigation of curricular differentiation
by the Consultative Committee which did much to demonstrate how
confused and contradictory were the ideas of educationists about
girls' schooling in the inter-war years.

The Consultative Committee to the Board of Education was a
body of experts to whom the Board referred educational questions
for investigation. In 1920 the Committee was asked to consider
whether *greater* differentiation was desirable in the secondary
curriculum for boys and girls. It seems more than probable that

having established a degree of gender-differentiated organization, and having stated quite categorically (as they did in 1919) that 'the educational requirements of boys and girls, like their capacities, are not identical' the Board of Education would have welcomed a definitive statement in support of their policy.[63] If so they were destined for disappointment. The Consultative Committee clearly found the evidence they collected both diverse and contradictory and it was this that led them to a series of 'ambiguous and evasive' conclusions.[64]

They focused mainly on the psychological differences between the sexes and whether there were inherent intellectual differences between girls and boys. Educational psychologists could find little evidence for this and psychologists and teachers alike agreed that there were greater variations between individuals than between boys and girls.[65] Nevertheless, teachers in particular were keen on the idea of curricular differentiation because of their feelings that girls and boys were very different in terms of emotion and temperament. Boys were more independent, girls more amenable, boys reasoned and analysed where girls were more intuitive and 'emotional'. Educationally these differences seemed to be reflected in the way boys showed a predilection for natural science and girls for literature and the arts.[66]

Rationalizing the contradictory evidence was difficult. The Committee began by tracing the history of the 'girls' curriculum' and, as I suggested at the beginning of this chapter, concluded that the Victorian pioneers had adopted a model of the male liberal curriculum so that 'if new strength was gained, old and delicate graces were perhaps lost, and the individuality of womanhood was in some respects sacrificed on the austere altar of sex equality.'[67] On the other hand, they found that school mistresses had been more prepared than school masters to experiment, not least because they were 'unfettered by tradition and prejudices'.[68] They felt that since 1902 girls' schools had been developing in many of the right directions yet they still seemed very unclear as to the real extent of curricular differentiation or indeed whether it was desirable at all.

So perhaps in despair the Committee turned to other criteria on which to base their conclusions. They decided that the fundamental question was whether boys and girls have 'a different function to perform at that period [i.e. at secondary school] and later'.[69] They decided the overwhelming weight of evidence was that they did, and that these different functions must dictate children's education. All children, they concluded, were to be prepared in school for two main ends: 'to earn their own living' and 'to be useful citizens'. But girls had an extra function: 'to be makers of homes'.[70] To make matters worse girls were 'liable to seasons of lowered vitality' (they referred of course to menstruation) and had 'a part to play in the home and its duties which can hardly be shirked'.[71] Both of these unavoidably placed an extra strain on girls in schools.

The Committee believed that one of the major influences on the development of girls' schooling over the years had been 'currents of social opinion'.[72] In the early twenties opinion about women's role seemed to flow in two directions. In the throes of the post-war slump women were experiencing the full force of the 'back-to-the-home' movement and all the consequences of the war-time agreements made with trade unions for the restoration of pre-war practices.[73] Yet the Census of 1921 showed that nearly one women in three had to be self-supporting. The huge loss of life in the trenches meant that opportunities for marriage were limited in one entire generation of women so that once again it was being assumed that there was a social problem of 'surplus' women. Simultaneously there was a big demand for domestic servants but women's employment was growing in other sectors too, notably in distributive, service and light industries and in clerical work.[74]

The social function of women was clearly diverse and since paid work and a domestic role were regarded as incompatible the most the Committee would conclude was that there should not be too great a divergence of curriculum for boys and girls and that the primary aim of a good general education should not be sacrificed 'for what are thought to be the special interests of girls'.[75] Yet while they argued that it would be fatal to prescribe separate curricula for boys and girls, they also assumed that these already existed and had very different functions.[76] For they stated quite categorically that there were many girls who 'will proceed to careers which involved economic competition with men, and no hindrance should be placed in the way of their following the boys' curriculum if they so desire.'[77]

The equivocal nature of the Committee's discussion made it possible to interpret the Report as evidence *for* psychological difference and curricular differentiation and in some quarters that was done.[78] It certainly failed to give any realistic guidance as to how girls were to cope with a curriculum which somehow had to prepare them for School Certificate (and paid work), domesticity and to nurture the cultural well-being of the nation. Yet at the same time the Report failed to provide the Board of Education with the definitive statement it needed in justification of curricular differentiation.

For all these reasons the Report set the scene for the battle that had begun to rage over the structure and regulations for the School Certificate which set the Board of Education and women teachers at odds with one another. This too involved the protagonists in equivocation and contradictory strategies.

The School Certificate examination was introduced in 1917 to replace the university 'Local Examinations'. Every university examining board agreed to operate under a single set of regulations. Under these the 16+ examination was divided into four groups. Each group consisted of a number of different subjects and to gain a certificate a candidate had to pass in at least five subjects from groups I (English, scripture, geography and history), II (Latin, Greek and modern languages) and III (mathematics and science). Group IV, which consisted of the practical and aesthetic subjects, could not count towards a certificate and it was this which caused all the controversy.

The principle at stake was the academic status of group IV subjects, and it is significant that these comprised music and art, which were areas of strength for girls' schools, and domestic subjects, the compulsory practical element for girls. Thus on two counts the women teachers had cause for wanting a change in the regulations. All the more so because everyone seemed agreed that it was necessary to emphasize the 'educative' dimension of all practical subjects. They had to be seen to have an intellectual as well as a utilitarian function.[79]

The AHM (joined by the Association of Assistant Mistresses) took up the cudgels in 1918 with a call for group IV 'parity'. The request was consistently refused until 1929 when it was decided that two group IV subjects could be the equivalent of one subject in any other group in accumulating the total needed for School Certificate.[80] Even the fundamental modification of the group system which came in 1938 did not give either aesthetic or practical subjects parity with the others so that the women teachers never won their fight.[81]

Although other bodies, including men teachers and local education authorities, also called for modifications in the group regulations the women teachers regarded it very much as *their* fight because of the particular effect the ruling had on girls, and this feeling was shared by the Board of Education.[82] However, the women teachers consistently refused to entertain the idea that the regulations could be modified for girls only.[83] For these women the dispute struck at the heart of the dilemma over the girls' curriculum, that of accommodating the apparently incompatible aims of preparing for work either at home or in office, factory or shop.

The modern history of girls' secondary education began with a conviction that women had a special role to play in the world. Frances Buss, Dorothea Beale and their colleagues believed that they could give girls a liberal education which would fit them for their life at home or at work, without compromising their femininity. They could do this because for them femininity had both an intellectual and a social dimension. The combination of a liberal education and the messages learnt in the corporate life of the school would ensure the fulfilled womanly woman in whatever sphere.

The rewriting of femininity as domesticity and the sacrifice of the principle of a general education upon the altar of practical training for life at home heralded considerable changes in the girls' curriculum. No longer a 'dual' but a 'divided' aim underpinned girls' schooling and the two aims were perceived as incompatible. The divided aim entailed a gender-differentiated curriculum and although many women teachers did not object to this in principle, in practice it brought about inescapable difficulties.

Not surprisingly the response of headmistresses and their assistants to these problems was not straightforward. They tried to contain the impact of domestic subjects (and indeed other practical subjects, as well as music and art) on the timetable and at the same time sought to raise the academic status of them all through the strategy of parity in the School Certificate group system. In contrast the Board of Education insisted on the compulsory inclusion of these subjects in the curriculum for girls, yet cast doubt on their academic status which was further emphasized by their refusal to permit parity for group IV. But if the women teachers argued an equal academic status for these subjects then it would seem contradictory to object to their presence in the timetable, while if the Board insisted on their inclusion in the timetable it seemed contradictory to refuse them academic parity.

The Board's attitude seemed to reflect, very closely, the widely held opinion that marriage and motherhood were incompatible with paid work, as well as the universal practice of valuing women's paid work lower than men's. Domestic duties, of course, were considered to bear no economic value at all. Educationally the result was an impasse which was never resolved and which left the post-1944 tripartite system with a legacy of gender-differentiated schooling and a curriculum sharply divided into 'feminine' and 'masculine' spheres of expertise.

Acknowledgements

My thanks to Charles Hunt, Sheila Fletcher, Cathy Michell, Peter Searby, Deborah Thom and Perry Williams for their helpful comments on an earlier version of this paper which was presented at the Annual Meeting of the American History of Education Society, Atlanta 1985. I am grateful to the British Council for a grant which enabled me to attend this meeting. Many thanks to Penny Summerfield for reading and commenting on this chapter.

Bibliographical Note

There are a small number of studies which consider various aspects of the relationship between ideology and girls' schooling in the nineteenth and early twentieth centuries, notably Carol Dyhouse, *Girls Growing Up in Late Victorian and Edwardian England* (Routledge & Kegan Paul, 1981) and Sara Delamont and Lorna Duffin (eds) *The Nineteenth Century Woman: Her Cultural and Physical World* (Croom Helm, 1978). Published material on later decades is minimal though Carol Dyhouse has an overview in 'Towards a "feminine" curriculum for English schoolgirls: the demands of ideology 1870–1963', *Women's Studies International Quarterly*, 1 (1978). Unpublished sources include Felicity Hunt, 'Secondary education for the middle class girl: a study of ideology and educational practice 1870–1940', PhD thesis (University of Cambridge, 1984) and Sarah King, ' "Our strongest weapon": an examination of the attitude of the NUWT towards the education of girls, 1918–1939', MA thesis (University of Sussex, 1986).

2

Miss Buss and Miss Beale: Gender and Authority in the History of Education

Carol Dyhouse

> Co-education is no panacea for the ills of education. It will produce no utopia in school or society . . . It will help a young man to mix easily with women when he enters the world, but it will not guarantee him a happy marriage. It will help a young woman to understand men, but she may still try to drive instead of using her art of persuasion.[1]

> Each sex has something to contribute to the world and to the life of a school, and their different contributions stem from different qualities. It is not impossible that authority rests more lightly on the shoulders of a man than on the tongue of a woman, and maybe the role of a woman is that of influence and persuasion, which can be more lasting.[2]

Although the sentiments expressed here are reminiscent of those of Ruskin the remarks are taken from R. R. Dale's three-volume study of 1969–74, entitled *Mixed or Single-Sex School*? This study has (hardly surprisingly) received short shrift from feminists in recent years, many of whom have begun to look with new favour upon the idea of single-sex schooling.[3] Co-education, they argue, can be seen to disadvantage girls and the promotion prospects of women teachers. Earlier in the present century the existence of separate schools for girls at the secondary level guaranteed the preservation of a career structure for women teachers; whereas headships and senior posts in the newer co-educational comprehensive schools go overwhelmingly to men.

I shall return to the debate over co-education and single-sex schooling at the end of this chapter, but here I am concerned with the subject of gender and authority in the history of women's education and I began by quoting from Dale's work – which sets out, of course, to be a work of 'objective' social science – in order to show how deep-seated notions of the incompatibility between 'femininity' and authority or leadership still are. Even today, women who do achieve authority or act authoritatively are not unlikely to be the subject of ridicule. Popular expressions ('you can tell she wears the trousers') illustrate a widespread conviction that authoritative women somehow unsex themselves.

If there are difficulties for women in authority today, the difficulties which faced women in positions of authority in the nineteenth century were immeasurably greater, and some understanding of the conflicts faced by women in authority seems to me to be absolutely necessary to an understanding of the social history of women's education since Victorian times. Furthermore, since education was (and is) one of the few areas of public life where women *have* achieved a measure of status and authority, the history of education is a good area in which to explore the social history of sexual politics, and that of sex and gender generally.

In my view there are at least three levels at which, or areas in which, the historian of women's education needs to be particularly sensitive to an understanding of the conflicts between gender prescriptions and authority. These are, first: *the level of women's self-image and behaviour*. The kinds of issues relevant here include the ways in which individual women saw themselves, and how they reconciled their ambitions – personal or social, or their reforming zeal – with their sense of what was fitting, or socially acceptable. Secondly, *the level of public image and public behaviour*. How and why did some women succeed in establishing themselves as authority figures, and what were the problems they encountered in doing so? Related to this is the question of how they were perceived by their contemporaries. Thirdly, there is *the image presented by biographers and in subsequent historiography*. The fact that there is a continuing conflict between dominant social definitions of femininity and authority means that the presentation of strong or authoritative women is particularly likely to be coloured by the value stance of the biographer or historian. Sympathetic biographers are not unlikely to 'play up' the qualities in their subjects which they know will recommend them to readers and to *understate* qualities they feel more dubious about.

That this can produce extraordinary distortions can be seen from a brief consideration of the case of Florence Nightingale. The image of the gentle girl, the tender nurse, the lady-with-the-lamp stooping gracefully to cool the brow of a dying soldier conveys nothing of Florence Nightingale's 'real' personality. The 'legend', born in her lifetime, speaks volumes about contemporary gender definitions and prescriptions about feminine roles. And yet arguably the qualities that made Florence Nightingale outstanding were, during girlhood, her bitter frustrations and restlessness with the feminine role (expressed in *Cassandra*), and later, her extraordinary strength, her dominance, ambitiousness and dogged determination. Finding an appropriate language to describe these qualities can cause difficulties.[4]

Indeed, I have twice rewritten this paragraph, because in seeking for words to describe the 'gutsyness' of Florence Nightingale I first wrote of her 'particularly *unfeminine* stamp of dominance, of sheer will', and so on. Then I paused and put inverted commas around 'unfeminine', to try to indicate that it was only popular sentiment or prevailing social definitions that would hold dominance of will to be unfeminine or wrong in females; it was not my *own* prescription. Finally, I jettisoned the reference to 'unfemininity' altogether. But this is, of course, an evasion in a society which has for the last couple of centuries at least, consistently polarized human personality traits into the categories of gender.

And this, of course, is precisely the point. The existence of the twin polarities 'masculine' and 'feminine' means that if not the one, then the other. Or if in between, then nearer the one than the other. So if women were strong, dominant, ambitious or determined then they were likely to be categorized as *un*feminine, and therefore masculine women. There was no easy escape, nor is there one today.

The implications of this can be shown by turning to some of the strong, authoritative women in nineteenth-century educational history. Even today we can find historians and popular writers eager to caricature such women as masculine. Jonathan Gathorne-Hardy, for instance, describes M. A. Douglas, headmistress of the Godolphin School at the turn of the present century in his book *The Public School Phenomenon*.[5] He criticizes her for organizing the school in the image of contemporary boys' schools, insinuating that she went through something approaching a personal sex-change in the process:

> And Mary Alice Douglas, the 'great' headmistress who oversaw these changes, has changed in tune with them. In 1890, it is certainly a strong face, but it is a feminine one, she has long hair, pulled back and piled up, a long skirt, fine bosom and a slender waist. In 1919 she is wearing collar and tie, a pin-stripe coat, a waistcoat, a skirt (or are

they trousers? It is impossible to see); she has the short-cut hair, greying at the temples, and the level gaze of a successful headmaster.[6]

It is difficult to know quite how to interpret this kind of remark. Can one instantly dismiss it as crude sexism? It would be impossible to imagine a headmaster being described as a woman in this way without the writer trespassing beyond the bounds of good taste. One has to ask oneself what kinds of models there were for women in authority that did *not* carry masculine overtones. I shall return to this theme shortly.

The mention of the names of Frances Buss and Dorothea Beale is enough to start everyone's heads buzzing with the little rhyme:

> Miss Buss and Miss Beale
> Cupid's darts do not feel
> How different from us
> Miss Beale and Miss Buss

Which is in itself a fair illustration of what I am saying although it goes deeper. The rhyme does not stop short of implying a lack of *femininity* or gender attributes. It goes further and questions the *sexuality* of the women by highlighting the fact that both Frances Buss and Dorothea Beale remained celibate. Sympathetic feminist historians of recent years (such as Josephine Kamm, Sara Delamont, and myself) have all taken pains to point out that both Miss Buss and Miss Beale received and rejected several offers of marriage. The point is a significant one because it shows how even twentieth-century feminist historians feel a need to defend the women against the latent and enduring accusation that their careers were only made possible by their lack of sexuality. The urge to point out that they rejected suitors is similar to the urge which provoked Emily Davies to plant the prettiest students in the front row when they sat the Cambridge local examinations in the 1870s, in order to forestall public opinion gleefully caricaturing them as freaks. The defence goes further than this. Kamm has pointed out that Dorothea Beale's strong – indeed exaggerated – sense of social propriety would never have allowed her to combine marriage with her work in education. Indeed, the social pressures against married women continuing with any kind of profesional career in the late nineteenth century were so enormous that one has to see the celibate life styles of many women in senior educational positions right down until recent times as as likely to have been dictated by conscious choice as by circumstance. There is still a strong public prejudice, however, which prefers to stigmatize spinsters as 'left on the shelf' rather than to see them as women who, faced with the unenviable *choice* between sexual liaison and professional status eschewed the dependence of the wife for what they perceived as the dignity and independence of the professional worker.[7]

It is interesting to look briefly at Frances Buss's and Dorothea Beale's own responses to the little ditty, composed during their own lifetimes, about Cupid's darts. Miss Buss is alleged to have been delighted by it, whereas Miss Beale was not amused. Josephine Kamm relates how Miss Beale was lunching at Government House in Guernsey when the Governor, in the course of the meal, 'waving a finger archly at his guest, said: "I've just been reading about you, Miss Beale",' and then proceeded to recite the rhyme. ' "Nothing whatever to do with me",' Dorothea is supposed to have snapped, ' "nothing whatever to do with me".'[8] These contrasting reactions are quite in keeping with the other evidence one can amass about the two head teachers, their self images and their public behaviour. I shall develop these themes in the next section, but first, a word or two about the social background to the public careers of these two women and their contemporaries.

Feminist historians have recently paid a good deal of attention to the ways in which nineteenth-century industrialism intensified the sexual division of labour in British society. Middle-class Victorian males worked *outside* the home to earn the wage that would support the household. Their wives stayed *in* the home and were economically dependent on their husbands. This pattern implied very marked divisions and separation between the *private*, domestic world of family life and the *public* world of 'work', business and the professions. Men belonged in the latter sphere, women in the former, and all kinds of social barriers helped to maintain the boundaries between the two worlds.[9]

Barriers which served to hedge women into the home were particularly effective in two areas, where a number of taboos operated: first, in the area of finance, and secondly in the area of what may be defined as public exposure generally. Women – or more accurately, 'ladies' – were supposed to be 'protected' from dealings with money or indeed from the very *possession* of it until the Married Women's Property Acts of 1870 and 1882.[10] Ladies were supposed to be ignorant of financial matters; a state of affairs which was easily enough achieved while they were denied opportunities of handling money. For a middle-class lady to *earn* money was felt to be contaminating: it unsexed her, or even more significantly, her provider. An excellent and well-known illustration of this attitude is found in the letter to Sophia Jex-Blake written by her father, in which he expressed horror at the thought of his daughter receiving a salary for teaching at Queen's College, London. It was not the work itself he found distasteful, but the notion of her receiving any emolument.[11]

Ladies were 'protected' from finance: they were also shielded (if they did not themselves retreat) from appearing too much in public. Sitting on public platforms was a little unseemly; speaking in public even more so. It is worth remembering how so many of the female writers of papers and articles on learned subjects in the early and even in the middle part of the nineteenth century had to sit in the audience on public occasions while sympathetic men read their papers for them. Emily Davies' famous lectures on women's education were always read out by a man. Sitting on committees or the governing bodies of institutions alongside men was felt in many quarters to be quite unacceptable.

Joyce Senders Pedersen has argued that one of the most important aspects of change in late nineteenth-century girls' schooling was the decline of the small, private, family-like school for young ladies (usually accommodated in the residential household of the Lady Proprietress), and the rise of the large public school for girls.[12] She emphasizes that this involved a radical redefinition of the school-mistress's role.[13] The untrained but genteel Lady Proprietress typical of the ubiquitous small seminary earlier in the century had little or no real authority. The Schools' Inquiry Commissioners of 1864–7 had observed that: 'the first noticeable fact in ladies' boarding schools is the subjection of the teacher's will in every instance to the wishes of the parents, in many instances to the whims of the pupils.'[14]

In contrast to this the headmistresses of the new, larger girls' High Schools and endowed schools of the last quarter of the nineteenth century enjoyed a greatly enhanced social status. They were often professionally-minded, publicly-accountable figures with consider-able authority in the community.

In order to achieve greater authority and a rise in status individual women teachers had to negotiate their way through the constraints of gender and the jungle of barriers and taboos 'protecting' women from the 'vulgarities' of money and public exposure which have been outlined. It is interesting to investigate the ways in which Miss Buss and Miss Beale did this and to attempt to measure their success.

It is not at all easy to explore beyond the rather superficial images offered by early biographers – Elizabeth Raikes in the case of Miss

Beale, Annie Ridley in that of Miss Buss – to try to work out what these two women were like when they were young.[15] However, from a reading of these texts, in conjunction with the study of the two women published in 1958 by Josephine Kamm one can piece together impressions.[16]

Dorothea Beale seems always to have been rather aloof and sober-minded, with a strong sense of her own dignity. She played on these qualities, which in turn played an important part in building up the tremendous authority and presence she manifested later in life. Miss Beale was profoundly religious, in the High Anglican mould, and was inspired by a sense of mission. She saw teaching as her 'calling', being moved by something very close to the conventual impulse, and dreamed of founding a teaching order. Her favourite saint was Saint Hilda of Whitby, with whom she felt a special affinity and after whom she named a number of her educational ventures.[17] Dorothea Beale capitalized on her religiosity and certainly on her aloofness, dignity, distance – her remoteness from the banality of everyday life – in establishing her authority. She rarely compromised her dignity in dealing with everyday problems; tending to give the impression rather of transcending them in a way which lost her no advantages.

Frances Mary Buss had an altogether different personality, and experienced many more difficulties in building up her authority. There was nothing lofty or aloof about her: she was affectionate, demonstrative and impulsive, with a strong sense of fun. There were always, particularly in the early years, times at which she found it difficult to get people to take her seriously. Precisely because she was more conventionally 'feminine' in some of her external attributes than Miss Beale, men tended to patronize her. There was the famous occasion, for instance, of the Schools' Inquiry Commission of 1864–7 when along with her friend Emily Davies, Miss Buss was summoned to give evidence on the state of girls' education. Both women were nervous, neither being used to speaking in public, and it was, after all, one of the first occasions that women had been heard before a Royal Commisssion. Emily Davies, however, had a much tougher exterior than Frances Buss, who was absolutely petrified. She was almost too agitated to speak and Emily Davies, who had given her evidence and was 'being regaled with claret and biscuits' in the Secretary's room, had to be fetched back in hurriedly to prop her up. This exhibition of feminine frailty was supposed to have gone straight to the Commissioners' hearts. ' "Why, there were tears in Miss Buss's eyes!" ' Mr Fearon, one of the Assistant Commissioners, is supposed to have mused, several years later.[18]

It is almost impossible to imagine Miss Beale – certainly in later life – being patronized. Kamm describes how she would transport herself around Cheltenham, a stately figure, on a tricycle. When she came to an incline she would get one of her girls to push her; if none were available, she had no hesitation in hailing a passer-by. She records that a former preparatory schoolboy remembered all his life how impressed he had been on one occasion, 'when his own headmaster was suddenly summoned up from the pavement with a call of "young man! young man! Push me up this hill!" '[19]

Probably the image most of us have of Miss Buss is that of her when old, a short, dumpy figure dressed in black with grey hair and a white cap, not unlike the aged Queen Victoria. Contemporaries remarked that she aged prematurely; the anxieties and strains of her hectic career weighed heavily on her well-being. Yet it is useful to recall the snapshot image recorded by one of her original pupils, who remembered her as 'an elegant, dark young lady with curls and a low-necked dress, and whose energy seemed to sweep me up like a strong wind.'[20]

Frances Buss had few if any 'role models' on which to pattern her behaviour, in almost every aspect of her extraordinary energetic and productive career she was breaking new ground. She had what Kamm describes as a 'simple, unquestioning' religious faith quite unlike the highly intellectual High Church intensity of Miss Beale. She did not herself conduct religious observances in her school. Where Dorothea Beale regarded herself as carrying out a work of divine inspiration, Frances Mary Buss's sense of mission was profoundly secular; she was firmly committed to work towards bettering the social and occupational chances of middle-class girls here on earth. Miss Buss was a woman with a fertile imagination, immense determination and remarkable practical abilities. In effect she possessed the qualities of a first-rate entrepreneur, although these entrepreneurial qualities are *not* those which her friend and 'official' biographer Annie Ridley chose to emphasize. Ridley labours to present Frances Buss as a 'motherly' figure: large-hearted, loving and loved. Although 'the world knew Miss Buss as a capable, energetic and successful public worker', she wrote in her preface to the biography: 'By her friends she was loved as one of the most womanly of women – true, tender and loyal.'[21]

Of course the maternal role was (and still is) the most publicly acceptable kind of role for women in authority. And yet it is a very limited one. 'Motherliness' as defined by our culture, is not about cool professional judgement or detachment. And more critically,

Frances Mary Buss, aged 33.

Dorothea Beale as a young woman.

mothers are supposed to be dependent on, or subject to, fathers. Miss Beale's projection of self as a sort of lofty Mother Superior did at least enable her to remove herself from the judgement of early patriarchs: she was answerable direct, as it were, only to the Heavenly Father. Miss Buss, however more she may have grappled with the real world, had a far harder time of it.

The contrast becomes clear when we compare the ways in which the two women negotiated their way through the male preserves of finance and committee management. Miss Beale avoided (perhaps one should say evaded or even transcended?) problems of finance to a large extent by ensconcing herself in a highly privileged institution. She herself was from a secure background; she knew nothing of personal financial anxiety. Her tastes were frugal and she devoted large personal sums of money to the College and towards helping needy students. But Cheltenham was a highly select institution from the beginning – the credentials of prospective parents were carefully scrutinized and the Council determinedly rejected the 'daughters of trade'. The enormous increase in prestige which the College achieved during Miss Beale's headship rendered it even more privileged and secure. Miss Beale did not need to sully herself with the dubious business of financial appeals and her social propriety remained untarnished.[22] Interestingly, she left an enormous legacy to the College when she died, which showed that throughout her life she had invested her money shrewdly. Josephine Kamm, musing over whether this represented Miss Beale's own business acumen or the fruit of good advice, remarked that in either case, 'the excellence of her financial arrangements show how far-reaching in practical matters the mystic can be'.[23] But Dorothea Beale knew how to present herself publicly. (It is difficult to imagine St Hilda of Whitby with a reputation for financial wizardry.)

In marked contrast to Miss Beale, Frances Buss constantly muddied her boots, her hands and her reputation with sordid public appeals. She knew all about penny pinching and the struggle to make ends meet: her background had not been so secure as Dorothea Beale's and her father's income had never sufficed to provide for the family. This is what had initially prompted both her and her mother to move into teaching. Frances Buss was, as I have mentioned, a good entrepreneur. The North London Collegiate School which she founded was a highly successful commercial enterprise and until 1872 her own property. By that time – at the age of 45 – her mother had died and her father had been wholly dependent on her for some years and yet as Kamm points out, 'despite her status as the head and owner of a prosperous school, she remained a dutiful Victorian daughter. She mothered her father; but she had never opened a banking account.'[24] But Miss Buss's restless ambitions and her zeal to do something about the education of girls not only of the relatively prosperous, but of the *lower* middle classes would never allow her to rest or to retreat into privilege as did Dorothea Beale. She went on to open a second school; the Camden School, which she determined would charge much lower fees than the North London to enable it to admit girls from lower down the social scale. She and a small group of friends begged and cajoled potential sympathizers for financial support swallowing all their pride and suffering agonies of humiliation in the process. This was decidedly *not* ladylike behaviour and the antagonism, contempt and scorn that the public fund-raising brought was immense. Neither was this compensated for by any spectacular successes: the campaign bore very modest fruit.[25]

When we examine the question of school government, it is important to remember that the whole idea of women being included on governing bodies was, in the middle of the nineteenth century, a highly radical one. Emily Davies, giving evidence before the Schools' Inquiry Commission in 1864–7 told the Commissioners that in her opinion: 'Where a school is for girls there ought to be some ladies on the governing board. In endowed schools generally the trustees or governors are all gentlemen, and the schools are apt to get neglected from their having so many other things to do. They do not give so much attention, I think, as ladies might.'[26]

The Commissioners evidently had doubts about this. Mr Acland asked Miss Davies whether a Ladies' Committee with advisory functions might not be more fitting? This was a much more common practice at the time – ladies would not therefore have to speak before, or even fight with, men on public committees. However, Emily Davies knew her ground. No, she insisted: where the school was one for girls, women must share in the government direct.

Both Miss Buss and Miss Beale had problems in defining and securing their authority *vis-à-vis* the governors of their school which they had to fight out in the arena of male-dominated committee meetings. Again, the difference in their *styles* of authority become apparent. Miss Beale had something of a tempestuous career before going to Cheltenham. She had *resigned* from an early appointment, teaching mathematics and Latin in Queen's College, Harley Street, during the 1850s, because she resented the fact that the government of the college was entirely in the hands of men. The women tutors, she complained, were given no real responsibility, and she believed that only ladies could truly understand and educate young girls.[27] However, Dorothea Beale's next career move brought her even more problems. She went as head teacher to the Clergy Daughters' School at Casterton – immortalized by Charlotte Brontë as 'Lowood' in *Jane Eyre*. Here, she found herself appalled by the low standards of religion, pedagogy and community life. She set to work at reform but found her zeal and intensity resented by the committee of six clergymen who were her governing body. Conflicts multiplied and in 1857 she was unceremoniously *sacked* by the committee.

No doubt these experiences fuelled her determination to have things her own way at Cheltenham. Finding herself thwarted by the attitudes and prejudices of the local gentlemen on the Council of the Ladies' College, Miss Beale decided that it would not do for her to be answerable to such a parochial body. She considered that it would be much more fitting to secure the representation of distinguished educationalists and public servants on her governing body. Dorothea Beale handled matters with skill, consummate tact, and relentless determination. She conceded unimportant points, manoeuvred herself into unassailable positions, and homed steadily in on her goals. In 1875 the Council was reorganized and enlarged, and the respective power of proprietors, Council and Lady Principal were redefined exactly in accordance with the wishes of the latter.[28]

Things did not proceed so smoothly for Miss Buss. It is important to stress that the North London Collegiate was entirely her own property up until 1870, so that the question of her power was scarcely in dispute. It was her own decision to relinquish personal control and to hand over the school to the public. She felt this to be the most socially responsible way to proceed. The property then became vested in trustees and a governing body. As Kamm has commented:

> The gesture was a most generous one. The school was flourishing, and Miss Buss was giving up the profits – present and future – for a fixed salary, of which for several years she drew only a proportion. More than this, she was giving up her personal freedom of action. It is true that, unlike other headmistresses, she was a school governor, but she was responsible to her Board. To a woman who had been independent for so long this was a painful sacrifice: it was one to which she was never entirely reconciled.[29]

It is by no means easy to chart the exact course of the conflicts between Miss Buss and her governors (she had a particularly difficult relationship with Dr Storrar). Annie Ridley tactfully played down the whole series of incidents in order not to arouse ill feeling. She suggested that Storrar (although she did not mention him by name) was insensitive to the history of the school and to the fact that both the North London and Camden foundations owed so much to the private generosity and donations of Miss Buss and her personal friends. At the same time she conceded that Miss Buss, like many women of the time, was unfamiliar with the procedures of committees. Ridley's account is worth retailing in full because it is telling. Storrar, she claimed:

> had been used to long-established foundations, where everything went by rule, and to committees where the word of the chairman was law. Miss Buss was used to supreme power over her own school, and she was, like most women of that day, unused to business routine. This was, moreover, one of the very first governing bodies on which women were elected on equal terms with men. Such an arrangement was too new as yet to go without hitch. It would follow, quite naturally, that men, out of mere force of habit, as well as in real kindness of heart, should adopt a paternal and authoritative attitude towards all women, even to those most competent to stand alone.
>
> Miss Buss was by nature one of the least self-assertive of women. She had always been helped by some strong man, and had accepted all help with gratitude. First Mr. Laing, and then Dr. Hodgson (with her father and brothers, as a matter of course), had been recognised as friends and helpers.
>
> But, at the same time, one of the most definite aims of her life had been to raise the status of headmistress to the same level as that of headmaster. For the sake of all teachers – not for her own sake – she deprecated the secondary place given to women who were doing the same work as men. She also thought that the internal management of her school should be left to her, as it would have been to a headmaster in her place, and for this she stood firm, even when, as a matter of mere feeling, she might have given way, for she was really one of the old-fashioned women who would personally endure anything for the sake of peace.
>
> It is more probable that she felt some things too strongly, and that she misunderstood others. In those days most women suffered quite needlessly from sheer ignorance of business routine. They lacked the training and discipline which carry men unscathed through the roughness of public life. Two men meeting on a committee may oppose each other tooth and nail, but these men may afterwards go home and dine comfortably together bearing no traces of the fray. At that date, two women, after a similar encounter, would have gone their separate ways, to weep over a solitary cup of tea, and when they next met would pass each other with the cut direct.[30]

A careful reading of this passage illustrates nearly every point I have tried to make in this paper: Ridley's presentation of Miss Buss as womanly, ('one of the least self-assertive of women'), when her own picture everywhere contradicts this; the tendency of men to patronize women on committees; women leaders resenting the fact that they are treated differently from men in comparable positions, being frustrated and torn apart by their own ambitions and by their internalized sense of the 'feminine'; men rubbing salt into women's wounds by accusing them of 'taking things personally', and so on. Poor Miss Buss. In vain did Emily Davies, Annie Ridley and Dorothea Beale counsel her to keep calm, to give way on small points, and to swallow her anger and hide her hurt so that her opponents would not once again insist that women could not be trusted in authority as 'they always took things personally'. Alas, Miss Buss's temperament was as she herself described it 'gun-powdery', and smouldering quietly was not her way.[31]

Nineteenth-century women educationalists therefore had a hard time of it: they were deeply embroiled in sexual politics at two levels. As well as fighting the uphill battle for girls' education they were involved in a very complex task of negotiating gender constraints and social taboos in order to forge new roles for themselves as professional figures and recognized authorities. Perhaps the most publicly acceptable style of authority which women could adopt was a style with strong overtones of 'motherliness'. However, in a strongly patriarchal society such as that of late Victorian Britain this 'maternal' style of authority brought severe limitations. Dorothea Beale transcended these limitations by styling herself as a kind of Mother Superior, answerable only to a Father in Heaven. Frances Buss grappled with his lieutenants here below.

It is worth remembering that the two women played a leading part in founding the Association of Head Mistresses, which met for the first time in Frances Buss's house in 1874. Frances Buss wrote telling Annie Ridley of their intentions. They would 'hold conferences occasionally, in order to know what we ought to assert and what surrender'.[32] The question of the power and the authority of the headmistress in her school was a major concern of the Association throughout its history, and it provided a crucial 'reference group' or forum for headmistresses all over the country who found themselves involved with similar problems and concerns. The Association expanded greatly in the early twentieth century to include the headmistresses of the newer state girls' grammar schools established during the period.[33]

If women teachers experienced problems of status and authority in late-Victorian girls' schools, such problems paled into insignificance besides those faced by their counterparts in the maintained schools catering for both boys and girls in early twentieth-century England. In the 1920s and 1930s, the National Association of Schoolmasters campaigned openly and energetically against what its members deemed to be the 'pernicious effects' of having women in authority in the schools.[34] Boys needed the authority of men, the NAS maintained; women teachers were accused of undermining the manliness of their male charges – even of having a castrating effect on their nascent virility. (One delegate to the NAS conference in 1936 spoke of 'spinster' teachers 'nipping out' the 'budding shoots of young manhood'.)[35] At best it was argued, female authority fostered the 'mother-dependent' type of boy.[36] And members of the NAS were adamant that mixed schools must be headed by a male – no 'real men' would willingly serve under a headmistress.

If styles of authority developed by women teachers tended towards the maternal, a climate such as that of the inter-war period massively exacerbated problems of leadership for women. 'Spinster teachers' were vilified by the NAS as a social perversion, whilst the widespread introduction (by local educational authorities) of the marriage bar during these years ensured that many women who entered matrimony were promptly sacked.[37] Hardly surprisingly, the Association of Head Mistresses consistently voiced a preference for single-sex schools for girls. Women heads were profoundly mistrustful of the suggestion often made by supporters of co-education from 1902 onwards, whereby a mixed school should be headed by a man, with a senior mistress to support him. They were not taken in by this 'happy families' model of school organization, and all too painfully aware of the limitations inherent in the 'motherly' senior mistress role.[38] It was not uncommon to find a senior mistress responsible to the headmaster for just about everything except the supervision of the girls' lavatories. The AHM predicted that women would lose authority in co-educational schools. The numbers of women in senior positions would decline and the great majority of headships would go to men.[39] They would not have rejoiced to find that history has proved them right.

Bibliographical Note

It will be apparent that I have drawn heavily upon the work of Josephine Kamm, whose biography of Miss Buss and Miss Beale *How Different From*

Us, published by the Bodley Head in 1958, is entertaining and illuminating reading. There is still a dearth of published material on the lifestyle and occupational culture of the first generation of women teachers in girls' secondary schools and in higher education. Undoubtedly one of the most important recent accounts is that of Martha Vicinus, whose *Independent Women, Work and Community for Single Women 1850–1920* was published by Virago in 1985, at the time that this chapter was being written. Chapters 4 and 5 of Vicinus' book focus upon women teachers and touch upon many of the themes with which I have been concerned in the foregoing pages. An 'official' history of the Association of Head Mistresses, entitled *Reluctant Revolutionaries: A Century of Headmistresses 1874–1974* was written by Mary Price and Nonita Glenday and published by Pitman in 1974. Other than these texts there are of course numerous biographies and autobiographies of individual women teachers. The quality of these is very variable; by no means all of them touch on more general themes. A useful list of these accounts was compiled by Barbara Barr in 1984 for Librarians of Institute and Schools of Education. This is entitled *Histories of Girls' Schools and Related Biographical Material* and is available from the School of Education Library at the University of Leicester.

3

The Ideology of Femininity and Reading for Girls, 1850–1914

Deborah Gorham

In nineteenth- and early twentieth-century England, the printed word was the chief public medium for the dissemination of ideas about femininity and about what was then defined as appropriate female behaviour. The images of womanhood that characterized Victorian fiction and advice literature played a central role in shaping as well as in responding to women's fantasies, and in reinforcing prescription about femininity. Such images influenced girls as well as adult women. Indeed, girls appear to have been the chief readers of the earliest literature designed specifically for children, and when a specialized genre of girls' literature developed, it found a receptive readership.

This chapter examines the influence of recreational reading designed for girls from the middle of the nineteenth century to the outbreak of the First World War. It traces the origin of a separate literature for girls, examines the intentions of those who produced such a literature, and analyses the messages it conveyed about appropriate female behaviour.

Books and periodicals for children were published from the eighteenth century, although it was only in the Victorian period that a large market was created. The rise of a literature designed specifically for children in the late eighteenth and early nineteenth centuries can be attributed largely to the proselytizing zeal of the evangelical movement. The growth of literacy among the poor was perceived by religious reformers as both a threat and an opportunity. It was felt that if left to their own devices, poor children might be corrupted by penny tracts filled with tales of violence, but that if children could be reached by wholesome literature, not only would they be shielded from the corrupting effects of 'wretched tracts', their minds and their souls would be improved. Sarah Trimmer's intention, when she began publication of *The Family Magazine* in 1788, was to produce 'a repository of religious instruction and rational amusement . . . designed to counteract the pernicious tendency of immoral books . . . which have circulated of late years among the inferior classes of people.'[1] Eleven years later, the Religious Tract Society (RTS) was founded by a group of evangelicals whose main purpose was to counter the effects of 'wretched tracts'. From its foundation, one of the chief endeavours of the RTS was the production of reading material specifically designed for the young.[2]

The 'wretched tracts' that so worried these earnest religious reformers were the publications that became known in the Victorian period as 'penny dreadfuls'. These publications, with their brightly coloured, melodramatic illustrations, were the forerunners of the twentieth-century adventure comic book. They gained a similar popularity with young readers, and were viewed with similar opprobrium by those who concerned themselves with the welfare of the young. Originally designed for a general working-class audience, by the Victorian period 'penny dreadfuls' were read primarily by working-class youths, and with their highwaymen heroes they were thought to contribute to male juvenile delinquency.[3]

In contrast, the little books and periodicals produced by the RTS and similar organizations featured short, didactic tales that emphasized the need for the child's obedience to authority. Tales involving the inspiring death of a pious child were common. While they were written with an audience of working-class children in mind, these tales were often given to middle- and upper-class children as well.

Although worlds apart in most ways, the pious didactic fiction of the early nineteenth century, and the 'penny dreadfuls' did share one common feature: their female characters served to reinforce similar views of appropriate female behaviour. It is evident that one of the purposes of the pious literature was to inculcate ideas about appropriate sex role behaviour. The message about such behaviour conveyed to girl readers of this literature sprang from beliefs about feminine nature and the female role that were to develop increasing strength in the Victorian period, namely the image of femininity as innocent, gentle and self-sacrificing.

Most 'penny dreadfuls' contain few female characters, but the moral lessons that these characters convey about femininity are remarkably similar to those of the pious Sunday School tract: female 'penny dreadful' characters fall into two categories. On the one hand, there are the damsels in distress, pure, innocent models of nineteenth-century femininity who are invariably rescued by brave heroes; on the other hand, there are the girls or women who have been led astray by passion, or by a desire for wealth or power, and who are invariably punished for their unfeminine behaviour.

The pious didactic fiction of the first half of the nineteenth century was designed to be read by both boys and girls; the 'penny dreadfuls' were aimed primarily at boys. It was only in the second half of the nineteenth century that books and periodicals began to be produced that were written deliberately and specifically with a female juvenile audience in mind. In the years 1850–1914, the period with which we are concerned, literature designed for girls went through three overlapping stages of development, the transition from one stage to the next corresponding to changes in the objective situation of girls of all social classes, as well as to developments in the publishing industry itself. The first stage, beginning c. 1850, can conveniently be described as that of literature for the 'daughter at home': the second, beginning c. 1880 that of literature for 'the widening sphere': and the third, which begins at the end of the century, that of 'the school girl'.

Literature for the Daughter at Home

In mid-Victorian England, ideas about femininity and about women's role came to play an essential part in the ideology of an expanding and newly powerful bourgeoisie. Along with a world view that prescribed for its male members the necessity for commitment to hard work, self-reliance and an ability to compete in the marketplace, an imagery surrounding the home arose, in which the home was seen as a refuge and shelter from the harsh world created by urban industrial capitalism. The modern distinction between the public and the private emerged, which was often expressed in the Victorian era as the distinction between two 'separate spheres'. The separate spheres corresponded to separate sets of rules for males and females and distinctive conceptions of masculinity and femininity. The Victorians believed that masculinity demanded the ability to compete in the public sphere, whereas femininity demanded qualities appropriate to the private sphere of the home. Historians have referred to this glorification of the home as the cult of

THE STUDENT.

Illustration taken from *The Quiver*, May–Oct. 1911.

domesticity, and have pointed out that at its centre is an image of woman as 'angel in the house', exhibiting a femininity characterized by innocence, purity and gentleness, capable of continual self-sacrifice, and committed to the spiritual as well as the physical care of the home.

This imagery both involved and affected girls as well as adult women, and a literary image of the 'angel in the house' in which the redeeming female figure is a child began to emerge in early Victorian literature. As is often true of images conveyed through childhood, this image appeared in an exaggerated form: female children in Victorian fiction tend to be even more pure, innocent, gentle and self-sacrificing than adult women. Thus, as fiction written mainly with girls in mind began to be produced, it frequently exhibited an even greater preoccupation with the home, and with a femininity associated with the cult of domesticity than did fiction designed for adults.[4] The home setting, indeed, is one feature that characterized mid-Victorian girls' fiction and set it apart from boys' fiction, which, in contrast, was characterized by action and adventure.

Among the large number of writers, most of them female, who produced such fiction in the middle decades of the nineteenth century, few are remembered and still fewer are read today.[5] At the time, one of the most successful and widely read was Charlotte Yonge, a prolific writer of tales that appeared both as full-length novels, and as stories in girls' periodicals. Charlotte Yonge's stories often revolve around family life. For example, in *The Daisy Chain*, one of her most popular stories, the reader is introduced to the Mays, a family of 11 children, the eldest a girl of 18, the youngest a six-week old baby.[6] It is a solid upper middle-class family, affluent although not ostentatiously wealthy. As the story opens, the reader learns that the centre of the family's life is the mother, who keeps the noisy, good-natured happy family in order with her 'watchful, protecting, guarding mother's love, a shadow of Providence . . . round them so constantly on every side.'[7]

But Mrs May is soon removed from the scene, when she, her eldest daughter Margaret and her husband are involved in a carriage accident. Mrs May is killed, and Margaret is badly hurt, sustaining injuries that will later cause her premature death. The remainder of the novel is concerned with chronicling the difficulties that this motherless family encounters as its members attempt to survive without the maternal guiding hand. One of Yonge's chief purposes is to underline the fact that the Mays' spiritual and moral survival will come not from the father or the sons, but from the daughters.

At first, the task of 'anxious headship of the motherless household' is taken over by Margaret,[8] but when she dies at 25, it is her younger sister Ethel who learns to take her place. Ethel, who at the opening of the novel had been a little girl whose petticoats were always bedraggled and who was more interested in studying the classics from her brother's textbooks than in learning such feminine skills as sewing, becomes the 'pearl of their home' replacing Margaret as substitute mother.[9]

A Victorian reader of *The Daisy Chain* would have learned several lessons about the ideal pattern of a girl's life, and about what she ought and ought not to expect from life. First, even in the early pages of the novel, before the tragedy has occurred, we learn through the author's use of characterization and of incident, that male and female patterns of life diverge. Brothers and sisters can and should be close friends, but the closeness must be based on a recognition of the differences between them, differences in nature, but more important, differences in roles and in duties. It is emblematic of the differences in roles that the brothers in *A Daisy Chain* go to school, while the girls are educated at home.

Readers of Charlotte Yonge's work would also have been exposed to the author's deep commitment to a morality rooted in religious belief. Charlotte Yonge's writings were less didactic in tone than were early nineteenth-century children's tales; she was a favourite with many young readers for several decades because her characters were not lifeless paragons, but believable people with flaws, foibles and peculiarities. None the less, Yonge was a devout member of the Church of England, and the moral lessons at the core of her writings were firmly based in religious belief. The fate of Ethel May in *The Daisy Chain* is meant to illustrate the author's conviction that to be truly moral we must put our trust in God's love, rather than in any human love, and that earthly love demands more forebearance from women than from men. A truly good girl or woman, we learn, must do her duty in life, but must not expect much in return. A spirit of feminine self-sacrifice is especially necessary if a girl is called upon to minister to others as an unmarried daughter – as was Ethel May, who by the novel's closing pages has learned that ' "duty brings peace" ': 'Home! but her eyes had been opened to see that earthly homes may not endure . . . She had begun to understand that the unmarried woman must not seek undivided return of affection . . . but must be ready to cease in turn to be first with any.'[10] Ethel, whom we first meet as an enthusiastic, eager little girl with a serious and determined interest in scholarship, is transformed into her

family's self-sacrificing 'angel in the house': Ethel's consolation for
the loneliness that her lot in life would bring with it, the author tells
us, is faith in God.

In 1856, when *The Daisy Chain* was first published, its ideas about
feminine girlhood and young womanhood reflected a pattern
assumed to be appropriate for upper- and middle-class girls. Girl
children were to be provided with a sheltered childhood, whose main
purpose would be preparation for the femininity associated with the
cult of domesticity. In contrast to her brothers, a girl was not to be
educated in order to prepare her for achievement or for gainful
employment. Instead, a girl's education was designed to prepare her
to develop the appropriate refinement and the inner strength that
would allow her to serve as manager and as moral guardian of her
future home. Because of this emphasis both on domesticity and on
the need to preserve daughters from the contamination associated
with the public sphere, education at home was seen as preferable to
formal schooling outside the home in the early and mid-Victorian
decades, and in fact during these years middle- and upper-class girls
were educated primarily at home. The usual pattern assumed that
girlhood would end with marriage, which was seen as the best, if not
the only fully acceptable role for adult women. If a girl remained
unmarried, it was assumed that her adult role would, in any case, be
performed in a domestic setting – perhaps as caretaker for ageing
parents, or as a devoted maiden aunt in the household of a brother or
sister.

Mid-Victorian domestic literature directed primarily at a young
female audience was written with a middle- and upper-class audience
in mind, and we can assume that the readers of the stories of
Elizabeth Wetherell, Charlotte Yonge, E. M. Sewell and others who
wrote in this style were usually middle class. What of girls of the
working classes? Although the Victorian notion of femininity did
transcend the boundaries of social class, it was clear even at the time
that only a modified form of the feminine ideal could be applied to
girls and women of the working class. Even the most conservative of
mid-Victorian commentators on the subject realized that a sheltered
life was not possible for the working-class girl: she would have to
earn a wage. In spite of this fact – a fact that mid-Victorian
commentators saw as unfortunate – it was still believed that a
modified form of the feminine ideal could be inculcated in working-
class girls, and that a modified form of the ideal pattern of
domesticity could be designed for them.

These ideas about working-class girls and femininity are reflected in the discourse and activities of reformers concerned with the welfare of working-class girls, and in the early and mid-Victorian literature that was specifically directed at working-class children, namely the pious periodicals and Sunday School tracts discussed earlier. Taken together they reflect a desire on the part of reformers to inculcate in working-class girls a twofold sense of subservience, one based on social inferiority as well as on the inferiority of gender. It was assumed that working-class girls needed only a minimal amount of formal education, and that the best sort of employment they could adopt would place them securely in a domestic setting.

Such a pattern did, in fact, correspond to the reality that many mid-Victorian working-class girls experienced. The education available to the majority of them was limited, and the most common occupation such girls assumed between childhood and marriage was domestic service. We know little about what working-class girls actually read in the mid-Victorian decades, but any Sunday School tract – assuming that real children actually read these dreary productions – would have reinforced the idea that both her sex and her class demanded docility, gentleness and obedience to authority; the middle-class domestic fiction, if it came the way of a working-class reader, would have presented the same message; and finally, female working-class readers would have received similar messages about femininity even from the 'penny dreadfuls' directed at working-class youths.

The Widening Sphere

By the final third of the nineteenth century, the dominance of the mid-Victorian conception of feminine girlhood no longer went unquestioned. It was challenged first of all by the earliest activists who created the middle-class women's movement. The central argument that these moderate reformers advanced for loosening the bonds of the constricting feminine role was that it was not only restrictive, but that it was in conflict with the reality faced by many middle-class girls and women, since a life of sheltered domesticity was not possible for all middle-class women. Gainful employment during the years between childhood and marriage was in fact a necessity for many middle-class girls: only an affluent family could support its daughters for several years as 'daughters at home'. Moreover, some middle-class women would never marry, and would therefore in most cases be forced to support themselves throughout their adult lives. In order to prepare the daughters of middle-class families to support themselves, reformers campaigned for changes in the education of middle-class girls. Under the influence of these reformers, formal schooling gradually assumed a more central role in the education of middle-class girls and the nature of the school underwent significant changes. The early Victorian girls' school had been considered either a second-best alternative to home education, or a place where families would send daughters for a brief year or two in late adolescence to complete their education for domesticity. In contrast, the reformed girls' schools established in the late-Victorian decades, while still committed to the ideals of Victorian femininity, modified that commitment, introducing programmes that rewarded achievement and prepared girls for gainful employment. In addition to the reforms achieved in girls' primary and secondary education, some educational reformers went further and worked to open up opportunities for higher education and professional training for middle and upper-class women.

Improvements in middle-class female education went hand in hand with changes in opportunities for female employment. These decades brought with them the expansion of the service sector of the economy, and with that expansion came a demand for educated workers who could do skilled work, but who were not in a position to demand high pay or opportunities for advancement. Lower middle-class women fitted this description better than men, and it was in this period that employers began to hire young women in preference to men for clerical and sales jobs, and that the feminine professions of nursing and teaching began to develop. This 'widening sphere' did represent a real improvement for middle-class women who needed or wanted to support themselves. The limits, so apparent to us today, were less apparent in the 1880s: employment as a nurse, clerk, 'lady typewriter' or teacher offered women more money, status and security than the early-Victorian occupations of governess, companion or needleworker. In addition, a few genuinely high status occupations, like medicine, began to open their doors to a small minority of women.[11]

The experience of working-class girls also changed for the better in the last decades of the century. Girls as well as boys reaped the benefits of the expansion in elementary education that followed the Education Act of 1870, and of the limited funding that was provided for the secondary education of a small minority of working-class children at the turn of the century, and in the Edwardian decade. As might be expected, the Victorian elementary school did attempt to inculcate in its pupils an acceptance of conventional gender divisions – just as it attempted to inculcate an acceptance of an inegalitarian social structure. Nevertheless, education did provide genuine opportunities for advancement for some working-class girls, just as it did for their brothers.

These late nineteenth-century modifications in thinking about femininity and in the experience of girls and young women were reflected in changes in the nature of the reading material provided for girls. There were changes in the scope and variety of such material, as writers and publishers for the first time came to recognize that girls, considered as a separate group, formed a legitimate market for literature written exclusively for them. This recognition came about just as the periodical publishing industry was undergoing expansion, resulting in a proliferation of a new kind of publication: the girl's magazine.

The most representative and influential late-Victorian publication of this type was the penny weekly *The Girl's Own Paper*, published by the Religious Tract Society. The RTS began publication of *The Girl's Own Paper* as an afterthought: a year earlier, it had decided to produce an attractive publication for boys, and in 1879 it had launched *The Boy's Own Paper*. The boy's publication was immediately successful, earning a substantial profit for the Society, and it was thought that a similar publication for girls might be equally successful. The Society therefore began publication of the *Girl's Own* in January, 1880.[12] As it turned out, the *Girl's Own* was even more successful than the *Boy's Own*. In 1884 it claimed to have attained 'a circulation equalled by no other English illustrated magazine.'[13]

Taken together, *The Girl's Own Paper* and *The Boy's Own Paper* illustrate the changes in publishing for young people that were taking place in the last decades of the nineteenth century. Although both papers were successful – they made a profit for their philanthropic sponsor, and they were widely read – they were not commercial ventures, like the contemporary 'penny dreadfuls', or the twentieth-century Amalgamated Press publications that would later supplant them. The *Boy's Own* and the *Girl's Own* represent instead a sophisticated style of improving journalism, a style that displayed a recognition that young readers could not be attracted by the dreary preaching of the tracts and periodicals that philanthropists had produced earlier in the century. Neither paper was the first of its kind, nor was it the only one, but both dominated their respective markets for several decades.[14]

Unlike the few earlier periodical publications for girls, which were designed exclusively for a middle- and upper-class audience, the *Girl's Own* aimed at a readership drawn from all social classes. The editor's intention was to produce a magazine that would act as a friend to its readers, and as early as the first year of publication the desired tone had been set.[15] The magazine offered a wide variety of different features, including fiction; articles about female education and women's work; tips on home decorating; advice about fashion; and an 'Answers to Correspondents' column. The latter is particularly valuable from the historian's point of view, because through it we can learn something about social and economic situation of the magazine's readers, and about their concerns. Taken as a whole, the content of *The Girl's Own Paper* from its founding to the first decade of the twentieth century, reflects both change and continuity in the experience of girls and young women during those years.

The late-Victorian *Girl's Own* was an attractive publication, with numerous black and white illustrations, a lively style, and a layout and format that reflected its intention to entertain and to inform its readers. Fiction always formed a major part of the magazine's content. There was always an illustrated feature story, serialized over several issues, as well as one or more subsidiary pieces of fiction. Of all sections of the magazine, its fiction adhered most closely to the values associated with the Victorian ideal of femininity. The typical *Girl's Own* story involved the struggles and dilemmas of a middle- or upper-class heroine, usually in her late teens or early twenties. The setting was more likely to be rural rather than urban; the plot usually revolved around a love relationship, and the story almost invariably ended with the heroine's marriage.

'Three Years of a Girl's Life', a tale that was serialized over several weeks during the magazine's first year of existence, can serve as an example. Much of the story is set in a European spa, where Cora, the heroine, is living with her selfish, invalid father, who unreasonably opposes her marriage to Ralph, a strong 'manly' man who is in fact well suited to be her husband. In spite of her father's unreasonable objections, Cora obeys him: 'without papa's consent I can promise nothing', she tells her lover, and she sticks steadfastly and calmly to this decision.[16] Cora reaps her reward for her filial obedience three years later, after her father's death. Having inherited considerable wealth, she becomes reacquainted with Ralph in England, to find that his family has suffered unexpected financial reverses. Cora is now able to marry the man she loves and at the same time to bring him financial security.

'Three Years in a Girl's Life' combines several features that were evocative of the Victorian feminine ideal. It has a romantic theme with a traditional happy ending, but it also conveys the message that filial duty is important, that a good daughter serves her father's needs, even if her father is unreasonable. The story's conclusion also serves to underline the idea that for a truly womanly woman, the best use of money, which she inherits rather than earns, is to benefit her lover. In other more subtle ways, the physical descriptions of Cora evoke imagery associated with Victorian femininity: she is 'gentle'; she has 'sweet serious eyes'; she feels deeply, but is at the same time able to control her emotions: when her father tells her that Ralph may not visit the house, she is described as entering 'the room like a drooping lily, her cheeks white, her soft, dark eyes tremulous . . . but she was trying hard to be composed and calm.'[17]

During its first 25 years, the fiction that appeared in the magazine changed remarkably little. Some stories that involved younger children and a school-girl setting occasionally appeared, and some of the fiction did include references to new educational and occupational opportunities for young women,[18] but most of the fiction adhered closely to the traditional romantic formula.

In contrast, in its non-fiction the *Girl's Own* reflected and often encouraged a recognition of the changing opportunities for girls and women. There were articles about new employment opportunities and about developments in women's education, frequent pieces about serious social problems concerning women – examples include discussions of the need for suitable boarding homes for working girls in London; the need for proper working conditions for young women working in the retail trades; the needs of girls in domestic service; and the shortage of suitable employment for educated women.[19] And although romance ending in marriage was the usual theme of its fiction, in editorializing, the magazine warned its readers not to view marriage as the only acceptable pattern for their future. The magazine's position was that a happy marriage might be the best future a girl could hope for, but it was not the only acceptable one:

> It is a great pity that girls are brought up to think that the only way in which they can dispose of themselves, that will give satisfaction to their friends, is to get married; and if, from various causes, they fail to achieve this end they will be looked upon more or less as social failures. True enough, a happy marriage is the best lot that can befall a woman, but surely an unhappy one is by a long way the worst; and how many miserable marriages would be prevented if woman only

had something else to do and think about, some other means of advancing themselves in life?[20]

While no radical protest, this position did, at least, offer readers an alternative to popular opinion which even in the last decades of the century often saw the unmarried woman as 'redundant'.[21]

In its articles and editorial comments, *The Girl's Own Paper* took a position that supported the more moderate goals of the emerging women's movement. But while it offered its readers a vision of a 'widening sphere', this vision had well-defined limits. The magazine did open up the possibility of new opportunities, but it also suggested that its readers should conform to the principles of Victorian femininity, in a modified but still recognizable form. The magazine's blending of the old with the new is illustrated, for example, in an article on 'University Hoods and How to Make Them', which begins as follows: 'University hoods have been hitherto a mark of distinction which only men were entitled to wear, and although the movement in favour of extending degrees and diplomas to women has spread with such wonderful rapidity . . . until within a recent date no distinctive mark of honour has been allowed them . . . The restriction has been to some extent removed. Women graduates of certain Universities and Colleges have an equal right to disport themselves in the distinctive hood of their degrees.'

After this bold beginning, with its forthright assertions about women's rights to higher education, the article changes its tone, and becomes a feature on sewing with instructions about how to make the hoods which, the author explains, make a 'most useful and acceptable gift [for] father, brother, or cousin'.[22] The article is illustrated with a (male) figure of 'an Oxford Bachelor of Arts'.

The content of the fiction and non-fiction, and the illustrations that filled its pages, suggest that the girls for whom *The Girl's Own Paper* was designed would have been middle class and in their late teens. The correspondence columns of the magazine give us an opportunity to discover who actually read the *Girl's Own* and they reveal a wider readership, both in terms of social class and age, than the content would lead one to expect. Readers wrote to the *Girl's Own* editor asking a wide range of questions.[23] There were queries relating to health and beauty; requests for information about home decorating and cookery; for advice about personal relationships; and for information about employment and education. While some of the queries did come from girls or young women in their late teens, the correspondents were often younger, and it is clear that they were often working-class girls, or girls from the lowest levels of the middle class. The following answer, for example, was written in reply to a 14 year-old girl, in 1880: 'Susannah H. – We advise you to banish from your mind all thoughts of being what you always call a "governess". Your spelling, writing, grammar and common style of expressing yourself render a girl already nearly fifteen, quite incompetent to prepare for such a situation.' Susannah is advised to fit herself for 'a good situation as a lady's maid . . . or learn to be a cook'.[24]

The fact that girls like 'Susannah H.' figure regularly in the 'answers to correspondents' column of *The Girl's Own Paper* suggests that for some two decades, its original combination of romantic fiction, entertainment and serious advice, proved successful in attracting an audience that was diverse both in social class and in age. The magazine's success in appealing to a lower middle-class and working-class readership, even though its romantic ficiton usually involved middle-class heroines, needs little explanation. Throughout the nineteenth century, literary images of courtship were drawn almost exclusively from middle-class experience. The hegemony of the bourgeoisie operated in this sphere, as it did in others, and this respect, the *Girl's Own* did not differ from publications designed for older women.[25]

By the turn of the century, however, the marked incongruity between the age of its younger readers and the magazine's content did present a problem. The fiction and editorial content of the *Girl's Own* in its first two decades treated the experience of the girl or young woman in late adolescence or early adulthood as universal, and provided no clear image of the girl in middle childhood or puberty. The magazine's very title, when contrasted with its contents and illustrations, reflects this loose definition of girlhood. But three decades of increased importance of formal schooling in the lives of girls of the middle and working classes had, by the 1890s, produced a change in consciousness. As school came to dominate the experience of an increasing number of girls, a clearly defined image of the schoolgirl emerged and there arose a demand for reading matter that would reflect this new image. The *Girl's Own* itself attempted to adapt to this new development after 1908, with limited success.[26] The fact that the most successful Victorian publication for girls found it necessary to attempt such adaptation is indication enough that a new type of girl reader and a new image of girlhood had emerged.

The School Girl

In one important respect, the school-girl fiction of the turn of the century was similar to earlier Victorian fiction designed for the girl reader: like mid- and late-Victorian domestic fiction, it reflected upper- and middle-class experience, rather than lower middle-class or working-class experience. In the years before the First World War, school-girl stories were not set in elementary schools, or even in day schools of the kind that lower middle-class girls attended, but rather in upper middle-class boarding schools.

In other respects, however, the new school-girl story represents a sharp break with the past. School-girl tales not only concerned themselves with characters who were considerably younger than those of domestic and romantic fiction – with girls of 12, rather than young women between 18 and 25 – they portrayed a world made up almost exclusively of girls and women. Moreover, the stories were set not in the family, as was earlier fiction for girls, but in a unisexual institution. Our brief examination of the evolution of the school-girl story will survey the work of L. T. Meade, and Angela Brazil, two authors who played a major role in the creation of the genre.

The work of the first, L. T. Meade, can be regarded as representing a transition from mid-Victorian fiction designed for girls, to the twentieth-century school story.[27] Meade usually employed a melodramatic plot, one that frequently involved the death or severe illness of one or more of the chief characters, and her primary focus was always on the moral development of the main characters. She set her tales in the kind of late nineteenth-century 'school for young ladies' that was an intimate, emotionally intense community of girls and older women. In several ways, the atmosphere evoked by her settings looks backward to Victorian values while at the same time it embodies new ideas. The exclusively female world she created has some of the qualities of the Victorian family, but also suggests to its readers that the community of the school has something to offer girls that cannot be provided by ordinary family life.

The feminine milieu of the Meade tales is evoked by the title of one of the author's most successful books. *A World of Girls*, which was first published in 1886. It is set in a small, select school to which the central character, 12 year-old Hester, is sent after the death of her mother.[28] Hester, who was at first unwilling to leave her home for school, finds herself in a new environment. As the headmistress explains: 'You will find a miniature world around you; you will be surrounded by temptations; and you will have rare chances of proving whether your character can be strong and great and true. I think, as a rule, my girls are happy, and as a rule they turn out well. The great motto of life here . . . is earnestness.' And Hester does learn from school. The reader is told that '. . . there was much in its monotonous, busy and healthy occupation to stimulate and rouse the good in her'.[29]

Several kinds of girls figure in *A World of Girls*. There is the genuinely good girl, who has a 'great heart'; the mischievous, but loveable girl; the shallow, superficially accomplished, but fundamentally immoral girl, who 'possessed in a strong degree that baneful quality . . . essential selfishness'.[30] Meade uses the weaknesses and strengths of each of these characters to teach a moral lesson. In the course of the story, when the characters are tested, the tests are not primarily tests of intellect or of physical strength and courage, but rather of moral character. Achievement in school lessons, for example, is valued not because it demonstrates intellectual ability, but because it reflects earnestness and docility. It is clear that the chief purpose of 'Lavender House' is to prepare girls for feminine domesticity, not for achievement in the public sphere, and that Meade's 'world of girls', while more impersonal than a family was, like the family, designed to foster the ideals of Victorian femininity.

L. T. Meade's *A Sweet Girl Graduate*, published in 1891,[31] while not strictly a school-girl story – it is set in a woman's college – provides an excellent example of the way in which this late-Victorian author continued to reflect Victorian ideals of femininity in her fiction, while at the same time portraying the adaptation of those ideals to changing circumstances. *A Sweet Girl Graduate*'s heroine, Patricia Peel, is 18 when the story opens and is about to go off to St Benet's College (a thinly disguised Newnham College). Although Priscilla is a good student, she is going to college not to further her own ambitions, but to best prepare herself to support her three younger sisters. Her kindly village rector had pointed out to her several years before, that preparation to attend college would in her case be a better way to do this than dressmaking which she had originally selected but for which she had no skill. He had said to her 'My dear child . . . when it becomes a question of a woman earning her bread, let her turn to that path where promise lies. . . . You must not give up your books, my dear . . . for independently of the pleasure they afford, they will also give you bread and butter.'[32]

In Priscilla Peel, Meade created a heroine who pursues a university education – a course of action that many in the 1890s believed to be both radical and unfeminine – not because she is driven by masculine ambition, or because she desires independence, but in order to serve the needs of her family. The combination of plot and characterization in *A Sweet Girl Graduate*, allows the author to describe the social and interpersonal side of life at a women's college in a way that reinforces traditional values. Meade's 'St Benet's' offers a domesticated and non-threatening picture of an early woman's college, one that served to enhance the respectability of the real women's colleges on which it was modelled, and at the same time tamed and trivialized the struggle for the higher education of women.[33]

L. T. Meade's tales retain the flavour of Victorian domestic fiction. With Angela Brazil, whose first book was published in 1906, and who was the early twentieth-century's most successful writer of school-girl stories, we encounter a new type of school-girl tale. Brazil's stories are set in upper middle-class boarding schools, but these schools are not the intimate enlarged Victorian home of the L. T. Meade tales.[34] Brazil's schools have prefects and her school-girls play organized games and write examinations. Moral choice does figure, but the moral tone is muted: instead, the stories focus on adventure. Vestiges of the feminine ideal do appear, but in a modern guise. For example, in *The Nicest Girl in the School*, (1910), the heroine, Patty, is a genuinely good girl, and the fact that her goodness has a beneficial effect on her selfish cousin Muriel, is a central feature of the story.[35] Muriel is from a wealthy family and is extremely spoiled, whereas Patty's family is less well off, and she is in fact attending the expensive boarding school in which the story is set only because her wealthy relatives are paying the fees. But Patty is a 'trump' not a redeeming angel, and the scene in which Muriel finally recognizes Patty's moral superiority involves Patty's rescue of Muriel from a dangerous cliff, an incident in which Patty exhibits the kind of physical courage that traditionally figures in adventure stories for boys.

Brazil's school-girl world undeniably struck a new note in girls' fiction. In many ways it offered its readers a feminine version of the world of the fictional boy's public school with its games, adventures, friendship and school spirit. But did the Brazil books present girls with an alternative vision of the female role? Can Brazil's image of the adventuresome school girl be seen as part of the Edwardian challenge to the Victorian conception of femininity? Did she see her heroines growing up to be women who would lead unconventional lives?

For the most part, Brazil simply avoided this issue by restricting the scope of her stories to the pre-adolescent years. In the cases where she does carry the tale beyond the school years of her characters, such events figure only in a final chapter. But in the stories she wrote before the First World War, there are some interesting variations in these final accounts of the future of her heroines. In her first book, *The Fortunes of Phillipa*, the heroine is a motherless child, whose father sends her back to England from South America, for her education. Most of the book is concerned with Phillipa's school experiences, but in the final chapter, Phillipa's father returns to England and Phillipa, having finished school, becomes his 'little housekeeper' – an Edwardian version of the Angel in the House. In contrast to the ending of this first book, in *The Girls of St Cyprian's*, published in 1914, just on the eve of the First World War, Brazil wrote a story in which she placed considerable emphasis on the importance of intellectual and artistic achievement. *The Girls of St Cyprian's* ends on a note that affirms the value of adult achievement for women. In contrast to the L. T. Meade book of 1891, *A Sweet Girl Graduate*, with its portrayal of a heroine whose self-sacrificing femininity was designed to withstand the rigors of preparation for the classical tripos, the central character of *The Girls of St Cyprian's*, is the musically talented and ambitious Mildred, whose gifts and hard work win her a music scholarship to Berlin, and her achievements and those of other characters in the story are summarized in a final chapter, 'Harvest':

> St. Cyprian's decided that Mildred's success was so far the greatest triumph the college had had and a worthy finish to a term in which they had beaten Newington Green at cricket and vanquished Marston Grove at tennis; and . . . later on came the news that Laura Kirby had won the Girton scholarship and even Kitty Fletcher had managed to get a second class in her examinations . . . All [the] Sixth Form girls were leaving, some to continue their studies elsewhere, and others to find their vocations at home, but all carried away the warmest recollections of the school which had laid the foundation of their education.[36]

In spite of such allusions to new possibilities for women, it would be a mistake to characterize Brazil's work as presenting a serious challenge to the fact that a modified form of the Victorian ideology of separate spheres was still expected to shape the lives of upper middle-class girls as they left childhood for adolescence. Brazil wrote to entertain, and her books do not acknowledge the deep conflicts that existed between the role that was still expected of the majority of upper middle-class daughters, and any serious commitment to further study, to a profession or to employment. Nor does she deal with the disheartening limits to power and achievement that middle-class women would meet with if they pursued such a commitment. Still, the fact that such references are included does at least indicate that serious study and professional work had become acceptable enough to appear as background colour in girls' stories of this kind.

If one contrasts Charlotte Yonge's *The Daisy Chain* with *The Girls of St Cyprians*, it would appear that in the 60 years between the publication of the two, literature designed for girls evolved to reflect the increased opportunities for middle-class girls that had emerged in those intervening decades. The chief message of Yonge's fiction had been that each individual must learn to accept limits, and that the limits of female experience are narrower than those of males; in contrast, Angela Brazil presented her readers with a vision of life that afforded seemingly limitless opportunities.

In spite of this important change, the success of stories of the Brazil type brought with it significant losses. Angela Brazil wrote stories that were designed to sell to the school-girl market, and her work suffers from the shallowness that would become characteristic of much twentieth-century children's fiction – as indeed it is characteristic of all fiction that is written primarily to comply to a formula dictated by the exigencies of commercial publishing. In contrast, the best Victorian writers of domestic fiction not only defined their audience much less narrowly, they wrote out of deeply felt conviction. The conviction may have been to values that were employed by Victorian society to oppress women, but these same values also infused them with strength and seriousness of purpose. In contrast, the simplistic world of the Edwardian school-girl story offered its readers less exposure to the complexity of human experience, or to the real dilemmas facing women.

In some ways, the school-girl story of the Brazil type can also be said to have widened the gulf between upper middle-class girl readers and those from less affluent families, as a contrast between the tone and content of *The Girl's Own Paper* and that of the Brazil tales illustrates. The *Girl's Own* did make a genuine effort to serve the needs of its lower middle-class and working-class readers, even though the magazine's content reveals few strong images of girls who were not comfortably middle class. But in the school-girl tales, the class distinctions are sharpened, and the horizon narrowed to exclude recognition of any reality beyond the horizon of the upper middle class. This hardening of class lines in Edwardian school-girl fiction may have been one of the developments that encouraged the emergence of a commercial market for girls' periodicals directed specifically at working-class girls, a development that has its beginnings in the Edwardian decade.

The books and periodicals that have been the subject of this chapter were written and produced because they were thought to be appropriate for the girl reader. They have provided the focus of the analysis because it is through writing of this kind that we can best understand the dominant point of view. But we should remember that girls were not restricted to such fare. While it is true that Victorian and Edwardian children were less free than adults to make their own choices – as indeed children still are – many Victorian and Edwardian girls read widely. There were some, for example, who read literature designed for boys. And for the minority of bookish girls for whom literature was a primary means of interpreting experience, there was the wealth of material provided by the adult Victorian novel. *Jane Eyre* may have been banned at L. T. Meade's fictional school Lavender House, but the biographical record reveals that many Victorian and Edwardian girls, who in adulthood refused to accept the limitations of conventional femininity, gained the strength that prepared them for their adult choices through reading in girlhood the works of Charlotte Brontë, George Eliot and other writers who presented an analysis of femininity that was far more complex than that to be found in conventional literature for girls. All girls were to some extent influenced by the images of girlhood presented in popular literature, but for those who strayed beyond those limits, reading could be an experience with radical implications. It helped to encourage a small but significant minority of girls to reject the conventional definition of Victorian womanhood.[37]

Acknowledgements

I would like to thank Phyllis Leonardi, Toby Gelfand, Naomi Goldenberg, and the librarians at the Osborne Collection for their help.

Bibliographical Note

For further reading on girlhood in the Victorian and Edwardian periods, see Deborah Gorham, *The Victorian Girl and the Feminine Ideal* (Croom Helm, 1982), in which many of the ideas touched on in this chapter are more fully developed, and Carol Dyhouse, *Girls Growing Up in Late Victorian and Edwardian England* (Routledge & Kegan Paul, 1981). For working-class girlhood, Elizabeth Roberts, *A Woman's Place: An Oral History of Working-Class Women 1890–1940* (Oxford, Basil Blackwell, 1984) has an excellent chapter on growing up, and makes a significant contribution to a subject that has been insufficiently explored.

On the subject of children's literature, Gillian Avery, *Childhood's Pattern: a Study of the Heroes and Heroines of Children's Fiction 1770–1950* (Hodder & Stoughton, 1975) and J. S. Bratton, *The Impact of Victorian Children's Fiction* (Croom Helm, 1981) are both helpful. On literature for girls see Mary Cadogan and Patricia Craig, *You're a Brick, Angela! A New Look at Girls' Fiction from 1839 to 1975* (Victor Gollancz, 1976).

On the complex subject of gender and reading see the collection edited by Elizabeth A. Flynn and Patrocinio P. Schweickart, *Gender and Reading: Essays on Readers, Texts, and Contexts* (Baltimore, Johns Hopkins University Press, 1986) which contains an extensive annotated bibliography, and has one essay on reading in childhood: Elizabeth Segal, ' "As the twig is bent . . . ": gender and childhood reading'.

4

Learning Through Leisure: Feminine Ideology in Girls' Magazines, 1920–50

Penny Tinkler

> If you would make friends with a group of working-class girls, you
> can create a common interest at once by offering to exchange with
> them some 'girls' ' books. These 'books' are what one would
> ordinarily call papers and magazines. They cost threepence and every
> little back-street tobacco or paper shop in every part of England sells
> them.[1]

Magazines for girls of ten to twenty years of age were in fact available
for girls of all classes in the decades after the 1914–18 war. With a
school-leaving age of 14 this age range included both school girls and
girls at work. Each magazine offered images of femininity and
prescriptions of feminine behaviour. While many of the characteristics of feminine ideology were shared between magazines,
representations of femininity varied according to the age and social
class of the intended readership, and these variations reflected
changes over time in social and economic conditions, and in reader
tastes and interests.

The representation of femininity in any magazine was to a large
extent dependent upon the editor. It was the editor who made
judgements about the likely readership and their collective tastes and
interests, the editor who decided how best to mediate the message of
femininity according to the readers' perceived background, age and
occupation. The editor's own attitudes were therefore very
important, but so too were the publisher's codes and prevailing ideas
about femininity.

The chapter is concerned with the representations of femininity in girls' magazines, that is the way in which a prescriptive ideology was portrayed to a readership which was very likely to be influenced by what it read. In this context I am adopting Susan Brownmiller's argument that a 'major purpose of femininity is to mystify or minimise the functional aspects of a woman's mind and body that are indistinguishable from a man's'.[2] Thus I would argue that femininity, as defined and described in these magazines, entailed an artificial differentiation of females from males. It also defined females as inferior to males and denied them the strengths of their biological femaleness.

Magazines for Girls

School-girl and romance papers were very popular in the period from 1920 to 1950, particularly with working-class girls. Most working-class girls did not have any real literary alternatives especially once they had left school: 'what with washing your stockings and your hair and giving Mum a hand and doing some shopping and going to the library – your half-day's gone, and if you go to the flicks you've got a great heavy book to cart round for hours and then when you get it home the chances are it isn't the sort of book you like.'[3] Unlike library books, magazines were always 'handy.'[4]

Girls' magazines provided entertainment and also advice on feminine behaviour and appearance. Magazine prescriptions of femininity were expressed in terms which suggested that the main aims of femininity were that girls should be different from boys and that they should desire marriage and motherhood. Subsequently magazines set up courting and love as primary interests for adolescent girls. Their advice, meted out through all aspects of the paper, was reinforced because magazines, like the romantic movies, were probably the only source of advice on courting, love and boyfriends to which girls had access. Pearl Jephcott's observation of working-class adolescent girlhood clearly portrays this need.

> The matchbox maker of fifteen, with her boy friend of sixteen, her two nights a week at the pictures and her most cherished possession still an old doll, searches *Silver Star* to see how other, rather older people cope with the problems of sex that are being so constantly brought to her attention now that she is a member of the adult world of workers. How can she get to know the things that older girls know?[5]

Evidence that magazines did affect their readers can be found in the correspondence columns where girls of 12 years and upwards sought advice on how to follow feminine prescriptions, and how to cope with the contradictions between their own lives and personalities and those described and prescribed in the magazines.

During the period there were a number of magazines available and read by girls. School-girl papers published mainly by Amalgamated Press were numerous in the 1920s (*School Friend*, *Schoolgirls' Own*, *Schoolgirl*, *Girls' Crystal*), but by 1950 only two remained in circulation. These magazines were written mainly for elementary school girls, though they actually attracted a wider readership. Jenkinson's study of school-girl reading in 1938 showed that girls from senior and secondary schools treated these papers quite differently. Whereas 14 year-old senior school girls read roughly four of these papers a week, secondary school girls of the same age read only one a week.[6] But while school-girl papers constituted a large proportion of the reading of secondary school girls aged between 12 and 16, senior school girls turned increasingly to romance magazines, especially once they had left school at 14 or 15 years of age.[7] School-girl papers, in comparison with the working girls' magazines, were very unsophisticated and offered no advice on how to cope with the new interests and problems of working life, namely dress, beauty, love and courtship.

The *Girl's Own Paper* was the only middle-class school-girl paper during this period,[8] but between 1927 and 1930 it was incorporated with the mother paper *Woman's Magazine* and had no identity of its own until it re-emerged as a quite distinct girls' paper in 1931. *Girl's Own Paper* was regularly delivered to many middle-class homes and it was frequently stocked by school and public libraries for its educational content and strong moral tone, and it was here that some elementary school girls became acquainted with the paper. *Girl's Own Paper* readers generally stayed at school until late in their teens hence the paper catered for a wider and older age range than the other school-girl papers. But at the same time it portrayed and generally treated adolescent girls as less sophisticated than magazines for younger working girls.

There were also a number of magazines written specifically for the working girl; these concentrated heavily on romantic fiction (*Girls' Favourite*, *Girls' Weekly*, *Peg's Paper*, *Poppy's Paper*, *Polly's Paper*, *Pam's Paper*). Nell Kennedy the founder-editor of *Peg's Paper* (1919–40) actually constructed the magazine around the dreams and ideas of mill girls. Her daughter, Pat Lamburn recalls clearly how

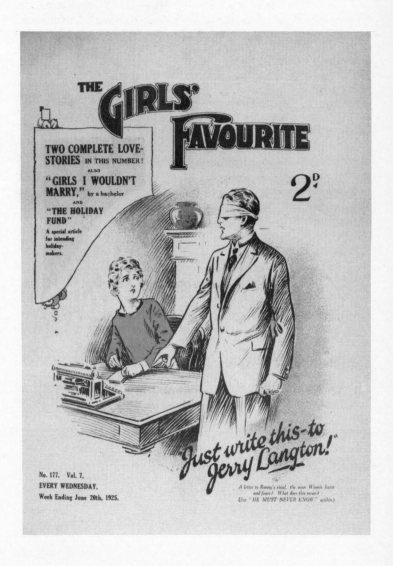

The cover of *The Girls' Favourite* magazine, 20 June 1925.

her mother, 'went up to Wigan and she stayed there – I remember vividly her telling me this – for six weeks. She used to go into the churchyard every day and sit and listen to the millgirls talking whilst they ate their sandwiches during their mid-day break . . . And she listened to them endlessly to find out what their dreams were, what their aspirations were, what they would want in a magazine'.[9] These magazines, which provided a mixture of passionate fiction, horoscopes and letter pages, continued to be popular with factory girls, servants, young wives and elementary school girls until they were phased out in the thirties and forties to be replaced by a new range of magazines (*Silver Star*, *Lucky Star*, *Glamour*, *Secrets*, *Red Star Weekly*).

The new mother/daughter magazines, which were very similar in content to the working girls' magazines, were intended for 'Mothers, Daughters, Sweethearts and Wives'.[10] However, by 1950, they had become more mother-centred and catered mainly for the mother and her children; they even provided toddler pages and school-girl fiction. These magazines attracted readers of 11 years and upwards, but they were not very popular with middle-class girls.[11] This could be because these magazines dealt with matters which were considered to be irrelevant to many middle-class school girls: 'A fourteen-year-old secondary school girl says that *Crystal* is the popular magazine with her friends, but that when she was evacuated and went to a village elementary school the girls were all reading *Red Star Weekly*, a more sentimental type of magazine principally intended for rather older girls'.[12] This girl thought these magazines 'daft' because they had too many love stories; in contrast many elementary school girls regarded courtship and love as very relevant as once they started work at 14 or 15, courting and marriage would become a major preoccupation.

Marriage and Careers for Girls

Marriage was an important feature in the lives of all girls, but magazines treated this topic differently according to the age and background of their intended readers. Attitudes to marriage portrayed in magazines were clearly related to the treatment of education and careers for girls. An understanding of the importance attributed to marriage and careers for girls by magazines is essential if we are to appreciate the mechanisms of persuasion and general content of girls' papers.

The working girls' and mother/daughter magazines portrayed marriage as the ambition and life career of a girl, but at the same time they encouraged their readers to train for work and to be prepared to support themselves if necessary. Work was discussed as a means of finding a husband and of developing skills useful to the potential housewife and mother. Considerable attention was focused on the clothes a 'business girl' should wear, how a girl could look smart; professional but also attractive. Throughout the period attitudes to work in these magazines changed very little. *Pam's Paper* in 1927 discussed careers in terms of the preparation it offered for marriage: 'The typist is qualified to make a good wife, because she understands men and their business troubles and is not inclined to be jealous if her husband is detained in town or is bad-tempered after a long day at the office'.[13] *Woman* in 1937 made a similar comment, 'If marriage is your goal, choose deliberately work which will prepare you for running a home of your own'.[14]

In the twenties these magazines expressed anxiety that girls were actually enjoying their careers and delaying or refusing marriage and maternity. Although editors believed a desire for a husband, home and family were innate they nevertheless felt the need to encourage these 'inclinations'. Magazines were prepared to accept girls working and even enjoying their jobs as long as they would eventually accept marriage, submission and maternity. Girls who did not want to marry were regarded as unfeminine, even unnatural. In the following extract taken from *Girls' Favourite* in 1927 entitled 'Is the modern girl different?', it is clear that magazines were compromising girls' work with prevalent notions of femininity. Esther Ralston wrote about how a girl's work really served very feminine ends: 'I admit we go out to business more. We have to; it's the fashion. And we've found its also so much nicer than depending on parental generosity for all the hundred and one necessities of our existence.'[15] The suggestion is that female work was for 'pin-money'; a trivialization of the social and economic importance of employment for girls. Ralston continued:

> The modern girl, it is true, no longer looks upon marriage as the one and only thing for her. That is all to her good, for she, being content to wait for the right opportunity, isn't nearly so likely to make a wrong choice as grandmamma was. And, on the other hand, if the opportunity never comes she sensibly makes the best of things and determines to be happy with her business chums and her business pleasures. Hence, she doesn't grow into that most unpleasant of persons, a sour old maid.[16]

Work gave the 'modern girl' the security to wait for 'Mr Right' thereby ensuring a more successful and stable marriage union. But it also ensured that the spinster would not become an embarrassing social problem by providing her with useful work and outlets for her 'inevitable' sexual and emotional frustrations.[17]

This attitude to work was clearly reflected in the magazine fiction of the period. During this time the heroine was quite independent and often had an interesting career, but the drama generally focused on her transition towards love and marriage. Work was treated superficially as a background for romance which was expendable when 'Mr Right' appeared. Stories often featured the heroine faced with the decision between a career and marriage; the latter always won. This theme was particularly common in the 1920s and 1940s. Shirley Smith was a happy air hostess who wanted to continue working and travelling the world until her single friend admitted to her how miserable she really was. Moved by her friend's story Shirley decided to accept an offer of marriage from a long-term admirer: 'Her mind free, she'd go out to the main gate, there to await the arrival of Peter Thorne – who was all that mattered in her life.'[18] Note that it was her mind that had always rejected marriage, not her heart; the implication is that every girl wanted to marry but only fashion and 'superficial' ideas of freedom distracted her. It is interesting that marriage was described here as offering Shirley real freedom even though she had to give up her work and financial independence on marriage.

In contrast, the school-girl papers, both the Amalgamated Press papers and the *Girl's Own Paper* rarely mentioned marriage. It would seem that editors considered their school-girl readers to be too young to be interested in love, courtship and marriage. They probably felt that school girls would not be able to relate to such topics and would be bored by them. Schools also received scant attention from papers and featured only as a backcloth for the drama, the attention being focused on the girls' adventures, their friendships and rivalries. Amalgamated Press papers also ignored the question of careers for girls, which seems strange as the majority of their readers would have been at the age when work was a major and exciting consideration for the near future. Career girls did appear in the fiction during the thirties but their work was usually glamorous and unrealistic. As Cadogan and Craig have pointed out:

> The authors' purpose is simply to crystallize the ten-year-old's image of herself at twenty; the author, if not the reader, is fully aware of certain 'socializing' pressures which will alter the child's view of

herself as she gets older. Thus, fantasies of rounding up a gang of thieves or a herd of cattle, or becoming an aerial photographer, are likely to give way gradually to the more limited, but more sensible and socially approved fantasy of 'getting married' – but by this time the girl will have shifted to reading papers of another type.[19]

In contrast, the *Girl's Own Paper* treated careers very seriously, it featured a careers advice article and, during the Second World War, it provided information on war work for its readers. Work was also portrayed more realistically in the fiction of the *Girl's Own Paper* than in the Amalgamated Press papers. In part this reflected the slightly older readership that the *Girl's Own Paper* attracted. It also indicates that careers for intelligent middle-class girls were increasingly acceptable from the thirties onwards; research by Edith Mercer in 1940 showed that all the girls she had interviewed from a girls' secondary school wanted a profession when they left school, the majority also wanted to marry.[20] In 1940 Dorothy Kirby wrote a two-and-a-half page article on the life and works of Margaret Bondfield.[21] Kirby described Bondfield's youth and education, her work as Labour MP and then Minister of Labour. However, only a brief mention was made at the end of the feature on Bondfield's attitudes towards marriage: 'In one of her speeches she declared that "home-making" was the finest career open to a woman.'[22] It would appear that the *Girl's Own Paper* acknowledged the importance of marriage and domesticity for women but felt that its teenage readers should be more concerned with building careers for themselves.

Girl's Own Paper's attitude to marriage and careers recognized women's intellectual abilities but it also paid attention to the belief that men and women should have different qualities and adult roles. Careers recommended by the *Girl's Own Paper* included nursing, teaching, veterinary work, agricultural work and shorthand-typing. These careers were either already defined as 'woman's work' or, like veterinary science, which was largely a male preserve, described as using 'feminine' skills: 'when it is remembered that nearly every girl is fond of animals and loves to care for them and nurse them, it is obvious that a large number of girls will be attracted to the profession which will give them the necessary knowledge and skill to be a doctor to animals.'[23] The treatment of veterinary science by the careers editor of the *Girl's Own Paper* suggests that she was eager to open up new areas of employment for middle-class girls even in work previously labelled as masculine. This she attempted to do by redefining veterinary work so that it would be compatible with femininity.

'Looks Feminine'

Of all the messages delivered, perhaps the most powerful was the emphasis laid on appearance. Articles and adverts constantly stressed the importance of this: 'in my estimation, and I'm sure you will all agree with me, details in dress and manners are the things that matter most of all.'[24] Even school-girl papers described to their readers how to keep fit and be attractive, a topic not discussed in the parallel boys' papers: the *Schoolgirl*'s readers were advised about 'good looks problems': 'It's no longer the thing to have a shiny, well-scrubbed look, and that horrid "starched" feeling your face gets if it is washed too vigorously' and 'rough red hands are admired by no-one'.[25] Although beauty featured in the school-girl papers it did not receive the attention nor the importance attributed to it by the working girls' and mother/daughter magazines. This was because readers of the older girls' magazines were considered to be preparing for, or already in the marriage market. At this stage, according to these magazines, femininity was vitally important; but girls did not just have to be feminine, they had, in a very real sense, to be seen to be feminine.

All aspects of the working girls' and mother/daughter magazines prescribed feminine beauty and appearance; they encouraged girls to create and maintain an illusion of femaleness. Adverts were often the most open about the artificiality of beauty: 'you're his dream girl. Don't disappoint him, give yourself a new look.'[26] This was a symptom of the direct links which developed in the thirties between capital interests, in the form of the cosmetics and fashion industries, and femininity.

The ideal feminine appearance did change over time but it maintained a remarkable consistency in its implications. Little Lil was a typical fictional heroine of the 1920s, she was described as 'golden-haired, young, pink and white and dimpled, with the wonderful freshness that England gives, with red, passionate lips'.[27] Later, in the 1940s, a typical heroine was described in the following way: 'She was so little and slender and breath-takingly lovely! She had dark, almost blue-black hair, and skin white as a camelia. Dark blue eyes and a sweet red mouth that seemed to invite him enticingly, even though, at the same time, she possessed a look of untouched freshness.'[28] Although separated by 20 years both girls were portrayed as dolls, very child-like, but at the same time extremely sensual although not actually possessing an independent and active sexuality. The emphasis of these descriptions was on fragility and passivity, the personalities of these characters was not discussed in any detail and it was not expressed through the facial descriptions. In contrast, male heroes had faces with character. Paul Grey 'carved his own way in the world, and won what he sought; it was the face of a fighter, of a man who only falls to rise again, stronger, more resolute, and undaunted than ever.'[29] Paul's appearance indicated action, independence and individuality, whereas the heroines appeared passive, weak and immature. It was in these ways that magazines artificially differentiated the sexes. On the basis of this, magazines allotted male and female characters different roles.

Magazine treatment of femininity, in terms of appearance, was full of contradictions and tensions. Girls were described by these papers as innately feminine, yet in spite of this romance magazines in particular, devoted considerable space to information on what constituted a feminine appearance and how to create it. In fact, appearing feminine was generally portrayed as an art form to be acquired by girls, rather than as a natural endowment. This contradiction posed a major problem for magazines; somehow they had to ensure that girls would adopt their models of femininity. The magazines seem to have invited their readers to collude in the creation of an illusion of femininity. But these girls were, in a sense, being blackmailed by a fear of failure as a person and as a woman. The main device used in these magazines to encourage girls to co-operate in the construction of feminine beauty was the argument that marriage and happiness depended on it. Girls were told that their looks were a commodity to be bartered in exchange for love, food and shelter. This was quite evident in the way girls were told to be feminine for men or to conform to male standards of beauty; such a policy rested on the assumption that the majority of girls would want to, or feel they should, get married.

The emotional and economic argument that if a girl wanted to get and keep a man, wanted a home and family, she must always appear feminine, was used throughout adverts, articles, fiction and letter pages in working girls' and mother/daughter magazines. During the twenties magazines paid lip-service to sex equality and promoted a reformed marital relationship based on companionship. Magazines also flattered girls' intelligence and spirit, and female heroines were portrayed as more adventurous, mischievous and plucky. In spite of this, fiction and articles continued to focus on looks; heroines were introduced face first and girls were constantly reminded not to be apathetic about their appearance. Companionate marriage may have been heralded by magazines but girls were nevertheless admonished for 'sloppiness' and clearly told that marriage and love depended on a wife remaining feminine in appearance. Referring to an extra ten minutes positioning one's hat, Louise Brookes wrote in 1927, 'He may love you with all his heart but when it seems that you don't value it enough to make yourself always worthy of it – well that's where the doubts begin.'[30] Clearly being oneself was not enough.

During the thirties the reader's confidence was more seriously and overtly undermined. Some magazines even denigrated a girl's capabilities in stressing the importance of appearance. Guest contributor, F. E. Bailey, writing for the monthly magazine *Miss Modern* in 1930 addressed the 18 year-old office worker and advised her to 'use your sex-weapons with discretion in the battle of a career . . .':

> In my opinion you would be foolish not to use your good looks discreetly in order to help your career, . . . Besides, if you want to carve a career, some day you must graduate from secretarial work to something more important, and then you may have to compete with men, and men have better brains than women. Consequently you must use your looks to supplement your brain.[31]

Readers were told that not only was a career likely to depend on good looks, but also their efficiency and self-respect. Many girls were greatly influenced by these messages, as the numerous letters to the correspondence pages prove. Often the correspondence editor had to contradict the powerful messages produced through other sections of the magazine. This could hardly have been reassuring for the reader.

Not only did marriage depend on looking feminine but, according to these magazines, so did popularity. Girls were clearly told that their posture, voice, clothes and body were reliable indicators of personality. A feminine appearance indicated a feminine personality. If a girl did not look feminine then she was not feminine and was therefore a disagreeable person. Throughout the period working girls' and mother/daughter magazines featured numerous articles judging personality from all types of physical characteristics; there was never any indication that personality may have been socially determined. Fiction reinforced the association between looks and personality. In school-girl papers the popular school girl always had curly hair and a round face, in contrast the bad girls had lank hair and sharp faces;[32] similarly the difference between the older heroine and the evil woman was manifest in their appearance.

Although a feminine face was vital as a sign of acceptability, the magazines also put considerable emphasis on clothes; the impression was that clothes and hair styles acted as a reinforcement to feminine behaviour. The link between clothes and personality was quite hotly debated in the magazines of the forties when girls were wearing trousers for heavy industrial and agricultural work. Derek Bond, a film star of the era, was asked to comment on whether girls should wear trousers. His reply is testimony to the restrictive nature of femininity for girls and provides a nice example of the way 'natural' was used to prescribe ideals of femininity: 'Let girls be girls and stop masquerading as some kind of male imitation. It isn't attractive. It isn't natural. It isn't even sensible because skirts are just as practical, and so much more becoming to the average feminine figure.'[33] Bond argued that Victorian girls had no trouble wearing long dresses even while they cycled, so why did the modern girl need to wear trousers? This is an interesting example of an illusion about femininity backfiring 50 years later; Victorian women were not comfortable in their long dresses and their movements were very restricted but no-one, or rather no man, was permitted to know this. Continuing his attack on girls wearing trousers Bond asked: 'You don't really want to be "equal" to men, do you? Wouldn't you rather remain a woman with all the respect and privileges of your sex? . . . Look like a girl and men will consciously regard you as such. That's the way it should be in the natural order of things . . . she provides a complement to my own sex.'[34] Dress, according to this statement, was vitally important for the way girls were regarded and treated, in fact their 'privileges' depended on it. But these 'privileges' merely allocated females a restricted sphere of activity which was labelled inferior to the public sphere occupied by males.

Physical Maturity and Sexuality

Presentations of femininity and feminine beauty in magazines were quite separate from female physical maturity and sexuality. While beauty was feminine and readers were encouraged to foster it, sexuality and physical maturity were labelled as unfeminine. Biological femaleness was either ignored, diminished or treated as abnormal, in its place magazines presented a socially constructed female as the norm.

Establishing femininity as the norm was a powerful argument to persuade readers to conform. For example, hair-free limbs were defined by magazines as feminine, hence heroines never had hairy legs or armpits. Throughout the period many adverts appeared in magazines selling depilatory creams, these referred to female body hair as 'superfluous', 'unnatural' and 'masculine'. This advert from *Poppy's Paper* in 1930 was a typical example: 'There is nothing more repellant to a man than a masculine growth of hair on the limbs and arms – it robs a woman of every vestige of daintiness and charm. Remove this disfigurement which breaks romance and spoils your happiness and joy.'[35] This advert clearly shows how a natural female characteristic was redefined as unfeminine, even as an exclusively masculine feature. It also points to the artificial separation of the sexes which was frequently used to justify the different and inferior status of women in society.

Magazines presented a very unreal picture of adolescent girlhood. Characters in magazine fiction did not manifest any physical changes during adolescence and articles did not deal with these matters. Letters concerning pubescence only occasionally featured in the mother/daughter magazines in the forties. It was not the case that magazines did not receive letters about adolescence. Evidence of the concern generated by puberty can be found in the study of letters addressed to *Girl* between April 1953 and March 1955. Although this study is outside the period being discussed its results and observations are nevertheless very relevant. James Hemming, education consultant for *Girl* and *Eagle* examined 3259 problem letters from girls. He noted that 16.1 per cent of problems were associated with anxieties about physical characteristics and deport-ment.[36] A major worry for girls was the size and shape of their breasts.[37] Hemming also discovered a 'continuing obscurantism' concerning the physical aspects of sexuality which resulted in many anxious letters about menstruation, sexuality and the 'facts of life'.[38] However *Girl*, like earlier school-girl papers, did not feature any discussion of the subject and heroines always conformed to the asexual ideal of the female adolescent. This insistence on an asexual adolescent model was most extreme in the Amalgamated Press school-girl papers whose artists were told to 'play down' girls' breasts, and in swimming scenes to keep the girls submerged up to their armpits.[39]

It would seem that magazines experienced tension as the needs of their readers could not always be recognized and catered for, certainly not in public. All magazines operated some form of censorship concerning which of their readers' letters to print. Nell Kennedy's letters editor selected 'suitable' letters for printing, this was done with 'an understanding of what would be acceptable within the social environment of that time'.[40] Even *Girl* implemented a selection policy with only 'safe' letters being published.[41] Personal problems were answered by letter; topics like periods and breasts were rarely discussed in public by the magazines.

In spite of the fact that the magazine readers were pubescent girls and newly matured women, menstruation was considered a taboo subject by girls' magazines and it was not until the thirties that letter replies concerned with menstruation occasionally appeared in working girls' and mother/daughter magazines. Magazine silence about menstruation was typical of society's reticence in discussing this matter. Many girls were quite frightened at the onset of menstruation as few received any comprehensive health and sex education from home or school.[42] Angela Rodaway suffered agonies from ignorance: 'I was almost certain that I should die. Everyone else in my form at school, next day, was almost certain too.'[43] Girls may have turned to magazines but with the exception of adverts for Dr William's Pink Pills and sanitary towels, which appeared in the mother/daughter magazines in the forties, periods were ignored. Adverts were the only sign that Fiona McFarlane had that periods happened to other women besides herself:

Through reading women's magazines – they never did mention it in those days, this would be 1946 to 1947, it just wasn't mentioned – I gradually worked out that these periods must happen regularly, because look at all the advertisements for sanitary towels there were, and if it only happened once in a lifetime you wouldn't need this massive advertising campaign.[44]

The advertising that concerned periods came in two forms with adverts for sanitary towels and iron tablets. In both, periods were treated as an ailment and handicap, rather than as a healthy sign of female reproductive maturity. Many sanitary towel adverts revealed ambivalence between recognizing girls as capable individuals in the social and employment spheres and feeling that females were inferior because 'handicapped' by a periodic loss of blood: 'Modern women cannot afford to be handicapped by Nature's disabilities. In the very full and active lives we lead there is no place for "woman's weakness", no room for "off" days . . . The freedom of full health for every day in the calendar is a stark necessity for every woman who works.'[45] It is strange that sanitary towels were advertised as if they were some sort of medication which would cure women of their 'natural' disabilities. Adverts for Dr William's Pink Pills similarly treated periods as a problem when they referred to the onset of menstruation as those 'perilous years'.[46]

Pregnancy was also a taboo subject in magazines in the twenties, although motherhood was often discussed in the women's magazines. Magazines appeared to be reflecting the attitude that pregnancy was 'low', an attitude endorsed by Miss Helena Powell in an essay entitled 'The Problem of the Adolescent Girl' in which she claimed that the 'beauty and the essence of motherhood lie not mainly in the bearing of children, but in the devotion, the patience, the understanding which makes the real mother'.[47] The realities of pregnancy were never discussed in the fiction or in the articles, although after the mid-thirties doctors and nurses gave advice in the mother/daughter magazines about mother and child nutrition and general health care. Even the few adverts which appeared in these magazines advertising pregnancy frocks did not have illustrations of pregnant women; dresses were modelled on extremely slim and shapely models.

During the thirties the editors of the working girls' magazines introduced the young, distressed, unmarried mother figure. Magazine editors appear to have been quite daring in their pursuit of new story lines and they probably recognized the semi-tragic appeal of the virtuous unmarried mother. They may also have been responding to the increased illegitimacy rate.[48] However, the editors kept the fiction and the heroines well within the bounds of prevalent feminine ideology through the use of several devices. First, and most importantly, the heroine remained innocent and ignorant about sex and her sexuality remained dormant. Secondly, the heroine's pregnancy was never mentioned or shown in the illustrations; one minute she was with a man, the next she was cradling a baby in her arms. Thirdly, the heroine was always a devoted and caring mother, repentant for her 'foolishness' and frequently loyal to the father of her child even if he was a scoundrel. It was important that no hint should be given of the girl's sexual experience or pregnancy.

In the forties correspondence features dealt more openly and in detail with maternity. Robin Kent suggests that after the thirties there was an opening up of sex discussion, what she calls 'the breakthrough into the bedroom'.[49] However, my survey suggests that many magazine problem pages continued to be reticent in discussion of sex-related topics. Letters dealing with such matters were often given only brief and cryptic replies. In reply to 'Curly Tops', in 1940, *Peg's Paper* replied: 'Yes; pregnancy can follow then just as easily as any other'.[50]

Virtually all discussions of maternity which appeared in the forties focused on the morality and economics at issue. In a letter to *Lucky*

Star's 'Ask the family doctor' in 1940, a girl wrote that her friend was having a baby outside marriage, the father having been killed before he could return to marry her. The doctor was quite sympathetic, but his major concern was for the child; he reminded readers to help girls who were pregnant outside wedlock because a harassed mother harmed the child she carried. Referring to the suffering of unmarried mothers the doctor revealed how strong opposition to pregnancy outside marriage remained in the forties: 'It is very terrifying for a girl who has always lived a straight life to find that she is going to be an unmarried mother. She knows she will lose her job, she realises that she will be blamed and probably scorned, and having a baby is quite a big and perilous enough adventure in itself.'[51]

Magazines may not have dwelt on the physical aspects of maternity but they were not completely silent, an indication that discussion was becoming more open. However it is clear that society generally ignored the biological aspects of maternity and instead focused on the socially constructed aspects.

Adolescent girls were generally not credited by magazines with a sexuality, in spite of the numerous letters to these magazines which indicated that readers did have an active sexuality.[52] School-girl papers did not feature love affairs and in the working girls' and mother/daughter magazines romantic heroines were usually over 18 years of age. By the late thirties working girls' and mother/daughter magazines did acknowledge female sexuality in their fiction but it was portrayed as latent until aroused by a man, except in the case of the overtly sexual and bad woman character. A favourite phrase of magazine fiction was a description of the heroine as a 'sweet untaught girl'. In magazine fiction men were usually treated as essential to female arousal. Female sexuality was invariably described in magazines as passive and it was often characterized as a fruit, nearly ripe and waiting to be picked and eaten. Because an active and independent female sexuality was labelled as unfeminine, fiction heroines became pregnant either through innocence or being misled; heroines rarely took the initiative in love-making except when seeking revenge. It is significant that a heroine in love was nearly always reduced to a child-like stature and behaviour; she was described with 'a glow of almost childish pleasure on the softly contoured face',[53] she had the 'face of an innocent candid child',[54] and after marriage she was frequently referred to as a 'girl-wife'. This was a very impotent, passive and innocent image of mature adult females and it would seem that her powerlessness was one of her chief attractions. For this reason the heroine was frequently portrayed in the presence of an over-bearing or bullying person because this enhanced her desirability in the eyes of the hero. It was not only her sexuality which was portrayed as child-like, but also her body, which was devoid of body hair and denied physical maturity.

The presentation of the adult female as emotionally, physically and sexually child-like was a clear denial of female adult status and power. The message of femininity portrayed in the magazines served to reduce the adult female from mature adulthood, thereby creating a wide separation between adult male and artificially child-like female, and implicit in this was an assumption of male superiority. Alternatively a woman's sexuality was described in maternal terms, that is, female sexuality was linked to maternity. This denied women a sexuality in their own right and once again reduced female sexuality to a controllable form.

In contrast to the treatment of the heroine's sexuality, male heroes had an active, often aggressive sexuality, which was frequently unrelated to feelings of love and family: there was 'nothing small, nothing tender about this love of his. It was a fierce desire, the passion of a lion for his lioness, a tiger for his mate.'[55] Similarly, the portrait of the evil woman's sexuality was active and aggressive. The active sexuality of the bad woman is an interesting example of magazine compromise. Characters like Cora Cripen and Sadie Bracken were introduced in the thirties to supplement the increasingly boring 'goody-goody' heroine in working girls' and mother/daughter magazines. Possibly editors felt that their readers desired power and sexual prowess – in fiction they could work out these fantasies without danger to the status quo. The fact that magazines felt that femininity was not totally entertaining raises interesting questions about girls and femininity. Bad young women had aggressive, masculine sexuality but they were not part of the feminine ideal. So as to ensure that the sexually independent woman was not adopted as a model by readers she was portrayed as an adulteress and murderer – not even her own mother was safe!

Conclusion

Contemporary commentators regarded girls' papers and magazines as very influential. *Girl's Own Paper* was believed to be a good influence on the young mind and was consequently stocked by school and public libraries. Certainly the Amalgamated Press schoolboy papers had a memorable effect on Robert Roberts and his contemporaries and it seems that working-class girls would have responded similarly to their school-girl papers.[56] A glance through a copy of the *School Friend* reveals how readers related to this magazine and its fictional Cliff House school; letters to the editor frequently adopted a tone more akin to the magazine's fantasy world than the reader's real life, particularly with regard to language.

Romance magazines received considerable attention and criticism during the thirties and forties. Social commentators regarded these magazines as harmful, particularly to the young ex-elementary school girl: 'If she were reading other matter as well, they would be relatively unimportant, but since generally she is not doing so, they are immensely important.'[57] Their main criticism was that magazines over-stimulated the young woman's sex interest and established unrealizable expectations of life.

These criticisms obscure the complexities behind magazine presentations of femininity and girlhood. Romance magazines did concentrate on love and passion but at the same time they reinforced current notions of feminine conduct in courtship and marriage through their fiction and problem pages. Magazines upheld a strict moral code and encouraged girls to remain virgins until married and to be submissive, monogamous and maternal within wedlock. Similarly magazine treatment of sex and sexuality reflected the commonly held belief that female sex instincts were directed towards love, children, family and security: females, according to this popular philosophy, were unfeminine and unnatural if they desired sex for itself or sex outside marriage. By presenting this restrictive view of female sexuality magazines contributed to the ideological pressures which curtailed the lives of girls and women.

The other main criticism levelled at the magazines, that they glamourized life, was true where marriage, courtship and sex were concerned. Nevertheless, editors were most concerned to ensure that their readers could relate to their magazines, hence editors paid close attention to the age and social background of their readers and to changes in society and girlhood. For example, magazines aimed at working-class girls deliberately limited the options available to their heroines, they did not encourage their readers to seek professional careers but rather to look forward to marriage and domesticity. In this respect, magazines were sensitive to the options available to girls from different backgrounds, though at the same time they did not challenge these often restrictive norms.

Magazines presented an unreal and glamorous picture of girlhood at school, at work and in relationships. They also presented readers with unreal images of adolescence and its problems. Problem pages throughout the romantic magazines showed that readers sought advice on how to cope with the contradictions which existed between the ideal of girlhood as portrayed in the magazines and their own lives. Readers also sought advice on how to satisfy feminine prescriptions for behaviour and appearance and how to reconcile these images with their own personalities, ambitions and bodies. Overall, magazines actively reinforced and reflected current notions about femininity and feminine roles and in doing so they revealed and reinforced the enormous contradictions which existed between feminine ideals and the realities of girlhood.

Acknowledgements

Many thanks to Felicity Hunt, Penny Summerfield and Mario Chin for critical comment and support. I am also grateful to James Hemming and Pat Lamburn for permission to interview and quote them.

Bibliographical Note

To date there has been no comprehensive study of magazines written for, and read by, girls in the period 1920–50. The body of this chapter is therefore based on a study of magazines and interviews with editors carried out as part of my ongoing research for a PhD thesis. However, a number of contemporary surveys provide invaluable insight into the reading habits and interests of adolescent girls. The most comprehensive survey was undertaken by A. J. Jenkinson, *What Do Boys And Girls Read?* (Methuen, 1940), in which Jenkinson assessed the popularity of magazines and compared the reading habits of secondary and senior school girls and boys in 1938. A shorter survey by L. Fenwick, 'Periodicals And Adolescent Girls', *Studies In Education* 2, 1 (1953), is also useful. Pearl Jephcott, *Girls Growing Up* (Faber and Faber, 1942), provides an interesting guide to magazine popularity and girls' attitudes towards these papers. I would also recommend Mary Cadogan and Patricia Craig, *You're a Brick, Angela!: The Girls' Story 1839–1985* (Gollancz Paperbacks, 1986), which provides an interesting and amusing study of school-girl papers. For further reading on girlhood for this period P. Jephcott, *Rising Twenty, Notes on Some Ordinary Girls* (Faber & Faber, 1948) and *Girls Growing Up*, mentioned above, are very useful. James Hemming, *Problems Of Adolescent Girls* (Heinemann, 1960), offers a rare glimpse of adolescent anxieties in the 1950s, much of which is relevant to girls of an earlier period.

In thinking about femininity, two studies by Angela McRobbie are particularly stimulating: 'Just like a Jackie story', in A. McRobbie and T. McCabe (eds), *Feminism For Girls, an Adventure Story* (Routledge & Kegan Paul, 1981) and 'Working class girls and the culture of femininity', in Women's Studies Group, *Women Take Issue: Aspects of Women's Subordination* (Hutchinson, 1978). Susan Brownmiller, *Femininity* (Paladin, 1986), is also thought provoking.

Part II

Inequalities in Education

5

Learning Her Womanly Work: the Elementary School Curriculum, 1870–1914

Annmarie Turnbull

This chapter will examine some of the ways in which the curriculum for girls and boys was differentiated between 1870 and 1914. Its focus will be on the effect of the development of practical subjects in the elementary school system where the schooling of the six-sevenths of the population considered to comprise the working class took place.

Before the 1870 Education Act the state of the working-class girl's schooling was in some ways similar to that of the working-class boy. It was short, generally covering only the years when girls could not be usefully employed; and in content very limited. It usually comprised only reading, religious instruction, and possibly writing. Children could be educated in schools run by voluntary societies like the Anglican National Society and the non-conformist British and Foreign Schools Society; organizations which received government grants from 1833. Also firmly under state control, were the schools produced as a result of legislation such as the Factory Acts, the Reformatory and Industrial Schools Acts, and the Poor Law Acts. These provided some compulsory schooling for very limited groups of working-class children. Outside the state aided system there was a plethora of dame or common schools, small private schools, charity schools and schools of industry. Here the similarities of provision between the sexes ended. There is a small but growing body of evidence suggesting, as Hurt points out, that 'the schooling of girls was both qualitatively and quantitatively more restricted than that of boys'.[1]

In all types of elementary schooling girls spent much time in tasks which anticipated their assumed adult domestic roles. These centered around sewing and cleaning. Codes of regulations from the Education Department to grant aided schools accepted and reinforced the differential treatment of girls and boys. For example, needlework regulations were enforced for female pupils and teachers alike, but not for males, and different standards of achievement in arithmetic between the sexes in elementary schools were officially sanctioned.[2]

The period from 1870 to 1914 saw the construction of a massive machine of state organized education in England and Wales, and by the end of the century there were well over five million children in public elementary schools. In these schools it was a period when the existing differences in the treatment of boys and girls were extended and increasingly formalized. In urban areas the school buildings themselves sometimes reflected this: there might be a floor each for the infants', boys', and girls' departments, while the grounds surrounding the building had different entrances for the sexes, and separate playgrounds. In contrast, the children of the ever-declining rural population, because of the smaller numbers and fewer teachers and resources, were more likely to be educated together.

By 1900 it was estimated that while 88 per cent of those under 12 were on school registers only 72 per cent were in average daily attendance.[3] Local factors such as the poverty of the neighbourhood, the availability of juvenile employment, alternative amusements, and even the weather, maintained a lively truanting population. Efforts to deal with this took up much of the time and expenditure of local school boards.[4] Although truancy was widespread among both sexes Davin's examination of its incidence in London board schools has revealed that, 'More boys would miss just one morning or afternoon a week, more girls would miss two or three or more.'[5] Girls' absences were condoned more readily than boys' by all concerned. Frequently references are made in contemporary writings to priority being given to domestic duties. One teacher, recalling her work, commented, 'A girl seldom came to school more than eight times a week because she had to stay at home and help on washing day.' (There were ten possible attendances.)[5]

The provision of schooling for working-class children was the centre of much debate throughout the period. Political and denominational controversies in the financing and control of education were not the only causes of concern. As the geographical extent and age limits of schooling were increased gradually to cover, theoretically at least, all the five to fourteen year olds of the working class, there was growing anxiety as to the purpose and therefore the content of their schooling. In the early 1880s for example, the alleged over-pressure of pupils in elementary schools focused attention on the content of schooling, and throughout that decade concern over the nation's technical inexpertise resulted in pressure on schools to include more manual and technical instruction in the curriculum.

Frequently these debates focused directly upon the assumed needs of girls and boys respectively, and much of the curriculum was consciously shaped to be sex-specific. The restrictions imposed upon girls by the Education Department's Codes of Regulations during the 1860s were reinforced as the curriculum expanded during the latter part of the century. With a growing number of subjects competing for timetable space girls spent increasingly greater periods of time in activities that separated them from boys.

Throughout the period most children experienced only the most basic schooling: reading, writing and arithmetic, with the addition of needlework for girls. Furthermore, there is evidence that gender differences were stressed and indeed increasingly encouraged in these basic subjects of the curriculum. Davin has examined the reading text books used in board schools, and has shown the rigidly sex-differentiated prescriptions of behaviour presented in them. Even in their naughtiness girls and boys were shown to differ. Boys were depicted as adventurous, daring and rough, but girls, if naughty at all, were only lazy or untidy. Children's adult futures were equally readily defined; 'Again and again girls who are tidy and diligent at home are rewarded with good places in service.'[7] For girls, work, whether paid – or more likely – unpaid, was always domestic. As one school reader proclaimed:

> Elder sisters, you may work
> Work and help your mothers
> Darn the stockings, mend the shirts
> Father's things, and brothers'.
>
> Younger boys, and you may work
> If you are but willing
> Thro' the week in many ways
> You may earn your shilling.[8]

Until the ending of the system of financing schools known as 'payment by results' in the 1890s, the Education Department (after 1899 the Board of Education) could encourage certain subjects by offering grants for their teaching. The Department issued Codes of precise regulations about the subjects which could be taught in schools, and the grants payable for their instruction. Their range expanded over the period until, by 1895, there were 30 possible subjects. Teaching of these was strictly regulated by the Department which grouped them into three categories – obligatory, class and specific. Leaving aside the complex regulations governing their teaching, it would be fair to say that what little effect this expansion had on girls was overwhelmingly that of differentiating their educational experience from that of the boys even further. If taught additional subjects at all, the boys might study a variety including animal physiology, mechanics and algebra. For the girls, it was first theoretical domestic economy, and later cookery, laundry work and housewifery, that occupied their time.

Boys did not receive practical instruction equivalent to the girls' needlework, cookery, laundry work and so on. It was more difficult in the case of boys to find tasks appropriate to the poor which were capable of being efficiently taught and which were acceptable to parents. There was no assumption for them of a uniform destination for their adult employment for which school should prepare them. Although needlework became compulsory for girls from 1862 there was no concerted effort to offer practical instruction to boys until the 1880s. By then there was a growing concern with the failure of a bookish elementary school curriculum to prepare boys for manual labour and as a result handicraft (or as it was variously called, workshop instruction, woodwork or manual work) began to make an appearance in the curriculum.[9]

In 1884 the second report of the Royal Commission on Technical Instruction described these beginnings and recommended the promotion of such teaching – but only after school hours.[10] Four years later the Cross Commission's enquiries in ten counties found that only 20 per cent of voluntary school managers, 31 per cent of school boards and 28 per cent of elementary school heads favoured the development of manual subjects for boys. Nevertheless, the commissioners noted that: 'It is urged by many persons that . . . we might early in life accustom boys to the use of their hands, and introduce some description of manual work for them, corresponding to the needlework and cookery provided for the girls.'[11] The Commission's final report gave a guarded approval to the teaching.

Finally in 1890 the Department recognized manual training for the purposes of grants, and made drawing a compulsory subject for boys, so that the 1890s began with a complete division of the sexes in practical subjects. From then handicraft teaching expanded rapidly, but domestic subjects had had a head start. Thus by 1913 while only 26 areas had no provision for instruction in domestic subjects (besides the ubiquitous needlework) 71 still provided no handicraft teaching.[12]

The development in schools of what in 1910 one educationalist called 'the domestic arts – *cooking, cleaning,* and *clothing*' reveals how persuasive and persistent an ideology of domesticity was in influencing girls' schooling.[13] This ideology suggested that domestic work and love of the home should be the focus of women's lives. The taken-for-granted, muddled teaching of adult sex roles in elementary schools was organized into distinct curriculum subjects and the progress of domestic subjects shows how the curriculum was moulded to encourage working-class girls to see their primary role as members of society to lie in serving others by sewing, cooking and cleaning, both in their own households and, as a result of society's 'servant problem', in the homes of others.

Clothing

Justifications for teaching needlework changed over the period. The original social and economic vindications of providing useful practical skills were gradually joined by claims for its educational significance in developing girls' minds and bodies, but from the outset practical utility was the motive *sine qua non* for its inclusion in the school curriculum. Plain needlework was constantly emphasized, all fancy work being deprecated in official pronouncements as inappropriate for the children of the poor. The comment of one HMI is typical of the Department's attitude to the subject:

> If we can teach them to darn and to mend, and patch with readiness and skill – if we can enable them to master cutting out to such an extent as is required for the ordinary work of a poor man's home, we shall have rendered to them, and at the same time we shall have rendered to society a lasting and incalculable service.[14]

This remained the primary aim of the teaching throughout the period, a 1912 text book, *The Aims and Methods of Teaching Needlework,* declaring its function to be, 'to fit the girls for the ordinary duties of the housewife'.[15]

Of course these 'ordinary duties' changed over the 50 years under review. Developments in the technology of textile and garment construction were to some extent acknowledged by the Education

Department. The advance of the sewing machine was accepted, albeit tentatively, and its use, where funds allowed, was encouraged in the classroom.[16] But the possibility that the poor might buy ready-made clothing was generally ignored. As a result of this, pattern-cutting and cutting-out were emphasized in spite of the increased availability of cheap paper patterns, or the possibility of making a pattern from an old garment. A growing awareness of the realities of working-class life was reflected, however, in the increasing attention given to patching and mending.

Indeed by the new century there was a substantial reassessment of the place of needlework in the curriculum. A 1909 circular is a good example of the Board's growing concern about the subject. It criticized the frequent waste of time spent on fine stitching, 'most of the stitching can be done as well if not better by sewing machines', and on elaborate mending. It acknowledged the increasing availability of cheap materials, and stressed that the only way needlework could continue to justify its existence in schools would be by becoming of real practical use. Nevertheless, it also noted that, 'It is however, equally impossible to deny that most people have two hands, and that a woman who cannot use her hands has deliberately neglected one side of her development.'[17]

There was another more insidious justification for the subject. *The Aims and Methods of Teaching Needlework* noted: 'Above all, it is hoped that the increased interest which enlightened methods bring to the subject will stimulate girls to take up needle.vork as a valuable form of recreation, so that it may become to them "that most effectual sedative, that grand soother and composer of woman's distress".'[18]

The use of needlework as a sedative was no new idea. It was a latent justification almost as pervasive as the manifest claims for its utility. An iron discipline in all subjects was considered essential for the smooth running of the schools, but the emphasis on the use of needlework here is interesting. The dampening of any high spirits on the part of girls was a quite explicit intention of the architect of the London School Board's scheme for needlework teaching in the seventies. Lousia Sara Floyer, the board's first salaried needlework inspector, found the image of the silent, motionless female, bent busily over her sewing a persuasive ideal of mature womanhood, and organized needlework instruction accordingly, believing that such a paragon could be moulded from infancy via the needlework curriculum. For example Floyer claimed that, 'Cleanliness in personal appearance is also indirectly cultivated by knitting, because a child cannot so well play in the gutter or knock her playfellow about, if she has knitting in her hand.'[19]

In his report for 1900, HMI J. Fitzmaurice was still emphasizing this function. School needlework was important he argued: 'Not only on account of its practical utility, but because it is a splendid training for hand and eye, and has also a great refining influence; and love for the needle encourages domesticity.'[20] The useful values of neatness, cleanliness, tidiness, self-respect and thrift so frequently eulogized throughout the whole elementary school curriculum, were to be specially emphasized in needlework, stressed the Board.

In spite of all this excellent practical and disciplinary value in the schooling of females, the thorny problem gradually emerged of finding some educational, as opposed to moral and utilitarian justification, for teaching needlework. As Fitzmaurice's comment implies, by 1900 the encouragement of refined and domesticated housewives was considered an insufficient aim. By then the growing professionalization of education meant that such justifications were much less acceptable, but the Board of Education had invested considerable time and resources developing needlework and sought to find examples of its educational merits. As a consequence, the Board's advice to teachers began to draw parallels between the teaching of needlework, handwork, handicraft and art.

Needlework was presented as a continuation of the Froebelian methods then gaining ground in infant departments.[21] Indeed from the 1870s Floyer had emphasized the need to link needlework with other subjects. She had suggested its teaching could be encouraged in reading, writing, spelling ('since words like "stitching" and "herring-boning" are quite as hard to spell as "abominable" '), diction, geography, and even in object lessons. Here she recommended a lesson on 'the parts, properties and uses of a needle'.[22]

By the turn of the century such claims were becoming commonplace. One of the most influential arguments was that needlework could develop artistic qualities. This gained impetus under the influence of Ann Macbeth and her colleagues at the Glasgow School of Art.[23] Macbeth's needlework books for schools emphasized neither femininity nor function, but design. Sewing became art just as cookery was to become science.

It is difficult to be specific about the proportion of their time girls spent sewing in school. Practice varied from district to district, and even from school to school. After needlework became compulsory in 1862, the time spent on sewing may well have increased. The London School Board's subcommittee on needlework reported in

1873 that sewing was taking up a quarter of the school hours devoted to secular instruction, that is between five and seven hours a week. HMI E. M. Sneyd-Kynnersley also attested in his memoirs to the large amount of time girls spent sewing. 'It was not unusual', he noted, 'to find five afternoons a week entirely devoted to sewing.'[24] Needlework's inclusion among the class subjects from 1875 compounded this situation. In the 1880s the Liverpool School Board advised that four hours a week should be devoted to sewing and HMI Reverend Byrne noted that the promotion of needlework to the 'payment by results' category, meant that in some schools: 'needlework was carried almost to excess, so that the school would seem not unlikely to relapse into the state of the old-fashioned industrial or sewing school of many years ago since [sic] where needlework was the main staple of instruction, with a little reading.'[25]

The demands of the needlework schedule set out in the Board of Education Code continued to be considerable throughout the period. Boys would usually be doing additional arithmetic as the girls stitched.[26] In 1894 partly in response to pressure from the teachers, some modifications were introduced to ease the burden. The Department believed that these afforded 'substantial relief to teachers'.[27] It is doubtful that this greatly affected the time devoted to the instruction, for a year later a witness to the Bryce Commission observed: 'Girls spend too much time on needlework . . . I have seen some time-tables lately in elementary schools and have found four or five hours often given to needlework.'[28] Traditional assumptions about the value of time spent sewing persisted. As late as 1901 one HMI mourned the lessening of time given to it: 'It is lamentable to see how the sewing lessons are curtailed by the attempt to teach smatterings of arts and sciences. It is with difficulty that three hours a week can be rescued for the subject; and I think this should be the irreducible minimum.'[29]

The new century, however, saw a determined effort by the Board to regulate the time spent on needlework and by 1904 the maximum time specified for its teaching was four hours a week. By 1905 worries about the effect of sewing on children's health led to the relaxation of its teaching to infants, and by 1909 the Board was actively discouraging this. In 1912 the chief woman inspector reported that the time spent on needlework varied from two, to occasionally four hours, the average being two and a half hours a week, in two separate periods. This average she recommended as the maximum time girls should spend on sewing, except in their last year at school.[30]

At first individual teaching had sufficed; the teacher had moved from girl to girl letting each work at her own pace. The inadequate work of the tardy or untalented would be compensated for by the output of their more productive sisters, and the inspector would never know whose work he examined on his annual visit, but from 1876 needlework began to be examined through the working of a series of graded exercises, under the eye of the inspector. The grant now depended on the expertise of each and every girl and a more efficient means of teaching them had to be developed. A 'systematic' or 'collective' method was introduced, especially into the large classes of urban schools.[31] In essence this was teaching by demonstration. The teacher stood at the front of the class and directed the girls by a series of step-by-step commands. The pupils performed each action necessary to the formation of a stitch in perfect unison. These 'drills' started in the baby class, where there were drills for threading needles (with 'baby threaders' – special needles with no points), putting on thimbles, and holding the work in the 'correct' position. In later standards knitting, hemming, seaming, pattern marking and cutting out were all taught by this method.[32] After two decades of emphasis on samples the 1894 Code introduced a major alteration: girls in the higher standards could submit a completed garment for inspection and the formal annual inspection was discontinued. The standard of work was still extraordinarily demanding. Instructions to HMIs recommended 12 to 18 stitches per inch for seaming and stitching at the turn of the century.[33]

School sewing was undoubtedly generally accepted by girls as part of a female's lot but there was some resistance to it. For example the pupils of one Devon School were reported to have 'struck against thimbles' and a Suffolk woman, recalling her schooling at the end of the century, explained how:

> The Headmaster's wife was in charge of the needlework class. She would never allow me to do anything worthwhile. Oddments of wool to knit, unknit and reknit – the same with needlework just odds and ends to stitch together, unpick and restitch. One afternoon, after taking the same little piece of calico, sewn, unsewn, and resewn for the sixth time, I just threw it on her desk, jumped the seat, through the door jumped the playground wall, and was away home.[34]

Perhaps the most interesting aspect of needlework teaching was its economic position in the curriculum for it had to be financially self-supporting. Thus there was a tendency to rely for practice on work required by local dignitaries. Materials would then be free. Sneyd-Kynnersley recalled the production line of one country school where household items for the local aristocracy would be made by one class and marked with coronets by another. He went on to explain how, 'In country schools there was not much fear of neglect, for Mrs Squire and Mrs Rector kept vigilant eyes on this branch of education, and the subscribers to the school funds often got back part of the value of their money by sending their household sewing to be done in school.'[35]

In towns, schools even took orders from local shops, and as late as 1912 the problem of selling completed work was such that the Board of Education considered the taking of orders 'acceptable within limits'.[36] Expenditure on other aspects of elementary school teaching was often the source of criticism and controversy, but in spite of needlework's severe costing problems there was no suggestion that it should be abandoned. Yet its teaching abounded with contradictions. The realities of a working-class home, where time and space would often be considerably restricted, were rarely acknowledged; the emphasis on the production of minutely-stitched white shirts, impractical underclothes or useless 'samples' continued until the end of the period, while the intention of producing sensible industrious women, resigned to their appointed station in life meant that a class could dress a doll in the most intricately detailed finery to demonstrate their skills, but were discouraged from adding the simplest of decorations to their own garments.[37] Such was the power and the illogicality of the ideology of domesticity.

Cooking and Cleaning

Before 1870 the Committee of Council for Education (the predecessor of the Education Department and the Board of Education) had largely restricted its promotion of practical subjects to needlework, but in 1870 the Education Department added theoretical domestic economy to the Code, as an additional subject that could be taught by the class teacher. In 1874 it became a subject for which a grant was available and in 1878 it became a compulsory specific subject for girls. So from the seventies onwards instruction in domestic subjects increased.

The widespread interest of the middle class in the expansion of such teaching in schools was revealed by the organization of a number of domestic economy congresses. The Society of Arts

Teaching the teachers – a cookery demonstration.

organized the first of a series of these in Birmingham in 1877 and 600 people attended. The congress included discussions on nutrition, thrift, needlework, housing and sanitation and numbered among its speakers Edwin Chadwick, public health pioneer, and T. H. Huxley, scientist and London School Board member. The following year's congress was held in Manchester and entitled 'Domestic Economy and Elementary Education'. The growing enthusiasm for the subject could not be stemmed and many speakers urged the immediate introduction of practical cookery instruction into elementary schools. The idea had taken hold so firmly that, in the words of one cynical observer, 'England is to be made regenerate under the auspices of Domestic Economy.'[38] Cookery teaching fired the imagination of many philanthropic middle-class women. In his study of women and philanthropy Prochaska has noted that 'a distinctive feature of women's work in nineteenth century philanthropy is the degree to which they applied their domestic experience and education . . . to the world outside the home.'[39] This practical crusade for the efficient training of females for work in their 'natural' sphere took many forms, of which support for school instruction in domestic subjects is only one example. The original aim of the developing domestic subjects movement had been to educate women of both the middle and working class but this was replaced by a new objective. One pioneer of the teaching explained: 'Experience has certainly taught me that it is really hopeless to teach the wives of artisans how to improve their cooking; they are utterly indifferent. Our only hope is to reach the children.'[40]

In 1874 the National Training School of Cookery was opened in South Kensington, London, and was soon training middle-class women who took their newly and rapidly acquired skills to other towns. Only two years later the School's Principal, Edith Nicolls, wrote in her annual report:

> There have been schools opened for instruction in Cookery, taught by teachers trained at South Kensington in Liverpool, Leeds, Oxford, Leamington, Shrewsbury, Birmingham, Edinburgh and Glasgow, and from all these satisfactory reports have been received; whilst other towns, such as Hereford, Bristol, Sheffield, Rugby, Dundee and Wickham will shortly have teachers sent to them to open schools in those towns also.[41]

It was these teachers who were to pioneer school cookery instruction.

The 1877 'Memorandum to the Education Department from the

School Boards of some of the Principal Towns in England and Scotland on the Subject of Instruction in Cookery' advocated the rapid introduction of practical cookery. In 1881 a Royal Commission on Technical Education was appointed: it too favoured the expansion of practical subjects and when in the same year, a deputation from the cookery schools submitted a scheme of instruction for teaching cookery to elementary classes and appealed for a grant to be extended to the subject they found a favourable response.[42] The following year saw the introduction of cookery into the Code's permissible clauses as a grant supported subject. It was increasingly accepted as an appropriate school subject for girls throughout the 1880s, and when the 30 witnesses to the Cross Commission were asked for their opinion on the instruction all but one approved its place in the curriculum.[43]

Again after pressure from the cookery schools, laundry work entered the Code in 1889 as a grant earning subject. If there was an obligation on women to feed others they faced an even stronger compunction to keep the home and its occupants clean. Cleanliness after all was next to godliness and, as with needlework, moral justifications mingled with utilitarian ones: 'The object of teaching laundry work is not only to teach girls how to wash and dry the clothes and to starch and iron them in the best way . . . but to train them to habits of neatness, quickness and cleanliness', claimed one of its promoters.[44] In 1897 housewifery too entered the Code, becoming a grant earning subject in 1900. The roles of housewife and domestic servant have much in common and illustrations and photographs of London's housewifery centres show the pupils dressed neatly in caps and cuffs – the perfect image of compliant servants. The connection between schooling and service that was implicit in much cookery and laundry work teaching was here made explicit.

The interest in technical education for women, in the limited form of domestic subjects instruction, escalated with the growing awareness of public consciousness of the issue of 'national efficiency', or rather, inefficiency. The mounting concern with 'maternal ignorance' in the period has been closely documented.[45] Fears about the supposedly unskilled British housewife and mother were fanned by the publication of the Report of the Inter-Departmental Committee on Physical Deterioration in 1904. This stressed the importance of well-organized and well-taught domestic subjects instruction in schools and its recommendations brought a prompt response from the Board of Education.[46] Robert Morant, Secretary to the Board, urged the appointment of a woman chief inspector and of more women domestic subjects inspectors. The resulting appointments increased pressure to provide more domestic instruction in schools. By 1910, when a 'Memorandum on the Teaching of Infant Care in the Elementary Schools' was published, it was apparent that the Board considered it essential that girls, under 14 years of age, should be receiving a thorough training in the practicalities of housework and mothering.[47]

Yet a structured and regular domestic subjects curriculum would not have been the experience of all girls. Cookery, laundry work and housewifery were costly subjects requiring expensive equipment, and this sometimes led to the opposition of local school board members who had an eye on the rates. There were wide regional variations and while the teaching flourished in many urban areas, the problems of accommodation, poor water supplies and cost, hampered developments in rural districts. Thus at the turn of the century, when London and Liverpool could claim to be instructing nearly all girls in domestic skills, only 24 girls in the whole county of Northumberland earned the cookery grant.[48]

Other factors hindered the development of domestic subjects. Initially many ordinary elementary teachers were hostile to them. In the early 1880s *The Board Teacher* reflected the scepticism of many London teachers to the claims made for domestic subjects. The pressure which the introduction of additional subjects would impose on mistresses already burdened by needlework requirements brought the despairing cry, 'What are the Mistresses going to do?'[49] What some of them did was try to oppose the introduction of cookery. In 1884 the Metropolitan Board Teachers' Association passed a motion suggesting that girls' attendance at cookery should not be enforced. The proposer 'contended that it was impossible to teach scientific cookery to girls. Far too much was being attempted during girls' school life.'[50]

By the end of the century, however a subcommittee of the London School Board investigating the relation of domestic subjects to other subjects in the school curriculum found that the necessity for *some* practical domestic instruction was generally accepted by women teachers. Their principal complaint was that the time spent on them hampered the more academic girls, who were destined for higher grade schools and teaching or office work. It was not the subjects themselves but the elementary teachers' lack of control over the amount and timing of the teaching that emerged as the central criticism.[51] While friction persisted between the elementary teacher and the specialist domestic subjects teacher the belief that women's inevitable burden of domestic work should determine the content of girls' schooling had been largely accepted throughout the profession by the end of the period.

In contrast, such a belief was not always accepted by girls' parents. They expressed some hostility to cookery, and when laundry work and housewifery joined it the authorities expressed concern over the mounting parental disapproval. These two subjects were especially associated with drudgery and manual labour. Unaware of or unimpressed by the growing educational pretensions of domestic subjects, for example their claims to develop hand-eye co-ordination or to develop understanding of scientific principles, some parents disapproved of their daughters spending school time on cleaning and cooking. Even in London, where the teaching was always closely supervised, the School Board frequently faced sceptical parents. Annually the reports of the domestic subjects superintendents noted that the subjects were finally growing in popularity with parents. However, these claims may be interpreted as indicating the depth and persistence of the antagonism still felt towards them.[52] In 1899 Bessie Skinner's parents ingeniously but unsuccessfully requested her exemption from laundry lessons on the grounds that she practised mandolin and guitar, and laundry work would soften her fingers.[53] HMI Hyacinthe Deane noted in her annual report for 1899–1900, 'Laundry work continues to be unpopular among the parents, who, I think fear lest their children should take up a trade which, from its almost unrestricted hours of labour and often bad conditions, is mainly undertaken by the roughest class of women.'[54] But the authorities were increasingly unprepared to countenance parents' objections. By 1912 the journal *Education* reports the prosecution of William Sanderson, farmer, for removing his daughter from cookery classes. The prosecution was successful and Sanderson was fined.[55]

Dissatisfaction was expressed about all domestic subjects and cookery was no exception. The criticism most frequently made of the teaching was its inappropriateness as a preparation for working-class womanhood. After retiring from her post as inspectress of cookery at the Education Department in 1896 Mary Harrison wrote a series of articles documenting the failings of the teaching. The disregard of pupils' home conditions was illustrated by the frequent baking of vendible cakes and buns that would help the subject pay its way, or of miniature meals. Alice Lewis, a London woman recalled, 'I remember making a Yorkshire pudding for one! "You

won't want a large family for that" Mum said.'[56] Towards the end of
the period the move to the provision of school meals also meant that,
in the interest of economy and efficiency, the syllabus was
sometimes abandoned and the pupils used to prepare the meals. One
teacher recalled how her class 'peeled thousands of potatoes,
prepared Cornish pasties and did the washing up.'[57]

The exact content of the cookery syllabus was often a problem.
There was always a tension among the leaders of the domestic
subjects movement as to whether they should restrict themselves to
the living conditions that their pupils would face as adults by using
cheap ingredients and 'homely' measures, or teach them the 'proper'
way. The Education Department stressed relevance at all costs and
were always severely critical of the failure of schools to use
equipment, fuel, and ingredients that would be found in pupils'
homes, or of the use of methods unsuited to the busy working-class
woman such as 'the picking of every single stalk from every single
currant'.[58] Text books and syllabuses contained a bewildering
number and variety of dishes, many entirely inappropriate to the
incomes or time constraints of working-class households, and often
specified an astonishing battery of utensils and equipment for their
production.[59]

Even the Board of Education was unable to ameliorate the
situation, as the failure of its attempt to provide detailed syllabuses
for local authorities shows. In the summer of 1905, exasperated by
the task and by the acrimony it had created within the inspectorate,
Maude Lawrence, chief woman inspector, illustrated the difficulty
with one telling example, 'a fishing village is usually the last place
where fish is obtainable, it is generally more plentiful and as cheap in
towns.'[60] In October the attempt was finally abandoned after she
pointed out to Morant that, 'It would be unfortunate if it should
come to the knowledge of the LEAs and teachers that there was a
difference of opinion on the matter of a syllabus between two
officials of the board.'[61]

In this period, as now, the curriculum was the focus for arguments
about the kind of society that was wanted. The belief that the sexes
should have separate but complementary adult roles found expression
in every aspect of schooling. Domestic subjects teaching played a
central part in this and during this period the haphazard teaching of
sewing and cleaning was transformed into a number of distinct
school subjects, each with its own structured path to expertise.
Originally aimed only at girls destined to become working men's
wives, the subjects in later years developed to encompass also the

supposed concerns of middle-class housewives. The inculcation of moral values and standards was an integral part of the teaching for all girls, but class differences produced a differing practical interpretation: the middle-class girl might be taught the 'science of cleansing' while her working-class sister learned 'laundry work'.[62]

How much any of them benefited from this use of their school time is questionable. Certainly, with regard to cookery, the Board of Education itself admitted in 1907 that in many cases there had been 'a serious waste of public money and a futile waste of time and teaching power, upon lines that made it almost impossible for the children to obtain any practical benefit from the so-called instruction in cookery to which they are submitted.'[63]

By the First World War elementary schools had largely accepted the assumptions of a Victorian domestic ideology now freshly cloaked in the guise of the new century's imperialist and eugenist ideals. Between 1870 and 1914 women were admitted in growing numbers to all levels of the education system. They were involved as pupils, teachers, higher education students, managers and administrators. As women featured more prominently in educational debates and decision making, and in educational institutions, so a concern with gender roles grew in schools. Yet their entry into the organization and management of the growing public sphere of education did not herald a rejection of the separate spheres doctrine. On the contrary, women's presence in this area often produced educational plans and policies in accord with the assumptions of the ideology of domesticity, and practices originating from the domestic sphere became educationally legitimated and institutionalized with the full support of women; many of whom contributed to this process in the belief that it provided opportunities for their sex to exert independence and authority in society.

There was, however, an enormous gulf between the intentions of those who promoted a sex-differentiated curriculum and aimed to ensure that every 14 year-old girl would be a skilled and resourceful housewife, and their achievements. The teaching was fraught with problems and despite the ambitious claims made for domestic subjects they made little impact on the practical household conditions of the nation. Goals were invariably unrealistic and ignored the material domestic conditions of the majority of the population. Nevertheless, the ideology behind the curriculum was powerful and provided school girls with an image of woman as servicing others. Schooling secured women's imprisonment in domesticity.

Bibliographical Note

In this period useful starting points for the history of the school curriculum generally are P. Gordon and D. Lawton's *Curriculum Change in the Nineteenth and Twentieth Centuries* (Hodder & Stoughton, 1978) and J. S. Hurt, *Elementary Schooling and the Working Classes 1860–1918* (Routledge & Kegan Paul, 1979). The work of Anna Davin, Carol Dyhouse and Jane Lewis cited in the notes to this chapter, provides a framework for exploring the school curriculum in terms of sexual divisions, but there is still much groundwork that needs to be done based on the wealth of as yet unexplored local school records. For domestic subjects instruction specifically the best introduction remains H. Sillitoe, *A History of the Teaching of Domestic Subjects* (Methuen, 1933). The chapter draws heavily on material presented in my PhD thesis, 'Women, Education and Domesticity: a Study of the Domestic Subjects Movement 1870–1914', Southbank Polytechnic, 1983.

6

Inequalities in the Teaching Profession: the Effect on Teachers and Pupils, 1910–39

Alison Oram

> Were it a question of 'teaching subjects' or 'managing' scholars, it might be conceded that men and women are to a certain extent interchangeable. But when it is a question of inculcating manly qualities in boys and womanly qualities in girls there can be no interchangeability.[1]

> Boys and girls would respond to any head teacher, man or woman, who was a sound educationalist. For a man to be at the head of a mixed school engendered in the boy a false idea that Nature had destined him, the lord of creation, for positions of authority, and it developed in the girl a cramping lack of confidence and ambition.[2]

Throughout the 1920s and 1930s, the National Association of Schoolmasters (NAS), a group of anti-feminist men teachers who had split off from the main teachers' union the National Union of Teachers (NUT) in 1922, pressed their demands for men teachers for all boys over seven, and for headmasters in mixed schools. They argued that a crucial part of the elementary schooling process was to instil gender characteristics, that is to say masculinity and femininity, into pupils. They were especially anxious that boys should be taught to be men. Their whole notion of desirable schooling arrangements and the significance of gender was forcefully challenged by the National Union of Women Teachers (NUWT), a small feminist teachers union, at the opposite pole of the debate. These women argued that the emphasis on masculinity and femininity should be broken down, and that girls' needs must be given more consideration by those in charge of the education system.

To support their demand for 'men teachers for boys' the NAS maintained that men and women should occupy separate spheres in teaching. They made a distinction in teachers' work between 'instruction' and 'education'. Instruction could be competently carried out by a teacher of either sex, but when it came to 'education', a crucial but somewhat mystical process, then a teacher of the same sex as the pupil was required in order to induce gender-differentiated characteristics. Thus only men could inculcate manly qualities in boys. 'Women could teach boys but the education of the boy required and included the manliness of character which was his birthright and which the nation would require when he grew up.'[3]

Although the different roles of men and women in society were assumed to be 'natural', the manly *instinct* had to be *taught*, a contradiction frequently expressed by the NAS. 'Men and women were fundamentally different; the man would find his work in the world, the woman hers in the home . . . If boys were to be trained to become men they must have manly instincts implanted in them, and these could not be produced by women teachers.'[4] So, boys could not become men by virtue of their biology alone. They had to be taught manly characteristics, not just by any male teacher but by a 'true man', thereby confirming the teacher's own masculinity as well as the child's. A delegate at the NAS's conference in 1930 strongly maintained that: 'It was essential today that boys should be taught by the most manly type of teacher that could be found. Many of the boys in this country had never come into contact with real men at school.'[5]

But feminists questioned the whole concept of teaching gender. As Winifred Holtby, the feminist writer and journalist put it in 1926, 'Should education be directed towards emphasizing or eliminating the differences that exist between the sexes.'[6] The National Union of Women Teachers, an organization firmly based on feminist principles, saw education as a tool for creating *equality* between women and men, both in the home and at the workplace, by *breaking down* sex roles. The union 'stressed the importance of inculcating in early youth the right psychological attitude of boys and girls to each other in preparation for the time when they entered the labour market.'[7]

The NUWT argued that the curriculum should be the same for both sexes. If domestic subjects were going to be taught in schools, they should be taught to both sexes equally. Boys should be given instruction in needlework and cookery, and girls in light woodwork as a 'more equal preparation for future home life'. In 1925 one leading member said that, 'they had often been told that woman's place was the home, but was not man's place the home too? . . . They did not want girls working for other things to waste time in acquiring a smattering of domestic knowledge which they would never need in their future life.'[8]

In particular, the union argued against mixed schools, on the grounds that they did not offer true co-education, but favoured boys and penalized girls. Their observation that 'in a mixed class the boys received the attention and the girls were not catered for' is one still made by feminists today.[9]

> We ask that in all schemes of reorganisation our predominantly male reorganisers shall remember they are catering for girls as well as for boys, and that the interests of neither must be subordinated to those of the other. The existence of the mixed school in which these conditions do not obtain is at best an unsatisfactory compromise, and in cases where women are excluded from the headships constitutes an abiding injustice to successive generations of girls trained in an atmosphere where one sex perpetually dominates – and that not their own.[10]

For the NUWT the first priority was that teachers should be good educationalists; their sex was less important. However the NUWT argued that girls needed to see women teachers in positions of power such as headships to provide positive role models and encourage them to aim high in life, while boys equally needed to be shown that authority should not always lie in the hands of men.

It was the NAS who took the offensive in the debate, framing the argument in terms of boys' needs and the importance of masculinity – boys were clearly seen as the most important group of children. The NUWT was constantly striving to get girls' interests and the issue of equal opportunities in education taken seriously. What was the reason for all this anxiety about masculinity (and femininity) in the schools and why should it have come up in the inter-war period?

As the demands of the NAS suggested, the debate over teaching gender characteristics to children reflected another battle within the elementary teaching profession itself between men and women teachers over equality of opportunity, pay and status. This battle had become so fierce that by the 1920s it was described as 'sex antagonism' and had caused huge rifts in the NUT. The NAS had left the NUT in 1922 because it disagreed with NUT policy for equal pay, while the NUWT had split off in 1919 because they believed (rightly as it turned out) that the male-dominated NUT would never put its weight behind this issue.

Women elementary school teachers suffered major inequalities, compared to their male colleagues, in three areas of their employment. They received approximately four-fifths of the men's rate of pay, despite doing equal work and possessing identical qualifications. After 1922, under most local education authorities, women teachers were obliged to resign their posts on marriage.[11] And thirdly, women were less likely then men to be promoted to a head teachers' post, especially in mixed schools. It was this contested area of promotion prospects which led to the fiercest arguments played out in terms of gender, that is, how areas of teaching and responsibility should be apportioned according to the sex of both teacher and pupil. This debate became most intense and acrimonious during the 1920s and 1930s. The NAS and to some extent the men in the NUT alleged bitterly that men were being driven out of the profession and that the headships of mixed and junior mixed schools were being given to women, when they were really men's jobs. The main policy of the NAS was expressed in their slogan 'Men Teachers for Boys' which not only sought to strengthen their claim to higher pay on the grounds that men were or should be doing a distinctly different job from women teachers, but also enabled them to try to extend men's position and opportunities in the profession. 'Teaching the boys and youth of the nation was a man's work', said the president of the NAS in 1929, 'does sex make no difference?'[12]

Since the standard qualification, the teaching certificate, was the same for both sexes, men teachers could only argue that they had special skills by emphasizing the sexual division of labour – the definition of different jobs as either masculine or feminine. 'Masculinity' cannot be constructed without a complementary idea of 'femininity'. The men's campaign to justify sexual inequality in the teaching profession rested on the reinforcement of these beliefs about gender. For example it was argued that men needed to earn a higher 'family wage' to support their dependent wives and children, and that they were naturally more suited to leadership roles like school headships, while women preferred to teach young children. At one and the same time, then, the NAS were promoting masculinity for boys, reinforcing their own masculinity, and defending – and indeed attempting to extend – their professional position.

The women of the NUWT and NUT claimed similarly that *their* chances of promotion were being blocked by the policy of amalgamating departments and giving the headships to *men*. It was the NUWT in particular who took up the women teachers' case strongly, arguing that: 'Men were an almost insignificant section of the whole, yet gradually the chances of promotion for women were becoming less and less. The practice was growing of combining infant departments with mixed schools and putting men in charge. That was how economy worked when coupled with sex prejudice.'[13]

The NUWT maintained that the headships of mixed departments should be open to men and women equally, and sex should make no difference. Equality of opportunity would improve the efficiency of schools, by ensuring that the best heads were chosen, and would also be in the interests of the children, who ought not to be taught that the male sex was the superior, as well as doing justice to women class teachers.

However the union did advocate that 'in the present stage of development' adolescent girls and boys should wherever possible be taught in separate departments each with its own head teacher in 'the cause of establishing right relations between the sexes', that is, to avoid the disadvantages suffered by girls in senior mixed schools.[14]

At times, the NUWT was forced to defend women teachers' position by supporting one aspect of the sexual division of labour, the female monopoly of infant school headships, although they stressed women's specialized training as much as feminine qualities in justification. The amalgamation of infant with mixed departments, often under a headmaster, reduced promotion opportunities for women teachers. Furthermore, 'The control of infant schools was an important and delicate work calling for special insight and sympathy and specialist training. The best men knew they were not qualified and did not apply for headships.'[15]

Strategies for Promoting Masculinity

The NAS condemned the appointment of headmistresses to mixed schools who, as well as taking posts which were rightfully men's, compromised the masculinity of the men teachers serving under them. They argued that it was bad for boys in the school to see a woman in charge of men, as well as being detrimental to the men's self-respect. 'Service under a headmistress is distasteful to the majority of schoolmasters. This distaste is based on an entirely healthy instinct, is strongly approved by the great majority of men and women, and reflects the normal and sane attitudes of the sexes to each other.'[16]

The men teachers' terrified concern for their manliness reflects its fragility in an occupation where women did similar work and which was often seen as a feminine profession. In 1930 a leading NUWT member strongly defended women's right to the headships of mixed schools.

> Men objected to working under women. Why should they? Prime ministers worked under queens, public servants worked today under Miss Bondfield, and soldiers followed Boadicea and Joan of Arc to battle . . . The man who could not work under a woman was not fit to teach young children, and the sooner he found another job the better for the unfortunate children under his care.[17]

At the NUWT conference two years later it was said that: 'Some local authorities would rather have the most colourless inefficient man as head than a Solomon of a woman.' In the same debate, 'Miss D. A. Davies said that she had for 12 years been head of a mixed school in Birmingham. She had three men in her school, and there was no question at all about the management of the men. (Laughter).'[18] When the same issue was discussed later in the 1930s, one member 'criticized the argument that "we cannot ask our young men to serve under women". "That false sense of masculine superiority", she said, "must be eliminated".'[19]

Indeed it is obvious from the NAS propaganda examined earlier that the schoolmasters' insistence on the importance of gender in teaching involved upholding masculine values as superior and positive against feminine ones as inferior and negative, and that they tended to hold women teachers in contempt. The NAS repeatedly said that they did not wish to attack women teachers – their work should be separate from men's but was equally important. 'They did not', said one member, 'attack women who had to teach boys. They were only saying that these women were not in their proper place.'[20]

These assertions were rather disingenuous, as the NAS constantly disparaged the work of women teachers, especially in boys' and mixed schools, and slighted their 'feminine' qualities. The women teachers of course clearly recognized NAS attacks as woman-hating and anti-feminist. 'What had happened to the virility of men that they should only assert themselves by insulting women?', they asked indignantly.[21] One NUWT member pointed to the importance of deeply embedded ideas of male and female power relations. 'There was in many people's minds, she said, a customary traditional feeling of the superiority of one sex. It was an intangible barrier, but it was one that was very difficult to break down.'[22]

The NAS argued for a more rigid sexual division of labour in

A male teacher with a mixed class at Bentworth Road School, Hammersmith, 1930.

teaching on the grounds of a need to foster masculinity in boys. The emphasis on teachers' sex was not only an attempt to reserve the more prestigious posts for men teachers and expand their promotion prospects but also helped to establish the importance of gender identity during a period of obvious anxiety, confirming 'masculinity' in opposition to and superior to 'femininity'. The NUWT recognized that men teachers' attempt to claim particular jobs for themselves in terms of masculinity was very much opposed to the interests of women, and they lobbied for equality of opportunity on feminist grounds. They pointed out that it was only by *minimizing* gender distinctions of masculinity and femininity that women would be able to achieve full emancipation.

However the NAS was able to reinforce its arguments by connecting them to other strands of educational and social concern of the period such as militarism, eugenics and psychology. The union's attacks on women teachers were strengthened by reference to and use of these contemporary social fears and prejudices, because they partly grew from the same set of historical circumstances.

The suggestion that if women taught boys the nation's future manhood would be damaged, was associated with nationalistic sentiments and militarism during and after the First World War. The debate about the desirability of women teachers for boys began immediately after the war broke out when many men teachers enlisted, leaving women to run boys' schools. It was said of these men that 'not all of them will carry back their shields. But those who do return will come back more virile than ever. There is little fear of the feminization of the boys who are afterwards to come under [their] influence.'[23] Masculinity was closely bound up with and indeed central to militarism. Even in 1929 the representative of one NAS branch expressed his opinion that: 'Personally, I think that if the men of the armies of the Great War had been taught in their youth by women, history would now be somewhat different.'[24]

Of course many of them *had* been taught by women! Shortly before the outbreak of the Second World War this theme was again revived. In order to combat the threat to democracy, 'the utmost efforts must be made to equip the future men of England with that virility of character, steadfastness of endeavour and sense of fair play which alone would enable this country to play its part in the struggle with any hope of success.'[25]

Closely connected with these ideas about manliness and nationhood was concern about the falling birthrate and the quality of the nation's children. The need for men teachers was often put in the language of eugenics. 'We could not produce an A1 race of men unless its boys came under the influence of men . . . an insufficient supply of men teachers must disastrously affect the future of the race.'[26]

Concern over juvenile delinquency led to a shortlived panic in the early 1930s, when women teachers, and particularly their alleged inability to discipline boys, were blamed for crimes by school boys. This led to headlines such as 'Are Boys Taught by Women More Likely to be Criminals?' and 'Boy of 13 Who Resented Women Teachers'.[27] The NAS pointed to American research which linked juvenile crime with the feminization of the schools. Many of the men teachers' arguments were derived directly or indirectly from the new, or newly popular, science of psychology. Psychology was a fashionable influence on both teachers and educational policy in the inter-war years. Teachers were encouraged to read books on psychoanalysis and child development while educational psychologists employed by LEAs justified moves towards streaming in schools. Crudely interpreted Freudian theory of the man as naturally dominant and the woman as submissive was also used to account for women's oppression in the family and at work. Thus NAS assertions that their policies were based on 'sound psychological and professional grounds' carried a good deal of authority.[28]

The men's attempts to establish a male sphere within teaching were reinforced by the way their arguments meshed with contemporary social fears and problems. But the NUWT were quick to counter their assertions, often using arguments drawn from the same sources. A Bristol delegate at the union's conference in 1930 insisted that 'it was psychologically wrong and vicious that any body of men should differentiate between the sexes in the teaching profession.'[29] Ethel Froud, general secretary of the NUWT, rejected the claim that women teachers made boys effeminate.

> If it is suggested that women make boys namby-pamby, how many army officers and men who have got on well will tell you they owe much to women who taught them when they were at school? It is a large number. This is largely a move to prevent women from becoming headmistresses at mixed schools. Under the new re-organisation scheme schools will be filled with mixed classes of boys and girls, and the men want to keep all the educational plums for themselves.[30]

The reorganization scheme she referred to followed the recommendation of the 1926 *Hadow Report* of a change in schooling at the age of 11, combined with a fall in the number of school-age children. Schools were increasingly separated into junior and senior departments, with a growing proportion of mixed rather than single sex departments. This process frequently led to a situation where girls' and boys' departments were reorganized into a mixed junior school, or where senior classes were taken away and junior and infant classes combined into one school, leading to diminished promotion prospects for all teachers.

The NUWT saw the displacement of women teachers caused by blocked promotion prospects in the 1920s and 1930s and by the marriage bar as part of a general attack on women workers resulting from the economic recession and political reaction.[31] Citing the events in Germany, where women had been barred from professional and public life and sent back to the home, the union expressed the fear that too great an emphasis on masculinity led to fascism and militarism. 'Stressing the so-called masculine qualities is going to lead Germany and other countries to serious things – possibly war. We do not want women to be mothers if their sons are only to be trained as warriors.'[32] The NUWT linked the growth of anti-feminism with the rise of fascism in Europe and one of their major feminist political activities was strong support for the peace movement. They protested against the compulsory celebration of Empire day by school children and against cadet corp training in schools.

The Policy of the Mixed Union

Perhaps the NAS was just a small group of atypical extremists. After all, the majority of elementary school teachers were represented by the NUT. What were the NUT's views on the appropriateness of teaching masculinity and femininity in schools? Did the NUT have the interests of men teachers or women teachers most at heart?

From the mid-1920s the NUT did adopt an equal opportunities position on the staffing of mixed schools. Its policy was that Local Education Authorities (LEAs) should appoint the most suitable applicants regardless of sex to the staff and headships of mixed schools, but should include both men and women to give adequate provision for the education of both boys and girls. In 1929, however, the Executive amended this policy, adding a proviso that LEAs should consider the individual preferences of members of their assistant staffs when appointing men teachers to serve under headmistresses or women to serve under headmasters.[33] This appears to acknowledge the refusal of many men to serve under a woman head and admits a considerable degree of leeway to the recommendation that the sex of the teachers should be unimportant. The union tried to avoid confronting the problem of men and women teachers' opportunities in mixed schools by recommending separate spheres, i.e. a sexual division of labour, in order to safeguard both men's and women's jobs. Boys and girls should, if possible, be educated in separate schools, and infant departments should not be amalgamated with juniors but should have a separate headmistress.[34]

The union did not clearly convey its policy to members, but it was certainly anxious to be *seen* to be protecting the interests of men teachers. In a pamphlet of 1924, directed at men, the NUT said that boys needed the influence of both men and women teachers. They rather confusingly argued that the application of the 'men teachers for boys' principle would mean that mixed schools and classes would be impossible and men would be displaced as heads, especially in rural areas. 'Infants departments now under headmasters would have to be placed under women.'[35] So the union's argument against the principle was conducted on the grounds that it was not in men teachers' own interests. Two years later however, the union declared that it agreed with the 1925 Committee on the Training of Teachers that wherever possible the older boys should be taught by men and the older girls by women.[36] By 1934, the NUT agreed wholeheartedly with the principle of 'men teachers for boys' but said that it was difficult to apply in practice. NUT policy was that 'men teachers should be provided for boys above the infant stage' but that, 'we can only expect to see it in practice when all who are actually dealing with the problem, daily, will accept it as "workable" and even "desirable" in their case.'[37]

The NUT came to endorse this view because of the strength of feeling among its male members. During the 1920s, the *Times Educational Supplement* frequently observed that the unwillingness of men teachers to serve under headmistresses was certainly not confined only to NAS members. The NUT feared that its men members might strongly sympathize with NAS policies, and was concerned to prevent more of them leaving the union.

On the local level there is plenty of evidence to show that NUT branches were more concerned about the position of their men members than their women members. There was controversy in 1927 when the NUT representative on the Torquay Education

Committee supported the appointment of a headmaster to a junior mixed and infant school.[38] In 1931 the Surrey County Teachers Association complained to the Education Committee that too many headships were being given to women.[39] Likewise the Kent NUT branch requested the Kent Education Committee in 1933 to ensure that vacant headships should go to men 'as it is an advantage to a locality to have a man in charge of the village school.'[40] So although the NUT did not go as far as the NAS and seek to extend men's sphere in teaching, it accepted the sexual division of labour and was anxious to be seen protecting the interests of men teachers, even supporting the principle of 'men teachers for boys' by the 1930s.

This was not, however, because the NUT *women* wished to uphold men's rights to headships, but because the union was run by men. Although two-thirds or more of the membership were women, there was only a handful of women on the Executive and rarely a woman President. Yet women teachers in the NUT did organize and protest against their subordination at work and they were constantly concerned during this period that their promotion prospects might be diminished. During the 1920s and 1930s the issue was sometimes raised by the women on the executive, and more often by the women's meeting at the annual conference. Women presidents, such as Leah Manning, who became the fourth woman president in 1930, also encouraged women members to become more active over the question of equal opportunities.

However the NUT was more concerned to assure men teachers that they were not losing out by school reorganization, so that women NUT members were consequently forced onto the defensive to make their case. After the secession of the NAS and NUWT the voicing of women's issues in the union was discouraged for fear of splitting the union further. Women members were powerless to affect the union's practice. In 1930 the Ladies Committee had to draw attention to the fact that many advertisements for men heads of combined junior and infant schools were carried in the *Schoolmaster*, the NUT journal, and it accused the union of not acting according to its principles. They alleged that between May 1929 and May 1930 over 200 such advertisements had appeared.[41]

By the time of the 1933 conference Miss Haswell, of the NUT's executive, had to remind a meeting of women members what union policy actually was.

> On the question of headships that policy was absolutely definite — that the headships of schools should be given, not on a sex basis at all, but that the best applicant, irrespective of sex, should be appointed.

She often found some hesitation on the part of women in pressing their just claims with regard to headships for fear of jeopardising the ideal of professional unity.[42]

So in theory NUT policy supported equal opportunities for women — that headships should go to the best person regardless of sex. In practice, the NUT really only helped women teachers by trying to protect their jobs as headmistresses of infant schools, thus emphasizing the sexual division of labour and avoiding any threat to men. Women NUT members were silenced and discouraged from fighting for their rights on promotion because the union was anxious to protect men's interests.

Official Policy and Equal Opportunities

The people who actually had the power to determine the sex of teachers and where they should teach were the LEAs and the Board of Education (the central authority responsible for public education). School staffing was officially the responsibility of the LEAs, but the Board was also concerned with it and could guide LEAs by the use of circulars and individual consultations. Was a deliberate policy articulated by the Board and LEAs over 'men teachers for boys' and the headships of mixed schools? And how was policy informed by the recurrent pressure to cut expenditure on education? During the early 1920s and again in the early 1930s economic crises caused the government to make cuts in public expenditure which fell particularly harshly on education. LEAs were keen to find ways of reducing their education budgets, and the weakest points were women teachers' jobs and girls' education. Men and women teachers were anxious to safeguard their jobs, men fearing that women's lower salaries might lead to their displacement. Public opinion also tended to support men's right to have the first pick of jobs during this period of unemployment.

For the employer, the sexual division of labour meant a cheap female labour force — women teachers were paid four-fifths of the equivalent male salary — which could be easily disposed of back into the home through a marriage bar if necessary. For men, the benefits were having the more prestigious and better paid posts reserved to them, for example the teaching of older children and a higher proportion of headships. However the interests of the employer and male workers in relation to women workers did not neatly converge and could clash. For example, cheaper female labour could be used as a substitute for men during periods of recession. The rigidity of the sexual division of labour normally prevented this from happening as men's and women's jobs were clearly demarcated but in teaching there were some areas of overlap, like posts in mixed schools.

During the financial cutbacks of the early 1920s the Board did try to limit the number of men teachers employed in some areas as an economy measure, for instance in London, 'men teachers of course having a higher rate of salary than women'.[43] However the Board was mostly able to absolve itself of responsibility for policy on 'men teachers for boys' by pointing out that discretion lay with the local authorities, although it did approve of the rise in the number and proportion of men after the mid-1920s. It was keen to reject the demands of the NAS which were increasingly pressed upon it in the late 1920s and 1930s. In an answer in the Commons in 1929 the President of the Board said: 'I must not be taken to accept their highly contentious statements that children of eight require "the influence of a man" and that "the womanly influence which is so valuable when dealing with infants becomes positively harmful when dealing with lads".'[44] In 1934 the Parliamentary Secretary to the Board of Education wrote to an MP referring to representations made to him by the NAS. 'I do not think I can accept the doctrine that all classes of boys should be placed under men teachers . . . but I do agree that generally speaking older boys are better under men than under women teachers.'[45] So the politicians at least were equivocal on the subject.

The Board did have in mind an optimum proportion of men teachers, although it did not specify a particular figure to LEAs. With the reductions in staff made by reorganization, this was one aspect which the Board thought should be taken into consideration: 'are men unnecessarily employed on the instruction of younger children, or are there too few men for the instruction of older boys?'[46] However there is no evidence to show that the Board indicated a policy on the headships of mixed schools to LEAs. That was a matter for local decision making.

Two sets of educational ideas, both based on gender distinctions, clashed in the mixed junior school – should children have a same-sex teacher, or should women teach the younger children and men the older? It was the suitable age of transition for the boy that was highlighted as a problem. Reorganization meant that there was an increasing distinction between the older and younger children, and the kind of teaching they required. This strengthened the common assumption that the education of younger children was women's province, an extension of their childrearing role in the family into the public sphere. This was voiced by one schoolmaster as: 'Women as well as men have their own particular advantages as teachers. Women teachers are particularly adapted for teaching small children, boys as well as girls.'[47]

The Board utilized this aspect of the sexual division of labour in the early 1920s when it encouraged high spending LEAs to save money on staffing costs without threatening men's jobs by employing unqualified women to teach younger children, which many did.[48] The Hadow Reports of 1931 on junior schools and 1933 on nursery and infant schools also proposed the use of girls of 15 to 18 year olds as classroom helpers. These policies were detrimental to the status of all women teachers because they implied that the work of teaching younger children was not sufficiently difficult or important to require proper professional qualifications and training. The Board of Education itself referred to this class of teacher as 'the "motherly person" type of teacher', suggesting that gender characteristics were more important than training for the work.[49] Lyrical comments on the 'natural' maternal gifts of infant teachers abounded. One HMI noted: 'Indeed this very mother-love is the most characteristic feature of the born teacher of "babies" – the hall-mark of her high calling. For true mother-love, often more discerning and more discriminating than that of an actual mother, is abundantly found in the heart of many a young unmarried woman.'[50]

There is evidence that some LEAs were susceptible to the ideas of the NAS, especially on the question of whether the headships of mixed schools should be reserved for men or open to both sexes. Women continued to be employed as the heads of most junior mixed schools because they were cheaper, but an increasing proportion of these headships went to men. After a headmistress was appointed to a junior boys school in Lancashire in 1938, the Lancashire branch of the NAS sent a letter of protest which led to the Education Committee deciding that for all future appointments, head teachers should be men.[51] The headships of senior mixed schools almost always went to men, and a decision such as one in Birmingham, where headships were open to both sexes and a woman appointed in 1934, was most unusual.[52]

The school was seen to be like a family, but a traditional patriarchal family with the father at the head. The sex of the head teacher not only depended on the age and sex of the pupils, but also very much on the sex of the assistant teachers. As one textbook for educational administrators in local government put it, 'it is not customary for a master to serve under a mistress.'[53] Women or men head teachers of mixed junior schools would have women asistants, while men heads of senior mixed schools would have a mixed staff. Men teachers were in little danger of being undercut by women in competition for the headships of mixed schools, since the idea that women should not be in positions of authority over men effectively reserved the higher posts to men. The local authorities were open to pressure to consider men teachers' interests, and over the whole country there was a growing tendency to appoint men to the headships of the increasing number of mixed schools.

Since government policy at both national and local level welcomed the increase of men teachers in the second half of the period, and would have liked more men for boys under 11, it is evident that the gender ideology that boys should have men teachers was as important as financial considerations, and in fact increasingly eclipsed them. This ideology allowed both the Board and the LEAs to follow policies which debased women teachers' status in order to save money without conflicting with men's interests. The changes in policy show how the sexual division of labour in teaching was neither a natural nor a static phenomenon, but needed to be constantly redefined and confirmed according to the conflicting interests of employers and workers, men and women teachers.

The authorities were at the same time concerned with the femininity and masculinity of the pupils in the schools. The Board accepted as unproblematic traditional ideas about gender roles.[54] During this period the curriculum in the elementary school also became more rigidly gender differentiated. Since the mid-nineteenth century girls had been required to learn needlework at school and cookery and other domestic subjects were added to the curriculum from the late 1870s. This trend was reinforced in the early twentieth century by fears about infant mortality and the nation's physical health. Boys meanwhile learnt arithmetic, woodwork and other technical subjects. The 1923 Consultative Committee *Report on the Differentiation of the Curriculum for Boys and Girls Respectively in Secondary Schools*, showed that this was still an important matter for debate after the war. At a time of unemployment, a falling birthrate and increasing emphasis on women's proper place in the home, the 1926 (Hadow) *Report on the Education of the Adolescent* again stressed the importance of teaching housecraft to the older working-class girls in the elementary schools. In this way gender roles were constructed and emphasized in the schools for both the teachers and the children.[55]

Fear and Anxiety in the Schools

The anxiety in the classroom around the issues of 'men teachers for boys', the headships of mixed schools, and the importance of masculinity and femininity, reflected wider fears connected with the changing roles of women and men in the outside world. These fears were enhanced by the social and economic changes of the inter-war period.

The First World War had created a disequilibrium of the sexual division of labour in education. Half of all male teachers joined the forces and there was a huge, though temporary, influx of women into boys' schools. Men teachers feared permanent replacement by women, while the women teachers felt they had proved their worth and capabilities by teaching boys.

Women had likewise entered other occupations and professions during the First World War, and right at the end of the war were in a position to challenge their economic and social subordination. Women teachers had got their demand for equal pay taken seriously and accepted as policy by the NUT. Women over 30 had won the vote. Women were attempting to enter occupations formerly closed to them, such as the legal profession, and extending their sphere in others, like the civil service. The emancipation of women, or the idea that this was happening, was feared and opposed by some men, and they sought to re-establish their economic advantage over women. The activities of the NAS are an obvious example of this. Women's apparent advance in teaching was threatening to men on two levels, first, on the economic level where women's undercutting would drive men out of the profession, and secondly, in the realm of gender identity where it was feared that women would take over masculine, i.e. men's jobs. The NAS clearly attacked 'the pressure of feminist influence' as being responsible for men teachers' problems. They presented themselves as, 'the only people who are organised to stand in the way of a flood of feminism which is gradually eating its way into the heart of the nation, already more hysterical than it has ever been before.'[56] At their 1930 conference, a resolution was put forward 'opposing the selection of the educational field as a battleground by feminists in their attempt to secure political domination.'[57] The NAS also attacked women teachers specifically as *spinsters*, revealing their fear that women who were outside marriage were particularly dangerous, undermining men's traditional superiority in the family as well as in employment. They maintained: 'Only a nation heading for the madhouse would force on men, many married with families, such a position as service under spinster head-mistresses.'[58]

Of course it was the same feminist movement that gave women teachers in the NUWT the strength to fight for equal opportunities and to challenge notions of femininity, whether applied to themselves or to their pupils. Now that women were emancipated they should be given equal opportunities in education and in their professions. The NUWT president reassured and warned her colleagues in 1930 that:

> On all sides women were bursting their way into new activities and spheres hitherto denied to them . . . These exploits marked the breaking down of barriers and the blazing of a trail towards full and free equality . . . There are barriers yet unsurmounted, prejudices yet rampant, artificial restrictions yet unremoved; but the new spirit of freedom and of power is leading us on cheerfully and confidently to the attack on the last remaining strongholds.[59]

The context of government cuts and reorganization of the schools in the inter-war period intensified the fears of both men and women teachers about their status. We have already seen how from the mid-1920s the post-Hadow reorganisation of the elementary school system together with the fall in the number of school-age children caused disruption for teachers. But were teachers' anxieties about their promotion prospects and status in this period justified? Did the situation worsen for men or for women? Looking back at the changes which occurred we can see that the fears of the men were not justified – it was the women teachers who suffered a deterioration in status.

Most men teachers did in fact teach boys, but not all the boys over seven, while women class teachers mainly taught girls and the younger children. Before the First World War it was rare for women teachers to be found in boys' schools. But even after the war, with the increase in mixed classes (to 70 per cent in 1938), there was still a very marked division of labour between women and men class teachers, as table 6.1 shows. A growing percentage of both women and men teachers taught mixed classes rather than single sex ones, but men were obviously preferred to teach the older children. Women predominantly taught infant, junior and girls' classes and

Table 6.1 Percentage of certified women and men assistants in charge of different types of class, 1921–38

	Under 11s				Over and under 11s				Over 11s				Total			Total no. of teachers
	Boys	Girls	Mixed	All	Boys	Girls	Mixed	All	Boys	Girls	Mixed	All	Boys	Girls	Mixed	
Women																
1921	5.9	8.2	42.0	56.1	3.9	12.4	9.8	26.1	0.8	13.1	4.0	17.9	10.5	33.7	55.8	62096
1925	5.2	7.9	41.2	54.3	3.0	12.3	10.2	25.5	0.7	14.8	4.7	20.2	8.9	34.9	56.2	61588
1930	5.4	10.8	49.6	65.8	1.0	8.1	7.4	16.4	0.3	13.2	4.3	17.8	6.7	32.1	61.2	67965
1935	3.5	7.3	50.1	61.0	0.7	5.3	8.2	14.2	0.4	17.2	7.2	24.8	4.6	29.9	65.5	70803
1938	2.8	6.6	54.1	63.5	0.4	4.5	7.7	12.5	0.2	16.4	7.3	23.9	3.4	27.5	69.1	69943
Men																
1921	7.5	–	0.9	8.5	30.8	0.1	8.3	39.2	38.5	0.2	13.6	52.3	76.9	0.3	22.9	20309
1925	7.7	–	1.1	8.8	28.7	–	8.8	37.5	38.1	0.1	15.5	53.7	74.5	0.2	25.3	23302
1930	15.0	–	4.3	19.3	21.8	–	10.1	31.9	34.3	–	14.5	48.8	71.0	0.1	28.9	25684
1935	9.8	–	6.0	15.7	12.4	–	10.1	22.5	42.5	–	19.2	61.7	64.7	–	35.3	28978
1938	10.0	–	9.0	19.0	10.1	–	11.7	21.7	39.0	–	20.2	59.2	59.1	–	40.9	29678

– indicates 0 or less than 0.1.
Source: Board of Education, *Statistics of Public Education* for each year

Table 6.2 Public elementary schools: percentage of men and women heads of different departments, 1927–38

	Senior				All Ages				Junior					Total	All		
	Boys	Girls	Mixed	All	Boys	Girls	Mixed	All	Boys	Girls	Mixed	All	Infants	Number	Boys	Girls	Mixed
Women																	
1927	–	1.0	–	1.0	0.1	18.5	33.1	51.7	0.2	0.4	8.2	8.8	38.4	17727	0.3	19.9	41.3
1930	–	1.8	–	1.8	0.1	18.4	28.8	47.3	0.3	1.8	11.3	13.4	37.0	17543	0.4	22.0	40.1
1933	–	4.4	0.1	4.5	0.1	12.2	26.1	38.4	0.2	3.7	16.3	20.2	36.5	17306	0.3	20.3	42.5
1935	–	5.2	0.1	5.3	–	10.6	25.3	35.9	0.1	4.1	18.4	22.6	36.1	16918	0.2	19.9	43.8
1938	–	5.8	0.1	5.9	–	8.9	23.4	32.3	0.1	4.4	21.8	26.3	35.5	16591	0.2	19.1	45.3
Men																	
1927	1.4	–	2.1	3.5	27.1	–	67.8	94.9	0.4	–	1.1	1.5	–	12941	28.9	–	71.0
1930	2.5	–	2.9	5.4	23.8	–	64.8	88.6	1.4	–	4.5	5.9	–	12837	27.7	–	72.2
1933	6.0	–	6.4	12.4	15.8	–	56.0	71.8	4.2	–	11.7	15.9	–	12641	26.0	–	74.0
1935	6.5	–	7.7	14.6	13.4	–	53.1	66.5	4.7	–	14.2	18.9	–	12663	25.0	–	75.0
1938	7.6	–	9.0	16.6	11.0	–	47.8	58.8	5.0	–	19.7	24.7	–	12623	23.6	–	76.4

– indicates 0 or less than 0.1.
Source: Board of Education, *Statistics of Public Education* for each year

men were concentrated in the boys' classes, particularly the older boys. This pattern became more rigid during the 1920s and 1930s, and was repeated among the head teachers.

Promotion prospects worsened during the period for both men and women certificated teachers but the chances for promotion to any headship were always less for women. While 66–8 per cent of certificated teachers were women throughout the period, only 56–7 per cent of certificated head teachers were women.[60] Given that promotion prospects for both sexes were declining there was little change in the *relative* position of men and women. The women held a fairly constant proportion of the certificated headships and at no point did they appear to be gaining any from the men or vice-versa.

But the *type* of headships they held did change. Table 6.2 shows that women heads were always most likely to be found in charge of infant and junior departments, and that this tendency became more marked with reorganization. Girls' and infant departments were invariably headed by women, while the senior boys' and all-age boys' departments virtually always had a male head teacher. The proportion of junior mixed departments with a woman head fell from 90 per cent to 60 per cent during the period, while the headships of senior mixed departments were practically closed to women.

The move towards separate junior and senior schools and mixed schools affected both men and women heads. Table 6.2 shows that in 1927 about half the women head teachers were in charge of junior and infant departments while half were in charge of departments containing children of all ages. The vast majority of men were in charge of all-age departments. By 1938 over 60 per cent of women heads held posts in junior and in infant departments, but men had clearly encroached on this area, holding a much increased 25 per cent of headships in junior departments. The fall in the number and proportion of women who were heads of infant departments shows that the fears expressed by women teachers that the amalgamation of infant with junior schools would displace women heads were to some extent justified. Furthermore, by the end of the period only 6 per cent of women heads had charge of senior departments, compared to 17 per cent of the men.

Conclusion

The work experience of both class teachers and head teachers was directly affected by their sex. Men were more likely to be found at the higher stages of the education hierarchy in charge of older children and boys, while women primarily taught younger children, and this pattern intensified during the 1920s and 1930s. The restructuring of elementary education evidently did facilitate this hardening of the sexual division of labour.[61] Although, broadly speaking, teachers' pay did not increase with the age of the children taught, their status did. On the whole it was regarded as more prestigious to teach older children, despite the emphasis of new educational theories on the importance of the earlier years. Reorganization lent added prestige to teachers in senior schools. Thus the deepening of the sexual division of labour in the profession tended towards lowering the status of women teachers generally.

Teaching was a major high status employment for women during the 1920s and 1930s, giving them some key positions within the education system. The profession employed large numbers of both men and women; approximately three-quarters of elementary school teachers being female in this period. It was a job seen as particularly suited to women because it involved working with children and using feminine maternal qualities. Men teachers felt threatened both by the number of women in the profession who were equally well qualified and capable, and by the labelling of the profession as a feminine one. Changes in the organization of schools combined with the powerful feminist challenge of the period endangered the benefits which they enjoyed by virtue of their sex, including higher pay and higher status posts. As a consequence men teachers hung on to and magnified the idea of masculinity in the education system by locking it into contemporary anxieties such as militarism and eugenics.

In educational terms teachers were role models for their pupils and they had considerable power to teach not only subjects like history and geography but also more subtle ideas about the world including the desirable roles for men and women. The idea of gender roles was accepted as common sense by the Board of Education, the NUT and most elementary teachers. Only the NUWT had a wider vision, based on an ideal of equality of opportunity for both women teachers and girl pupils, and they constantly resisted gender stereotyping in schools. At the same time as inevitably falling into the feminine role, for example as teachers of infants, women teachers subverted it by their very existence. Mostly single women, they represented an alternative way of life from the normal feminine role of dependence on men. For women, teaching was a relatively highly paid career. Few other occupations offered women similar salaries, and certainly not in such large numbers, so that women teachers, active in a job which carried status and some influence in the local community, were a visible challenge to traditional roles.

Bibliographical Note

Although important work has been done by feminist historians on women teachers in the nineteenth century, for example Frances Widdowson's *Going Up Into the Next Class* (Hutchinson, 1981) which deals with the social origins of women teachers, the twentieth century, particularly the period after the First World War, remains relatively neglected. Geoffrey Partington's *Women Teachers in the Twentieth Century* (NFER, 1976) remains a useful narrative account, as does P. H. J. H. Gosden *The Evolution of a Profession* (Basil Blackwell, Oxford, 1972), especially for equal pay. Miriam David sets the scene for a feminist analysis in *The State, the Family and Education* (Routledge & Kegan Paul 1980) in which she links changes in women's role in the teaching profession and girls' education with contemporary ideas concerning women's domestic role. The antagonism between women and men teachers over equal pay and the marriage bar has been discussed in my articles 'Serving Two Masters? The Introduction of a Marriage Bar in Teaching in the 1920s', in London Feminist History Group, *The Sexual Dynamics of History* (Pluto Press, 1983) and ' "Sex antagonism" in the teaching profession: the equal pay issue 1914–1929', *History of Education Review* (Australia & New Zealand) 14 (1985) pp. 36–48, as well as in my MSc thesis, ' "Sex antagonism" in the teaching profession: employment issues and the woman teacher in elementary education 1910–1939' (Bristol University, 1983). A fascinating, though less accessible account of the NUWT's activities can be found in A. M. Pierotti, *The Story of the National Union of Women Teachers* (NUWT 1963).

7

Better a Teacher Than a Hairdresser? 'A Mad Passion for Equality' or, Keeping Molly and Betty down

Deborah Thom

We know quite a lot about what it was like for girls to rise, by the process of education, from the working class into the middle class. The autobiographical accounts of life for girls in the 1950s published in *Truth, Dare or Promise* include several accounts of the significance of the transition from primary to secondary school; the ambiguity of it as a change in career prospects as well as, for some, a major change in social possibility. Valerie Walkerdine summed it up, 'Leaving one's class was to be admired and scorned.'[1] Julia Pascal described her feelings thus: 'I feel happy that I am one of the chosen . . . Many of the others are crying. It's as if someone had ripped the class in half, and those small children thrown out from the chance of grammar school education know deep in their hearts that this is the crucial moment in their lives.' What it meant to those children was 'that for the rest of their lives they will feel secondary.'[2]

Although such description was available, and used in the political polemic against selection, it did not inform writing about selection, all of which was about boys, about whom we know a great deal more. Literary and biographical accounts of the experience of education have largely focused on the advantages of the transition between classes, the advantages of the grammar school education in widening horizons and improving job chances and enhancing, often through the work of gifted teachers, the enjoyment of life. What is lacking is any comment on the effect of the grammar school selection process, and of any subsequent mobility, on gender divisions.

Turning to other accounts of the effects of education by people professionally concerned with education, the same omission can be seen. The assumption of most sociological studies has been that boys and girls are affected in the same ways by the processes of class formation and by the discourse of meritocracy. For example, in the book by the Centre for Contemporary Cultural Studies Education Group (CCCS), *Unpopular Education*, the index entry on gender goes first, 'absent questions' with three entries, secondly, with one entry each, 'construction' and 'new categories'.[3] The debate over schooling in wartime and post-war Britain excluded the question of gender. Yet this was the heyday of discussion on equality and there were ways in which such discussion could have dealt with gender as seriously as it did with social class. Gender was raised, but it was raised as a general social question, that is, the issue of whether girls and boys should receive a separate sort of education as a whole, not whether one girl should receive a different sort of education from another. No one asked what the implications were for equality in this; rather, whether boys and girls required a fundamentally different organization of education.

In investigating one inequality, the different norms established for boys and girls to go to secondary school, it would be possible to explain why such discussion as there was on the question of gender difference only took place at a local level, (although this was the crucial level for local administration) and as a technical question. Why was the conclusion to the discussion nearly always to diminish the advantage that girls had over boys? Whether this inequality was also an injustice will depend on one's beliefs about equality, parity of treatment and psychology. I think it was, as it presumed a dominant force in the lives of women, that one role should supersede all other general social principles. This may in fact have been the case in the lives of most women, but to treat it as an overriding educational imperative was to beg a fundamental question that could, and should, have been discussed.

The Second World War emphasized motherhood in public discussion, accentuating the pre-war emphasis on motherhood as the major factor needing change to alter the declining birthrate.[4] Women had been recognized by demographers as the crucial factor in any change in population. This recognition married to social reform rhetoric to provide a strong impetus to a package of reforms aimed at improving family life and the quantity and quality of the population.[5] Women, it was thought, needed convincing that motherhood could be morally and materially desirable. Hence the education of girls was particularly strongly described at this time as the education of future mothers. I have found little discussion of the question in the literature on educational organization but, as was recognized by the Royal Commission on Population during the 1940s, the spread of birth control meant that it had now become possible for girls to envisage choosing a life without motherhood.[6] Lower mortality among combatants and higher mortality among civilians in the Second World War meant that war made this not a matter of necessity as in previous wars, but of choice. Also the number of men dying relative to women did not greatly exceed the number who died in the natural course of things, so there was no drastic reversal of the sex ratios as there had been after the First World War. The Women's Group for Public Welfare, who perhaps most represented these strands in the social reform demands of the time, had summed them up most explicitly in their damning indictment of poor housing, poor health provision and low levels of welfare in their 1939 book *Working Class Wives*. They argued that the differences between social classes of the effects of the depression and changes in industry could be read directly in the lives of women.[7]

This rhetoric was not just the speculation of pressure groups. It represented a general ideological shift which can be traced through educational administration, British eugenics, feminism and even in the Conservative Party.[8] Reconstruction hopes built upon such rhetoric when politicians and journalists talked and wrote of 'equality of opportunity'. That equality was not discussed in terms of gender, although it was gendered. One of the commonest phrases used to describe the future was 'when the sons of Dukes and dustmen sit side by side'.[9] Although there were debates about equal rights for women, particularly in the crucial wartime debate on equal pay for teachers, women's rights were not discussed during the war in any analysis of girls' education.[10] Women's rights were subordinated to their social role, or the rights of society. In fact, girls as waged workers in the future were also rarely discussed in this social reform rhetoric.

When the question of girls' education was discussed it was often within the constraints of a discussion of the mothers they might become rather than as citizens of a post-war Britain. In 1943 such a debate was held in the pages of *The Times Educational Supplement* on 'Molly the non-intellectual and Betty the maths scholar'.[11] The difference between them was based exclusively on intelligence. 'It is not impossible to separate the Mollies from the Betties at the age of 12 or 13; intelligence tests can, and do, measure with fair accuracy a

girl's reasoning power or "G" – inborn general *intellectual* intelligence' [emphasis in original]. The article went on to advocate testing
for 'g', that is, doing intelligence tests, at the age of 12 or 13.

In the early 1930s and the late 1940s selection for existing
secondary education by a special places examination took place in
most cases at 10 or 11. Girls who passed this examination by which

TEST 12

The sentences given below are all jumbled up, you have to try and think
out the words in the right order to make sense of them. After you have done
this, you must put a cross under the last word of your sentence. Here is an
example:—

"**Summer** go people to many seaside the in." You can soon find
that you make sense of this by reading it either like this . . .
" **In** summer many people go to the seaside." or like this . . .
" **Many** people go to the seaside in summer." You would be quite
right therefore in putting a cross under "seaside" or "summer."

Remember.—Do not write anything, but only put a cross under
the last word of your sentence.

1.   Good us for milk very is.
2.   230 were school children there in.
3.   Their clean should teeth children.
4.   Run trams rails trains and on.
5.   Cars of hundreds see week we every.-
6.   Class child can every write our in.
7.   Eight to ought at be bed o'clock in we.
8.   Much others questions than easier are some.

TEST 13

Here are 6 lines of words, with 4 words in each line. 3 out of 4 words
in each line contain the same letter. You have to cross out the word which does
not contain the letter. Look at the example given, the only letter which is
contained in 3 out of 4 words is the letter "i," so that the word "Cork,"
which has not an "i" in it, is crossed out.

EXAMPLE :—   Will - Cried - Cork - Night.

ll

A page of the Ryburn Group Intelligence Tests, H. V. Clark, 1926,
Glasgow.

they had shown 'ability to profit by secondary education' went to academic schools to do a grammar school course leaving at 16. Those who did not stayed on in elementary schools until they could leave at 14. That is, the major difference between secondary education and elementary education was the length as well as the fees paid for secondary education by parents or through an assisted place under the special places scheme. A few, in some areas, could go to technical schools or colleges and were selected for vocational courses at 12 or 13. There was a great debate throughout the 1940s as to when children could be identified as clearly showing aptitude, that is, special inclinations or skills, as well as ability, that is, general all round intelligence. It had been believed for some time that ability could be identified at the age of 11. Since 1926 this had been incorporated into policy when the Hadow Committee's recommendation that primary education be separated from secondary at that age became approved practice. However, very few were prepared to argue that any special aptitude, such as that required for technical education, could be identified this young, and many argued that it could not be seen at all by any comparable measure. The question of when separation was made affected the length of secondary courses and therefore also affected comparability with private education which tended to segregate primary from secondary at 13.[12]

The conventional wisdom of the day was that if you looked at the children in the classroom there was little difference between them when young. The *Handbook for Suggestion for Teachers* recommended in 1937, first, that 'the range of differences in either sex being greater than the differences between the two sexes, they should not therefore be treated in any distinctive way'. It also argued, 'there is as yet no settled conclusion that has been reached as to the manner and extent of the resemblances and differences'.[13] If this was what teachers were recommended to do in practice facing a mixed classroom of children, the only way in which they could argue that the difference should matter was in the difference of outcome – and this was to affect the curriculum, particularly in secondary schools.

Girls were provided with less technical education. They were not encouraged into apprenticeships or any other technical training as young adults, and did not find many technical schools specially devoted to their jobs at the age of 13. Commercial education and domestic subjects could be taught as 'technical education' but in practice tended to be taught in the central or senior schools. This was the way in which some local authorities dealt with the Hadow recommendations that required the separation of children at 11 by taking off the next layer of ability after grammar school selection had taken place. The argument about girls was quite simply the one expressed in the *Times Educational Supplement* (TES) article; 'The majority of our pupils find their fulfilment in life not in careers, nor in institutions, but in relationships.' Seventy per cent of the population, said the writer, should be selected at the age of 13. At this stage they should choose more maternal or feminine professions, like nursing or kindergarten teaching. A girl would therefore be following her own 'practical, intuitive, creative, artistic approach to life'.

This argument ignored the realities of 1943 when it was written. It also ignored the realities of life in the 1930s and any possible future that could be envisaged after the war. A cursory glance at employment statistics shows that even in the period when women's commitment to paid work outside the home was lowest, the late 1940s, women who worked for wages did so in largest proportion in factories, followed by commercial activities, not in the service trades of nursing or kindergarten teaching.[14] In 1943 itself a large number of women were directed under compulsion into war work in factories, if they were between the ages of 18 and 30. Yet the discussion of girls' futures ignores this majority of young women in favour of the reproduction of rather empty abstract arguments about their social role.

This article did not meet with a warm welcome by those who responded to it. The editor of the TES, H. C. Dent, wrote disapprovingly that the article made two wrong assumptions: first, that there was any contradiction between femininity and equal chances in employment, and secondly, that some women would always need careers for which they should be trained, because they would not be able to marry.[15] Another correspondent argued that the description of what made a good mother was also mistaken. One said a good mother should be a good citizen too; 'there are no essential feminine qualities except the production and rearing of children. Surely this requires more than half educated cow-like females.'[16] Leaving aside what a half educated cow would be like, it is clear that this writer could be seen as arguing that good mothering was the superior goal of education.

This was not a new argument. Pre-war discussion had emphasized the need to improve mothering practice and to make motherhood more attractive to compensate for the declining birth-rate. In *Parents Revolt* by the Titmusses, it was argued that the way to achieve this improvement was to give child-bearing and child-rearing more material help and a stronger political voice. Education of the mothers of the future in motherhood was not seen as part of this process. The education of all girls as citizens was seen as relevant to encouraging a social change in attitudes to motherhood. War provided a new emphasis on making social change by state action although it was an emphasis added to pre-war arguments for social engineering through education most forcefully expressed by R. H. Tawney.[17]

There were other forces working for a change in attitudes to women as mothers. Women's position in the economy had changed in the inter-war years. Historians have debated long and hard about how far the so-called 'new' industries were new but none have disputed the increased employment of women in the factories of West London and the Midlands in light engineering, food processing, electrical goods and manmade textiles. War increased the numbers of women in factories and also made their labour much more visible. 'Women's work', said one *TES* correspondent, 'was in the process of being rationalised as men's was in the last war.' Correspondents in the TES and elsewhere thus rejected the timeless arguments of essentialism in favour of a highly biologised notion of civic progress. The editor summed up the debate, 'Many, perhaps most, girls entering employment will not be visualising a lifelong career in it. Second, the future of women in industry should be a complementary and not a rival one to that of men.'[18] Thus the debate on differentiation between particular types of girl, Molly and Betty, had shifted to a discussion on all girls – a phenomenon observable in most discussions of this sort.

Such discussions continued through until the mid-1950s when there was a shift in emphasis. But the assumption that girls were primarily future mothers and home-makers and its corollary, that boys were breadwinners and secondarily fathers, continued to dominate discussion until the 1960s. Girls were either described as deviants from the general analysis of childhood – needing special treatment – or they were not described at all, as if the category 'child' would cover all divisions. John Newsom's book *The Education of Girls* of 1948 takes the first view. He was then Chief Education Officer of Hertfordshire. He began by saying that he assumed there is a clear-cut, fundamental difference between boys and girls, that the differences are complementary and that education should take account of them rather than either ignoring them or trying to make them go away. He accepted the social engineering role for education but argued that it must depend upon existing structures, not set up new ones. So he concluded that, 'the vital educational objectives for women are to enable them to become accomplished homemakers, informed citizens and to use their leisure intelligently.' And that, 'this mad passion for equality has masked the fact that men and women are different.'[19]

There were contradictions in Newsom's view which bedevilled any discussion on equality. Equality of access does not necessarily provide identity of provision, or even parity of provision. Equality between boys and girls subsumes equality between girls and girls, as if they were the same thing. Yet equality and justice were the battle cries of the movement for comprehensive schooling and the particular focus of the attack was on the selection exam for grammar schools, the 11+. Why was the question of gender not much discussed in this wider campaign? Why did it remain a local technical matter rather than an issue along the same lines as social class? After all, gender divisions are administratively organized, and can be seen with the naked eye, unlike those of class which rely on political insight or the work of a trained observer, a sociologist. First, I shall describe what the inequality was and secondly, attempt to explain why, although widespread as a phenomenon, it did not become a *cause célèbre*.

The inequality lay quite simply in the relationship between grammar school places and selection procedures. The 1944 Education Act had provided 'secondary education for all' but this did not mean that all children now received what had before the Act been described as secondary education. What they got was allocated 'according to age, ability and aptitude'. In effect, the government recommended that the local authorities who administered education should adopt a tripartite scheme on the lines approved by the Norwood report, *Curriculum and Examinations in Secondary Schools*, published in 1943 by a committee set up in 1941. The committee had heard evidence largely from school teachers and ignored educational psychologists and egalitarians alike in defining children as belonging to one of three types, and was much criticized for this. What went unnoticed was that in the classification scheme the child was male. The first type 'was [the child who is] interested in learning for its own sake, who can grasp an argument or follow a piece of connected reasoning.' The second, 'whose interests and abilities lie markedly in the field of applied science or applied art. A boy in this group has a strong interest in this direction.' The third, which was all the rest, of course, 'deals more easily with concrete things than ideas'.[20]

Psychologists objected to this clarification scheme because, they argued, it was impossible to allocate children at the age of 11 to technical schools, that is, to type two. Technical ability was simply not measurable independently of general intelligence 'G'. There were not three types at all, they argued, but one continuum on which all children could be placed, a scale of general intelligence. Egalitarians were outraged by the way in which Norwood ignored the chance of change and sought to perpetuate the existing organization of secondary education. Norwood has been described as influential, but of all the LEA records investigated for a research project on mental testing only two showed any interest in Norwood at all; only one LEA referred to its recommendations as requiring any innovation, and this was that the LEA should provide some technical education in their schools.[21] Norwood represented thinking that had little influence on the Education Act itself or on the local authorities. The three divisions of children already existed in fact in the secondary schools, as did the class divide they represent. The report might be said to have ratified the principle of organization but the fact was that comments on Norwood generally described it as an *ex post hoc* rationalization of existing organization, and therefore theoretically inadequate. Technical education was already weak, and generally acknowledged as needing strengthening. Either local authorities already divided children in three ways at 11 or took from the already divided 13 year olds a further subdivision to go into technical education, or, if it was not already set up, the LEAs provided technical education anew, not because they believed in Norwood's three types, but because they could now, for the first time, afford to do so.

Specific technical education for girls was anyway much more limited than for boys, something which was not queried much. Girls were required to learn certain social skills, which were in themselves varieties of technical education, and all of them needed these skills according to the Norwood Report's formulation of 1943. On the issue of domestic subjects in the curriculum (in schools up to 18, that is the existing grammar schools) the report argued first, that all girls needed the knowledge of such subjects, which was necessary equipment for potential makers of homes; secondly, that the subjects had the advantage of 'offering a practical approach to theoretical work', that 'they teach thinking through doing and awaken interest in other subjects'; and thirdly, for girls who were likely to go on to domestic science colleges 'they are necessary subjects'. The Norwood Report further argued that these domestic subjects should be differentiated for different types of girl but the differentiation seemed to be on an additive basis, that is that there should be a common core of domestic subjects to be added to for specialists in home economy. Norwood assumes too that this is the one subject area in which the pupil is female. Though the report does allow that boys in mixed schools may want to use the equipment, this is expressed in such terms of doubt that it seems unlikely that it would have happened. The implication throughout the report is that most schools are not mixed but segregated by sex anyway.[22]

By the time the Crowther Report, *15–18*, appeared in 1959, there had been a major change in the way girls' education was viewed. First, it was assumed that most children were in mixed schools, not segregated ones. Secondly although the distinction between bright or able girls and less able remained, there was no longer any assumption that this meant any would not marry or would not have children, and would concentrate on a career as an alternative. All women, it was assumed, would want both marriage and motherhood as well as whatever work they could do. This view reflected demographic change. More women were marrying, marrying younger and having fewer children.[23] The post-war baby boom had confounded the prophets of demographic decline so that the problem was not to encourage people to have children, but to encourage all workers back into employment, including women. For a few post-war years women had been encouraged to remain at work as long as possible. In education there was a severe shortage of teachers, particularly women teachers, and married women were being urged to return to work part-time; in some areas they were even given housing priority and nursery places to do so. The report suggested that a wider range of employment outcomes be borne in mind when planning the curriculum for older girls. It also pointed to the difficulty of finding time in school to give 'intellectually able girls . . . any education specifically related to their special interests as women.' Less able girls were described thus: 'their needs are much more sharply differentiated than those of boys of the same age than is true of the academically abler groups.' They were 'to study subjects based on direct interest in their personal appearance and problems of human relations, the greater psychological and social maturity of girls makes such subjects acceptable – and socially necessarily.'[24]

Thus this repeated the refrain common to all such reports when they mentioned girls. Girls have special needs related to their social function outside school but they differ from boys in terms of

growing up earlier. Girls did reach puberty earlier but puberty was
seen as important for them in a way that it was not for boys. They
were seen as peculiarly subject to the imperative of ageing, not, as in
Victorian times, physiologically, but sociologically. Gender determined girls as it did not boys. It might have been put the other way
around as 'the problem of the immaturity of boys' but it was not.
Boys are the norm, the standard against which girls are measured.
Crowther's recognition of sociological and demographic difference
does represent a more sophisticated analysis of the differences as
they exist – but it also takes the current occupational structure and
turns it into norms, in a way which Norwood, with its attempt to
present timeless truths about sexual difference, did not do.

Crowther is at once the first attempt to make egalitarian
statements about girls in the positive discrimination with which it
raises the issues, and at the same time the worst example of the
acceptance of the limits of a functionalist approach in making
political statements. The result was that girls were always described
in terms of 'should' rarely in terms of 'are'. Extensive attention was
paid by these reports and by politicians to the inculcating of
domesticity into all girls and the recognition of their social role by
the curriculum at secondary school. Very little was paid to other
factors of much moment in the lives of the girls concerned.

Yet there was an issue of difference between the sexes which
underlay another of great contentiousness – the entry of girls into
grammar school and higher education. Girls did better in selection
tests at 11, particularly the verbal reasoning (intelligence) and
English tests. Opinions differed as to when this advantage fell away.
In Cambridgeshire it was noted by a member of the Education
Committee with concern in 1951 that girls got much better School
Certificate results overall, but they were worse in mathematics and
got fewer passes in science.[25] The psychologist J. J. B. Dempster,
Chief Education Officer for Southampton, wrote a great deal on
secondary selection. He argued that girls' superiority over boys
lasted until university.[26] It was obviously crucial in any discussion
on access to secondary or higher education to decide whether girls'
superiority did last or not and, if it did not, when it altered. The way
differences could be measured was by looking at exam results at the
end of secondary school. This had been done in the past when people
wanted to assess the effectiveness of secondary selection in general,
but the comparison presented major problems. It was often
impossible to tell why someone had not got any exam results, or
done less well than expected.

The first reason for not passing exams on leaving school was early leaving. The Central Advisory Committee for Education had been asked to investigate this in 1954 to find out what the causes were. They noted, oddly perhaps against expectations, that it was less of a 'problem' with girls than with boys, but drew from that conclusions about the boys rather than the girls.[27] It is probably the case that the single major difference between boys and girls over the question of leaving was that there was great demand for teachers, with the expansion of the education system. Intending teachers provided a large new group who wanted to stay on at school to take the new 'O' and 'A' levels. Far more girls tended to train as teachers, particularly for the primary schools, and they added to the few going to university in the sixth forms. (This sector was also expanding, particularly for previously excluded girls.) The second reason for an exam absence was lack of facilities or staff. In many single sex girls' schools there were fewer and less well qualified science and maths staff than there were teachers for English and the humanities and in old schools there were far fewer laboratories and less technical equipment. The third reason for exam absence was the influence of factors outside school, which could be said to apply particularly to girls whose own desires for adult life outside institutions could well inhibit their aspirations and for whom life in school might make it difficult to achieve their potential.[28]

The literature of sociology and psychology in the 1970s is full of accounts of the way in which teacher expectations, cultural attitudes and material provision all worked towards encouraging girls to lower their academic sights. It was difficult to measure outcome by GCE results since 11+ selection could not be compared directly to validate or invalidate the selection choices for individuals, still less for the two genders. People had recognized that other factors intervened to affect secondary schooling as well as the qualities of the individual. The literature on maturation thus worked sociologically against favouring girls when applied later in the school career, and was used to explain away their early academic superiority. On the one hand, girls mature earlier than boys at 11, which means they have an 'unfair' academic *advantage* at 11. On the other hand, they mature earlier than boys which makes them *disadvantaged* at 15 by their disinclination to set their sights on academic achievement. However, this sort of investigation in the sociological and pedagogic implications of attitudes on exam results was not done at all in the classrooms of the 1940s or 1950s.

The group responsible for the book *Unpopular Education* (CCCS) has criticized the Labour reformers of the 1940s for a narrow concentration of the politics of access. This represents excess hindsight. The politics of access were not that narrow in the 1940s nor was the reworking of them in the 1960s in educational sociology. One of the limits of the discussion was the omission of girls. The CCCS group points to that omission in the political arithmetic tradition in Britain in sociological studies of social mobility running from David Glass in the 1940s to Halsey, Heath and Ridge in the 1980s.[29] (The last study omitted girls because they had not been dealt with in the earlier ones.) The comparisons made are between groups of boys only. So were most of the interview-based, qualitative studies of the effect of class on achievement and on the persistent success of middle-class boys, like the one by Jackson and Marsden which shows the alienation of life out of class in school; and the work of Halsey and Jean Floud which investigated the variation within groups of children.[30]

This absence is even more striking in English psychology. There were only two articles throughout this period on the difference between boys' and girls' performance in the verbal reasoning tests that were a consistent feature of 11+ selection whether done formally through examination or informally through teachers' records.[31] One, W. G. Emmett's of 1949, was a response to worries expressed by clients for Moray House tests in those local education authorities who found consistently more girls than boys reaching the mark which qualified them for access to grammar schools. In most LEAs of course this mark was not fixed. It was directly related to the number of places available in grammar schools. That is, to pass the exam was not to qualify in terms of intellectual standard, it was to qualify relative to one's peers.

Before the 1944 Education Act the Spens report of 1938 recommended that there be slightly more grammar school places for girls because boys had more technical education available to them and that this provision of extra grammar school places would compensate.[32] By the time J. W. B. Douglas followed his group of children through for the study published as *The Home and the School*, he found that this slight surplus had in fact been achieved, that is, that 22.2 per cent of girls and 18 per cent of boys in his study were receiving grammar school education, while 4.4 per cent of girls and 5.8 per cent of boys were in technical schools.[33] However, if one compensates for the tendency of boys to leave earlier in greater numbers this advantage is not as great as it appears, there were more girls in more sixth forms around the country getting ready to train as teachers than there were boys and it was there the numerical advantage lay. Douglas also, interestingly, found that parents were more concerned about the progress of their daughters than of their sons.[34] And it might be the case that this precisely reflected the narrow range of occupational opportunity for girls and therefore their greater dependence in the market for skills measured by School Certificate than for boys. Allocation to grammar schools in the thirties had, however, been much more uneven, that is, if you looked at the number of children in grammar schools there was a great majority of boys, at approximately 20 per cent to 15 per cent, boys to girls. The result was that over the late thirties and early forties girls had improved their position relative to boys and relative to their own position in the past.[35] Allocation to secondary education remained broadly the same as selection for grammar schools had been before the 1944 Act. Authorities used the same sort of examination papers, and they marked them in the same way, but they found themselves faced with a much bigger demand for places. Now people did not have to pay fees and did have to stay at school the difference between types of education after 11 was not that great. Demand for a full course of secondary education, in a grammar school, therefore rose greatly and outran supply of places. The only cost to the family was now deferred earnings, which could be heavy, but full employment meant that staying on at school did not mean loss of any chance to get a job at all.[36]

Before the 1944 Act the disparity between boys' and girls' marks in the grammar school entrance exam, as it was often known at the time, or common entrance exam, had not been commented on by psychologists or local education authorities at all, or if it had it did not reach the written records of the LEAs or the test producers. People had known for some time that there was a different distribution of intellectual abilities (as they were called) among boys and girls. This was one of the earliest topics investigated by Cyril Burt in a long career of psychological investigation. He argued in 1912, in one of his first published works, 'with few exceptions, innate sex differences in mental constitution are astonishingly small – far smaller than common belief and common practice would lead us to expect.'[37] By 1962, in the fourth edition of *Mental and Scholastic Tests*, Burt was still arguing, as he had done in the first edition of 1921, about differences in general ability due to sex, that 'at almost every age the girls outstrip the boys. Their superiority, though, is a very modest one. On average the girls appear advanced by about three-tenths of a year. The difference swells to a maximum at about the age of six or seven; at ten it is raised in favour of the boys; towards fourteen the superiority of girls is again visibly mounting.'[38] The 1964 edition adds the point that this recovery is transient. He says 'in this book it is hardly needful to compile age norms for the two sexes separately.' Other work by leading psychologists made the same point. Terman and Merrill, the American authorities who did quite substantial comparisons of the intelligence of girls and boys, came to the same conclusions, that is, that girls were superior to boys until six, boys above girls from six to 13, then the girls again. Others pointed to an explanation of this which lay in girls' superior verbal fluency. The man most responsible for spreading the word about mental tests, P. B. Ballard, pointed out that girls read better than boys: 'generally speaking they are 5 marks or 3 months ahead.'[39] However, if this was the psychological wisdom it did not make sense of the disparities between boys and girls in secondary selection. All these people argued that girls' superiority was at its lowest in the years of selection, and that it improved again in the years preliminary to School Certificate. Others pointed to girls being more industrious than boys. Fewer girls were 'misfits' after secondary selection because it was suggested that 'the drags and pushes of the social environment whose resultant was directed away from full secondary education have more effects on girls than boys.'[40] The result was that when this disparity was commented upon it remained a matter of social concern. People discussed what it meant in terms of girls' future after school, not in terms of what it meant in relation to girls' behaviour in school or girls' legitimate aspirations for further education.

In looking at the results of the Scottish Mental Survey (which attempted to survey the nature of the child mind for the whole of Scotland), the Scottish Council for Research in Education had designed the research to show whether children were on average less intelligent than they had been when the first survey was done in the 1930s, and in 1953 produced their report on the social implications for 1947. They commented on sex differences in test scores only in so far as it affected the comparability of two sets of test figures in the summary of changes over time. Another volume on the same material and in the same series said 'girls have converted what was a very slight inferiority in 1932 into a significant superiority over the boys in 1947' but no further comment was made.[41] Vernon, the most prominent writer on intelligence testing in the 1950s, identified the same phenomenon directly but assumed it to be temporary, caused by social factors.[42] He argued:

From about 1940 to 1950 girls usually did better than boys at the intelligence and arithmetic group tests in 11-year selection examinations, as well as in English, and different borderlines often had to be drawn for entry to grammar schools. It seems likely that boys were more seriously affected by war-time relaxations of home discipline and upsets to schooling. By the later 1950s, boys had generally caught up in intelligence tests and regained their superiority in arithmetic.

He commented in 1960 that 'girls do a little better on most verbal tests . . . boys on tests of inductive reasoning and arithmetical ability. The most marked difference occurs on spatial and mechanical tests', citing Emmett writing in 1954.[43]

These comments are perhaps surprisingly casual, to 1980s ears; less so if set against other contemporary comments. They do not reflect the same careful and detailed discussion of fine points seen in any discussion on social class or linguistic ability which filled the technical journals of education and psychology in the 1950s. In many texts there is not even a reference to the issue. Perhaps the most surprising of all these absences is in the summing up of the use of intelligence tests in selection in a major professional statement made in 1957, the British Psychological Society's *Secondary School Selection*. Psychologists argued that they were opposed to selection on psychological grounds because it could never be perfect. They argued that at least one in ten children would be misplaced under the best possible selective system, which, they argued, the 11+ exam was.[44] The only mention of the difference between the sexes was the comment, 'sex differentiation is highly controversial' – and there the matter is left.

This is not an argument about a prolonged conspiracy of silence, of exclusion or of secrecy. There was discussion on the issue in the local authorities themselves, and quite extensive discussion on particular years' mental test results. The earliest example I found was the report of the examiner to the Wiltshire County Education Committee in 1944 who noted girls' superiority to boys and raised the issue as grounds for a serious and elaborate discussion. The chief examiner's argument was that, 'possibly present day conditions with their favourable influence on child development had affected the girls more than the boys.' Apart from the Education Act which had been passed in August, it is hard to see why Wiltshire, with four years of war behind it and a major recipient of evacuees, should present particularly favourable conditions for child development. However the councillors expressed a variety of points of view, all of which could have been taken as a summary of more serious accounts written 20 years later. First, they said, girls learn to read earlier than boys. They went on to state that: 'Junior schools are practically bereft of men teachers and boys do not advance under women teachers as well as under men.' 'Girls take the job and treat life more seriously than boys.' 'Boys develop at a slower rate than girls but may outdistance the girls at a later age.' 'Girls have to accept responsibility in the home and this is carried on into the school.' The discussion concluded that this question would be raised as part of the general review of borderline for admission.[45]

There we have almost a paradigm of such discussions as there were in local authorities. This is the fullest account I have found so far in which, by and large, it is common sense and social observation that are used to explain the disparity between boys and girls. This disparity is not seen as a product of the test. It is not seen as a question of innate difference. Although these two factors are used to explain other phenomena, they are not used to explain the difference between the sexes.

Such discussions were most evident in the years 1947 and 1948, at any rate for the clients of the Moray House test-agency which supplied many of the LEAs with their 11+ exams. Several of them wrote letters to the test producers and asked if there was anything unusual about their children that year, or about the test. The head of the test agency investigated the question in response to the clients' requests. He concluded that it was not the test that was responsible. Most of the tests used that year had already been used elsewhere, except for one test battery, new that year, but the difference recorded was evident by use of new and old test alike. He also pointed out that the questions in verbal reasoning tests were carefully selected not to favour one or the other sex, and, in conversation with me many years later he said, that if they favoured anyone, they could be said to favour boys. He correlated test results with School Certificate results and concluded that the difference did not endure beyond the age of 14.[46] This was to be the explanation and the solution at once for anybody who took the trouble to look into question in any detail. One of the chief workers on the tests at the National Foundation for Educational Research (NFER) which began to produce tests in the late 1940s made exactly the same point in the British Psychological Symposium on the 11+ in 1957 and recommended that LEAs simply set up different norms.[47] That is, because the difference did not endure, it should not be accounted for in the selection process. Again the solution is one that actually says this is not a real phenomenon, it is to do with differential maturation, it is not real because it does not last, it is not a phenomenon produced by the test, it is a phenomenon produced by 'nature'.

In practice this meant that girls had to do much better in the 11+ exam in order to go to grammar school. In Essex, for example, girls had to get 190 in the combined examination marks to be even considered for the borderline group who needed further tests to get a place. Any boy who got 189 or more was in the category of those automatically accepted, while girls had to achieve 203.[48] In the Isle of Ely the difference in 1948 was as great, and in most years girls had to get 30 more points out of a possible 300 to obtain a place.[49] In some authorities rather than set up different norms a new test was added – a spatial test which did not correlate very highly with grammar school success (although it did with technical education), but it did favour boys rather than girls. This was introduced, for example, in Lindsey in Lincolnshire in 1952 in order to make up the number of boys. It was in this same year that the problem of the unevenness of girls and boys was raised in Parliament.[50] It was raised, not in itself as an issue to be dealt with immediately, but as a supporting example in the broader campaign against testing in schools, as yet another way in which testing was unfair.

The interests of equal justice were thus increasingly seen as being served by equalizing not opportunity and the chance to do well in the exam, but by equalizing provision. In Huntingdonshire, for example, girls had gone to grammar school in larger numbers until 1954 when the LEA said they would equalize them 'even if it means admitting some boys whose performance at the age of 11 is inferior to the performance of some girls who are excluded.'[51] The test had become visibly what it had always in fact been, a selective filter to fill the places available on a variety of social as well as educational grounds, not, as it had been initially argued it should be, a qualification for entry to grammar school. Successive debates on selection had raised public awareness that this was the case and it helped to emphasize the issue of justice rather than equality of opportunity in the rhetoric. In the early 1950s the work of sociologists had underlined psychologists' conclusion that complete fairness was impossible by pointing out how free secondary education for all had provided the elite form of education in grammar schools to the middle class in proportionately more numbers than were in the population at large.[52] What the discussion missed in ignoring gender was yet another inequality to add to that of geography, social class and political interests, so aptly described by the successive reports of the NFER on Allocation Procedures. Gender of course was compounded by these inequalities. Areas short of grammar school places were often especially short of girls' places, because they were areas which tended still to have sexually segregated secondary education in old buildings, and the weight of history had favoured boys. By December 1958 there were questions in Parliament on the shortage of girls' grammar school places.[53] The minister promised to remedy it by the end of 1959, but the complaint re-emerged in the 1960s, indicating how slow such response to political demands was in terms of providing bricks and mortar.

This was not a major inequality – it ment that 10 per cent of the 20 per cent of an age group who went to grammar school did not have access to grammar school education because of their gender (i.e. 2 per cent in all). But it was an equality all the more glaringly absent in discussions of Right and Left alike and it is that absence that needs explaining. A part of the explanation is what has been described as the 'absent feminism' of 1940s and 1950s Britain. But the inequality leaps to the eye in the comparison of entrance to various forms of education (see table 7.1).

Table 7.1 Percentage of boys and girls entering various forms of educational institution

	Boys	Girls
Entering universities	5.5	2.5
In grammar school at 17	11	10
In grammar school 11–13	20	20
Independent efficient schools 11–13	3.5	3

Source: A. H. Halsey, *Trends in British Society Since 1900* (Macmillan, 1979), p. 182.

In other words, girls were roughly parallel to boys in the state sector until the 'O' level stage, but they did not progress further. And this was not perceived by those who argued about the political future of education as a problem at a time when such arguments were bitter and long. The problem was viewed the other way round. It was seen as a problem of the disadvantage to boys, rather than the wastage of educational talent of girls.

The first reason for any lack of discussion is that the problem was a statistical artefact in many ways, dependent on the results of tests.

Tests were highly technical exercises, conducted in an arcane way by the procedures of factor analysis, by skilled experts not by ordinary teachers or even education officers, so that by the 1940s testing had become a professional matter for psychologists. The final selection process was seen as an arbitrary matter and it was not until the early 1950s, when the campaign against intelligence tests in education became a major public issue, that the arcane, secret and inaccessible nature of tests began to be questioned and began, to a certain extent, to be dissipated.

Secondly, it is quite true that, as the Wiltshire education committee observed, girls' success was a phenomenon partly created by improved social circumstances. It was also created by population growth, that is, the demand for secondary school places did not match the supply. It was partly a phenomenon to do with the increased social aspirations created by the years of war and the long delay in raising the school-leaving age from the late 1930s to 1947. It was also a phenomenon created by the post-war baby boom, which meant that at exactly the time when people had grown used to having education accessible to them in whatever form of school they were allocated to, there were the most children seeking such education. The 1934 special places scheme had provided fewer places for girls than for boys. It is not clear to me why this was so. It might have been again due to aspiration, but even if this was true it did not present a problem because there was decline in school population at the time. There was no great pressure on secondary school places. It seems quite clear from literary evidence – although no sociological studies of the issue have been done – that it was girls who tended not to take up places that they felt they could not 'afford' in the thirties. As a result, the 1940s saw girls taking the same attitude to secondary education as boys, and they did so increasingly as much before the Act as after it, as much under the special places scheme as they did under the free secondary education for all. Hence wartime did create improved expectations. It did create a diversity of hopes for the future in girls perhaps even more than boys. It also created a much greater reliance by local authorities on tests and, as had been observed by Burt all those years ago, girls were better at doing tests particularly tests involving verbal factors. The thing that correlated most highly with grammar school success was verbal fluency, at which girls were better. All these aspects came together in the late forties, but they could be solved by a technical adjustment and they were so, and as a result the inequality was to a certain extent invisible. It was only made manifest when a local authority scrutinized its figures carefully or when concern over places in grammar schools actually showed that girls were getting a poorer deal than boys.

The third factor in this discussion was quite simply what we would now call sexist assumptions. That is, this problem was always viewed as one for boys not for girls. It was not seen, as I have said, as grounds for improving the after selection life of girls in grammar schools, it was seen as grounds for attempting to improve the performance of boys, hence the substitution of the spatial tests for verbal tests in the selection tests, hence the establishment of different norms for boys and girls. Quite simply, what happened to boys at 11 was seen as slightly more important as what happened to girls. This simple ideological assumption was common from Left to Right. All political organizations, all educational pressure groups, were more concerned with inequalities between classes. This was partly due to the foundation of the anti-testing movement in its early stages in the Left of the Labour Party and the British Communist Party, neither of which were at this time notable for their feminism. It also related to the generally rising standard of life throughout Britain, the change of political attitudes among large sections of British society which were summed up as those of the 'age of affluence'. Compared to the hungry thirties and the austerity ridden early forties, the 1950s seemed much better. As a consequence, people did not see that some inequalities were being perpetuated and entrenched despite considerable improvement in the overall standard, and because of the improvement in the overall standard, inequality no longer seemed such an issue.

The small girls in tears because they had been adjudged failures may well have included some who, if they had been boys, would have gone to grammar school. They may have been only a few, but that few would have added weight to the clamour of voices from those who disliked the selective system. They did not. Nor did their misfortune lead to any investigation by psychologists, sociologists or educationists. Girls were a social issue, and the differences between them hidden by their basic difference from boys. Perhaps this example should provide a lesson for us in investigating the effects of gender – if we fall into the same trap our analysis loses its edge. At the same time the injustice within the system to those few who stepped down and were replaced by boys, was not as great as the injustice which turned 80 per cent of all English children into failures.

Acknowledgements

I am grateful for the support of the SSRC who funded the project from which this material comes. I would like to thank Sally Roberts for her help with word processing.

Bibliographical Note

There is really very little historical material on the relation between psychology and schooling or on girls as such for this period; and sociological studies of inequality are particularly blind to sexual difference (as it was called) in this period. There are some vivid accounts of girlhood; Pearl Jephcott, *Girls Growing Up* (1942) is one and the recent Virago collection edited by Liz Heron, *Truth, Dare or Promise* (1985), provides a fine analysis (I derive the first part of my title from Alison Henegan's piece). B. Jackson and D. Marsden, *Education and the Working Class* (1962), provides useful insights into the effects of social mobility. There is a huge literature about selection and comprehensive reform; and a large though less accessible range on psychometric technique in relation to the 11+. Brian Simon's *Intelligence Testing and the Common Secondary School* of 1953 describes most of the issues very clearly and deals with the techniques of selection as an opponent; the British Psychological Society's report on *Secondary School Selection* of 1957 puts the case for the 11+ as formal, standardized tests very clearly while showing the unease developing among psychologists about selective education itself.

Part III

Experiences in Education

8

Cultural Reproduction in the Education of Girls: a Study of Girls' Secondary Schooling in Two Lancashire Towns, 1900–50

Penny Summerfield

Schools, it is said by sociologists, play an essential role in cultural reproduction.[1] That is to say, they are engaged in a constant process of transmitting ideologies, values and attitudes such that dominant social relations between classes, sexes and ethnic groups are maintained and perpetuated. Research into the operation of these processes as far as gender is concerned suggests that schools teach girls that their main objective in life is to fit themselves for a caring role, primarily as wives and mothers, but also within the occupational world and within society more generally. By definition this role is a secondary, servicing one, and in learning the role girls learn to regard themselves as secondary to men in terms of ability, capacity to lead, and social importance.

Such analyses of schooling in 'femininity' have been of major importance in opening up for debate the impact on girls' educational opportunities of schooling in all its aspects, particularly within the dominant form of secondary school in Britain today, the co-educational comprehensive school. Feminists have concluded that single sex education, either within a mixed school or separately, is the answer for girls (if not for boys), because it protects girls from the subjugation which boys' training in masculinity requires of them, and maximizes their opportunities in terms of choice of subject and access to resources.[2]

A criticism of the debate has, however, been that it has tended to ignore both social class and the lessons in 'femininity' taught to girls in single sex schools. The burden of the argument about social class advanced for example by Madeleine Arnot is that the radical feminist view that women form a common class in relation to patriarchal domination has obscured class differences between women, and the class bases of the various forms of schooling for girls which developed over the past century. Feminist historians have emphasized the challenge to dominant gender relations represented by the demands for 'higher' education for women and by the establishment of the new girls' schools and colleges in the late nineteenth century.[3] Class differentiation between different types of institution has been acknowledged by these writers,[4] but little attention has been paid to the interconnected reproduction of both class and gender relations within the new girls' secondary schools. According to Arnot, class-specific forms of femininity have been taught by the various schools, with the aim of fitting girls for matrimony through domestic training suitable for their social position. In short the role of the girls' secondary schools established in the late nineteenth and early twentieth centuries was to prepare girls to become the wives of the bourgeoisie.[5]

This chapter seeks to subject this view to critical scrutiny through an exploration of the intentions as far as class and gender relations were concerned, of the secondary schools for girls which developed between the late nineteenth and mid-twentieth centuries. It is based on a case study of schools for girls in two Lancashire towns, Preston and Blackburn, which has involved analysis of official documents relating to the schools as well as oral history interviews of old girls and mistresses. The exploration involves the pursuit of answers to three key questions. First, were the schools aiming to produce middle-class women; secondly, were they intending to turn out potential wives; and thirdly, if not wives, then what sort of women did they want to produce? Aims of this sort are unlikely to have been overtly stated with any regularity, but they may have been revealed by those in control of the schools in various other ways. Three aspects of school life likely to yield information on their class and gender intentions are investigated here: the academic objectives they defined as important, the post-school destinations they wanted for their pupils and their prescriptions for their pupils' sexuality. It should perhaps be emphasized that this is not a study of the class composition of girls' secondary schools as such, nor an analysis of the 'afterlives' of their pupils. Its focus is on intentions rather than outcomes.

The six schools for girls in Preston and Blackburn which called themselves 'secondary schools' between 1900 and 1944, include a range of different types. In origin two, Preston and Blackburn High Schools for Girls, were founded by limited liability companies in 1878 and 1883 respectively, on the Girls' Public Day School Company model (though they did not belong to that organization). One, the Park School for Girls in Preston, was a municipal venture launched under the 1902 Act, which made it possible for local authorities to spend the rates on secondary education for the first time. Three of the schools were attached to Catholic convents, Winckley Square and Lark Hill House in Preston, and Notre Dame in Blackburn. All were day schools, although the convents ran small boarding departments in addition to their day secondary schools.[6]

The relatively large number of convent schools is explained by the high concentrations of Catholics in both towns. The Lancashire Catholic population was of long standing, and was swollen in the early nineteenth century by Irish families seeking remunerative work, especially during the potato famine of the 1840s. By 1912 between one-sixth and one-quarter of the Blackburn population and as much as one-third that of Preston was said to be Catholic.[7] Initially incoming Irish Catholics formed the lowest stratum of the working class, but within the Catholic population there was considerable class differentiation, and the role of middle-class Catholics in 'taming' the Irish poor through the agency of the church and the school became increasingly important.[8]

In terms of funding, the Catholic schools could not get grants from the local education authorities (LEAs) under the 1902 Act, since neither would support 'sectarian' secondary schools themselves, but the local authorities were keen to support 'waivers' of Secondary School Regulations relating to the teaching of 'religious formularies', so that the Catholic schools could obtain direct grants from the Board of Education. The convents were seen as making an important contribution to secondary education which the LEAs would otherwise have had to provide themselves.[9] Only two of the schools, the Park School, Preston and Blackburn High School (BHS), received local authority as well as Board of Education grants. Preston High School was never 'recognized' for grant purposes, and closed in 1918.

Apart from Preston High School all the schools were successful ventures. Numbers rose between 1900 and 1939 imposing consider-able pressure on accommodation. BHS had 139 pupils in 1908 and 436 in 1939. Notre Dame's numbers stood at 170 in 1908 and 390 in

1939. The Park School began with 220 in 1908 and had 530 girls by 1939. Winckley Square had 138 in 1908 and 379 in 1939, and Lark Hill had 92 in 1920 and 361 in 1939. Preston High School's numbers were around 120 in 1905 and 110 at its demise in 1918.[10]

In both towns the schools were resting on an industrial base. Cotton spinning and weaving mills dominated Preston and Blackburn, though the industrial scene was in both cases diversified by engineering, with brewing and iron in Blackburn and industries associated with the port in Preston where further industrial diversification took place between the wars. The dense networks of terraced housing in both towns bore witness to their 'proletarian' character, but a relatively small middle and lower middle class also developed, housed by the end of the nineteenth century in the leafier suburbs of Fulwood in Preston and Revidge in Blackburn and in the surrounding villages, its prosperity based on cotton, engineering, retailing and commerce, and the professions.[11]

Academic Objectives

If the intentions of girls' secondary schools were primarily marital, it would not seem necessary for them to have prioritised academic achievements. However, though the schools under consideration varied as to the manner in which they pursued scholarship, in none of them was it totally subordinate to the task of preparing girls for domesticity. All six schools aimed at teaching the same curriculum and entering girls for the same public examinations as those taken by boys at grammar and public schools, which in the 1900s were mainly the Oxford and Cambridge Locals and Higher Locals, superseded in 1917 by School Certificate and Higher School Certificate.

In terms of gender the decision to undertake the same syllabuses and public examinations as the boys' grammar and public schools was an unmistakable challenge to patriarchal control, given the long exclusion of women from academia, and was responded to as such by male commentators from the 1870s to the 1940s.[12] For some women it was experienced as a form of liberation in contrast to the intellectual confinement of home life. Many of those interviewed who attended the Park and BHS spoke with appreciation both of stimulating teaching and even of the piles of homework they were given, two or three hours' a night by Higher School Certificate level. Comments about enjoying the 'challenge' of difficult subjects, being 'well taught', feeling they were getting a 'good grounding' and of being 'thoroughly interested in all these essays and questions' were made by interviewees who had been at the school from the 1910s to the 1940s, including some of those who did not pursue the academic route into higher education but left at the earliest possible moment.[13]

The kind of academic education pursued at these schools also conveyed messages concerning social class. The influence of the Oxford and Cambridge Local Examinations, the Board of Education's Regulations for Secondary Schools and later the School Certificate examinations, ensured that the schools defined themselves as offering a 'liberal education' (as Felicity Hunt has demonstrated in an earlier chapter). This was the education of a 'gentleman' not a practical preparation for occupational life and it was predicated upon a moneyed background which permitted the leisure to pursue a non-instrumental course of study. Secondary school girls experienced the class meanings of their academic education through the division from their former class mates at elementary schools introduced by the new subjects they studied like Latin, French, algebra and trigonometry, and particularly by the restriction on their free time imposed by homework.

There were however differences in the academic atmosphere of the various schools, influenced by the post-school destinations on which they set their sights, and by the qualifications and personal dispositions of heads and assistant mistresses. Notably, although papal dispensations were obtained for Catholic women to take degrees at London University (1893) and Oxford (1906),[14] it was unusual for the nuns who taught in convents, and even their headmistresses, to be graduates, in contrast to the majority of the teaching staff at Blackburn High and the Park School where, by the 1900s, recruitment of schoolmistresses was deliberately focused on those who had successfully pursued the academic route through secondary school and university. Academic rigour was important in the convent schools but it occupied a different place within their ethos from the university oriented BHS and Park.

In contrast at Preston High School for Girls, a private foundation like Blackburn High School, academic results were less important than the social cachet conferred by attending the school. A Board of Education Inspector wrote in 1913, 'The school is scarcely of first grade character but owes its existence and such success as it attains to social considerations rather than to any superiority in the range and character of the educational advantages which it offers.'[15] As Preston High School was to discover, however, social kudos was coming increasingly to depend on academic status. The school had been established in 1878 by a limited liability company as a Church of England school charging high fees for the daughters of 'leading citizens' of Preston and took by the 1900s about 120 pupils. But it could not survive competition with the Park Secondary School in spite of the apparently inferior social standing of this municipal school established by the Borough in 1907, which charged relatively low fees and accepted free place pupils from public elementary schools. The key factor in the Park's success was its academic reputation, firmly established by its highly intellectual first headmistress, Alice M. Stoneman, ex-pupil of North London Collegiate School, graduate of Girton College Cambridge and Master of Arts of Dublin. Preston High School entered a period of financial uncertainty in the 1910s, was unable to obtain grants, and experienced dwindling numbers. In July 1918 its buildings were taken over by the Local Authority. September 1918 saw the four youngest forms of the Park School housed there.[16]

Although non-instrumental in itself, academic education could eventually lead, via higher education, to the ranks of the nation's professional elites, which were of course predominantly male. However, the Sex Disqualification Removal Act of 1919 made it illegal to deny women with the right qualifications access to any profession except the church and the administrative grades of the civil service on the grounds of their sex alone. The academic education offered by the girls' secondary schools gave girls the preparation they needed in order to challenge male predominance in the professions. In class terms it represented preparation for a slot within the professional middle class, while in gender terms it represented a challenge to male supremacy in this occupational world.

However the challenge to the dominant form of gender relations represented by the schools' academic endeavours was tempered by other activities in which they were engaged. For example, all the schools cultivated an ethos of service which found its main expression in voluntary work by pupils for charity. It emphasized the 'caring' role expected of women in society and could be seen as a counter to the competitive individualism of the exam-bound academic spirit of the schools. It was especially strong at BHS. Here charities dedicated to reforming the working-class poor on a model of self-sufficiency, temperance and purity were the favourites, such as the Charity Organisation Society and the Girls' Friendly Society. Both made requirements of their beneficiaries concerning deference, gratitude and respectability which served to reinforce bourgeois class and cultural control. BHS pupils experienced directly through their involvement in such charities their location within the class structure, at the same time as learning that their duty as women was to be of service.[17] Other schools were more inclined towards work for hospitals, orphanages and homes for crippled children and, as one Park School girl remembers, visiting unmarried mothers with clothes for their babies. The convents specialized in fund raising for missionary activities, epitomized by 'black babies weeks'. Such activities taught similar lessons in rather less overt ways.[18] Though reducing the gender challenge of the schools, the ethos of service strengthened their role in reproducing dominant class relations.

Service was a particularly 'feminine' aspect of the ethos of these schools, but it was not seen by headmistresses as at odds with the academic purpose of the schools. This was not the case, on the other hand, as far as the introduction of domestic subjects was concerned. The demands of the Board of Education from 1905 that 'housecraft' should be a compulsory part of the secondary school girl's curriculum was, as Carol Dyhouse has argued, part of a movement to 'feminize' the curriculum springing from eugenist concern over the quality of the race in the early twentieth century, and as such was a threat to the schools' primarily academic objectives.[19] Domestic subjects did not belong within the 'liberal' academic curricula fostered in these schools, in that they were practical and vocational. The Board itself as much as admitted this by not giving domestic science the same weight as academic subjects in the School Certificate Examination in 1917.[20]

In order to obtain the Board's grants, headmistresses had to introduce domestic subjects after 1905, but there is evidence that they found ways of doing so which left their academic objectives unscathed. For example, Blackburn High could not find an adequate domestic science room at the school and throughout the 1910s and 1920s His Majesty's Inspectorate (HMI) complained that 'cutting out' in needlework was virtually impossible because of the sloping desks at which pupils sat and that 'the time allotted to the subject is barely adequate'.[21] Eventually girls were sent a mile away to a local authority cookery centre at Whalley Range, used by elementary school girls in the town. 'You went out across the town to another school for Domestic Science' remembers Barbara Tomlinson who was at the school in the late 1930s and wartime. Her comments indicate the position girls understood domestic subjects to occupy in the school's order of priorities: 'It was regarded as a bit of play as I look back. It was a sort of afternoon when we weren't at School as it were.'[22]

Contrary to the image of 'domesticity' which is often attached to Catholic girls' education, the two convent schools in Preston were even more uncompromising. 'It is not intended to teach cookery', wrote Winckley Square's 'correspondent' to the Board of Education in 1907, 'This is sufficiently advanced on the entrance of the pupil.'[23] Like many high school headmistresses, the governing bodies of the Winckley Square and Lark Hill Convent Schools believed that the subject was better learnt at home. Neither school had a special domestic science room, though nuns in both taught needlework up to School Certificate level in the 1920s.

In contrast domestic science was much more firmly institutionalized at the Park School for Girls under the controlling influence of the Preston Education Committee. By the First World War a two-year cookery course had been added to the needlework which all forms were required to do, the school kitchen being used as a 'combined lecture and practical room for the Cookery Classes' and by the 1930s a separate Housecraft Room had been created.[24] All the same, the Park School's heads had a clear view of the sub-academic status of the subject, which was, said the second headmistress unequivocally, for the 'duds' only.[25] By the 1930s only those in the lower streams who were taking Domestic Science in School Certificate had to do cookery beyond the first year. The lesson that an inverse relationship existed between domestic competence and academic ability was absorbed by the girls. For example, Edith Berry, at the school from 1927–32, explained that she 'made bread and marmalade and cakes' for only about twelve months, 'because we were streamed you see, and I wasn't in the cookery stream after the first two years. I went in the Science form, and the Domestic Science was more for the – well when I say lower form, I'm not being derogatory, but some are better with working with their hands and they were streamed accordingly.'[26] The Board of Education's Inspectors supported such differentiation, recommending to the convents in the 1920s 'the custom which is fairly common in girls schools of providing a special course in Housewifery for the less able girls.'[27]

Not only were domestic subjects regarded as inferior, but many old girls' memories of needlework and cookery do not suggest that they learnt anything very useful. Margaret Adams attended the Park School 1916–21 where she was rewarded with 'very good' for patching, but made knickers that 'were no use to me at all'.

Elizabeth Smithies who attended the school more than 30 years later had a similar experience:

> We had to make a cookery apron – a white linen cookery apron, a cotton cookery apron. And we also had to make a pair of pants, knickers. And you had to do the pattern yourself on squared paper, to teach you how to make a pattern. Now when I had finished mine, they were not so much knickers as bloomers. And indeed, when the elastic was taken out of the legs, they served as football shorts for my brother![28]

However interesting to some individuals and genuinely important for society these subjects might be, it was clear that the schools themselves relegated them to a secondary position. In so doing they conveyed a message to girls about the relatively unimportant place which preparation for domesticity occupied in the schools' agenda. What is more the class connotations of the academic objectives of the schools implied that domestic science was not only a subject for less able girls but also for those from lower social groups, whatever the actual class composition of the groups that took it within the girls' secondary schools. Girls from higher social groups could in any case expect to live in homes where domestic servants were employed, at least until the Second World War. But even the decline of domestic service did not herald the disappearance of the association between emphasis on domestic subjects and the low social and academic standing of a school. It was reinforced after 1944 by the demarcation between grammar schools (in which domestic subjects were relatively neglected) and secondary modern schools (in which they assumed more importance).

The emphatically academic orientation of the girls' secondary schools of Preston and Blackburn also placed the objective of marriage and family in the shade. Miss Green, first headmistress of the Blackburn High School from 1883 to 1898, felt it necessary to redress the balance, when she realized that old girls were marrying without informing her: 'May I say that I think my girls should not let me hear casually, from other people, that such a momentous change in their lives is going to take place. Do you think I don't understand how much more it means to you, for your whole life, than any University Honours could do?'[29]

Her twentieth-century successors made it clear, however, that University Honours meant a lot more to the school than the regular succession of marriages reported in the Old Girls' Newsletter. The same was true at the Park School. Catherine Tipping, who was there from 1915 to 1920, replied to the question 'Do you think you were expected to get married by the school?', thus: 'I don't think as far as I can remember, that ever came into any discussion or – no, you always felt that you were supposed to go on and further your education. The girls that left, who just left school after they'd finished and got married and so on, they weren't thought anything very much about at all. No. Just let slip.'[30]

Post-school Destinations

If wife- and mother-hood were not highlighted as suitable targets for secondary school girls, what were the approved post-school destinations? BHS and the Park School emitted strong indicators, by, for example, inviting heads of women's colleges to preside at Speech Days and celebrating academic successes in ways which girls would not forget. For example, in 1904 when Agnes Mackie of BHS 'gained an Open Scholarship at Oxford, the highest honour which has hitherto fallen to the School' the whole school had 'a day's holiday to mark the occasion'.[31]

Unlike those who 'just left school after they'd finished and got married', old girls at university were certainly not 'let slip'. Their progress was monitored and reported on. In contrast to Miss Green's complaint that she was not told about marriages in the 1890s, Miss Porritt who taught geography at Blackburn High School from 1924 to 1955 remembers getting into trouble with Miss Gardner, her head until 1932, for failing to pass on the news that an old girl had obtained her degree:

> One of the two occasions on which Miss Gardner was cross with me was, I had a girl in my form that year, called Margaret, whose sister Mary, if I've got them the right way round, was at Liverpool University taking her degree. And Margaret came up to me on Wednesday morning or whatever it was, and said, "Oh Mary's got her degree", you see, and I said, "Ooh, how lovely", and I didn't go straight after prayers to Miss Gardner and tell her. And she heard about it in a round about way the next day and on Friday she sent for me, and she said, "Why didn't you tell me that Mary McCarthy had got her degree?" She was so cross with me because I hadn't handed in a piece of really thrilling information about one of her old girls.[32]

Not surprisingly from the earliest point girls developed a strong impression that academic success and entry to higher education, especially university, but also teacher training college, were what these schools required of their pupils, and that any other objectives they might have were of little interest to the heads and their staffs. If anything the university bias became more extreme over the years, even though the numbers going each year remained small. About three girls a year went to university and between six and twelve went into teacher training from the Park School in the 1930s. Figures at BHS, which was smaller by about 100 pupils, were slightly lower, about two and eight, though rather more entries to Oxbridge colleges were recorded.[33] Meanwhile the schools grew in size and social heterogeneity, and simultaneously opportunities for girls in paid work, especially clerical work, increased.

Family plans for daughters in this context were often at odds with school objectives. Joyce Gibson who attended the Park School in the 1920s was encouraged by the school in her ambition to become a maths mistress, but her parents were neither willing nor sufficiently affluent to send her to university (her father was a skilled engineer) and Joyce took and passed the civil service exams, in which the school showed little interest. Muriel Cowperthwaite followed the same path in the 1930s with no more help than Joyce: 'In a way you were kind of finished with if you weren't going to go on', she explained. Edith Berry's parents decided that she should be trained for dairy work in the 1930s because this coincided with the needs of the family business. The school dismissed her with no more advice than, 'Make sure you do it scientifically.'[34] Even though teacher training was a well recognized and approved destination, the Park and BHS girls who pursued it tended to feel that it was second best. Olive Hamby left the Park in 1943 and went to Whitelands College, where her mother had been before her, to train as a primary school teacher, but remembers: 'I think the school, we always used to feel that they were biased towards university, and latterly as you went back, they really only seemed to be particularly interested in university-trained people. Perhaps that's because they were on common ground. They were all graduates, in the main subjects, except the gym mistress.'[35]

Things were slightly different at the convents where the staff were not 'all graduates'. University was seen as the goal for an exceptional girl, rather than the norm, as it was at BHS and the Park (even though the figures show that it was in fact by no means a typical destination). Teacher training college was the target for the convents, in the context of an urgent demand from the Catholic elementary schools for a steady supply of women teachers, and the Board of Education's requirement that intending teachers should be educated at a secondary school from 1907, instead of serving a pupil-teacher apprenticeship during their teens in an elementary school.

Marriage was also a more acceptable goal at the convents, presumably because of the central place in Catholicism of the Virgin Mary as an ideal mother figure, and the importance of rearing the next generation within the faith. In contrast to girls at non-Catholic schools, Barbara Cairns who attended Lark Hill Convent from 1948 to 1952 remembers being advised by a nun on how to be a good wife: 'I remember Mother Monica telling us before we left that if we did get married we should look after our man. Always have your meal ready and if you must have an apron on always have a nice clean one on when he comes home. But always have the tea ready.'[36]

Other personal objectives, especially in clerical work, received no more encouragement than at the non-Catholic schools. Doris Watkinson, who went to Winckley Square Convent in the 1920s explained:

> Their attitude was, oh yes, that you either got married, or perhaps became a nun, or a teacher, a teacher was practically the same in those days as becoming a nun, they didn't seem to get married much. You know – and these were all very worthy things to do, to be a teacher, to be a nun, or to be a married woman. I think that there was a general despising of the other things some girls, awkward, obstinate girls might wish to do, like being typists, in particular. I remember that described as drumming your brains away on a typewriter. It was despised. And a girl in the sixth form in my year was going into the civil service, they have to give a sort of special tuition for the civil service entrance exam, and I remember that that was given, not exactly reluctantly, but as if not one hundred per cent approved, they didn't think it was a sort of very wonderful thing for her to be doing. I don't know what the attitude was towards nursing, I can't really remember, but that was what we picked up, that the best thing was to be a teacher and eventually to – you'd get married or not.[37]

Things had not changed much by the 1940s and 1950s, in spite of the expansion in the number of women doing clerical work during the Second World War, and their retention after it. Women formed 17 per cent of the labour force in national and local government in 1931, 46 per cent in 1943, and 38 per cent in 1948. Two sisters who left Lark Hill in 1945 and 1952 respectively remember that 'if you did this shorthand typing they wiped their hands of you.' Both went into clerical work. But whether the focus was on university or teacher training college, the comment made by Mary Robinson about Lark Hill in the 1930s can stand for those made by girls from all the secondary schools under consideration throughout the period: 'The only career they ever came up with seemed to be teaching.'[38]

In gender terms teaching was obviously a 'sensible' target for educated girls. Women formed 66 per cent of the total teaching force by the 1940s, numbering 134,000, and they had predominated in the elementary schools since early in the century: 75 per cent of elementary teachers were women in 1914, 71 per cent 1938. In no other profession except nursing were women so prominent, and teaching salaries were considerably higher than those received by nurses. Even in the 1940s women constituted only 16 per cent of those working in public administration and medicine, and they did not top 10 per cent in any other profession.[39] Heads and mistresses were delighted when unusual girls achieved more remarkable career goals, such as becoming a doctor, lawyer, architect, accountant or joining the administrative (as opposed to the executive or clerical) ranks of the civil service. But to have emphasized these careers as alternatives to teaching would have required the schools to take a more challenging stance as far as gender relations within the professions were concerned, and even if teaching was somewhat sex stereotyped, any career which provided women with the means to be self sufficient struck a blow against conventional norms for women.

Teaching was also a fitting destination in terms of class, though secondary teaching, for which a degree was necessary rather than the two-year course at training college required of elementary teachers, had higher status as a professional goal. Elementary teaching only gradually shook off its nineteenth-century working-class image, deriving from the pupil-teacher system of training and the assumption built into the 1870 Elementary Education Act that these were the schools of the labouring poor.

Lessons in Femininity

The argument so far has been that though the girls' secondary schools intended to reproduce dominant class relations, their insistence on providing a largely undiluted academic education designed to prepare girls for higher education and the professions, especially teaching, challenged dominant gender relations. The schools stood for the idea that girls' intellectual capacities were the equal of boys', and the possibility of female economic independence (even in the absence of equal pay for women) was part of the life-plan they advocated. Preparation for wife- and mother-hood was overshadowed by these aims, even in the convent schools, which as we have seen were less dismissive of matrimony. Nevertheless, it is possible that concurrently the schools were transmitting lessons in femininity which would prepare girls for bourgeois wife and motherhood.

The convent schools in particular were renowned for the inculcation of a refined femininity bound up with the Catholic faith. This aspect of convent schooling persuaded a minority of non-Catholic parents to send their daughters to the Catholic schools in both Preston and Blackburn throughout the period.[40] Even when they were critical of the academic standards attained in the convents, the Board of Education's Inspectors always commented favourably on the ambience of the schools. For example, they wrote of the Convent of Notre Dame, Blackburn, in 1906, 'The discipline and tone of the School are of a high order, and the frank and pleasant manners of the scholars and their cheerful activity testify to the sympathetic and refining influences with which they are surrounded.'[41] Old girls remember the methods by which mistresses still sustained such a tone forty years later: 'A lot of them tended to put on "you are offending Our Lady" you know. I mean today they wouldn't buy that would they? They always tended to put that before you, and you were a sort of sinner against your religion as opposed to the school.'[42] Examples of 'sins' came readily to the minds of many of those interviewed, for example, Barbara and Kathleen, the sisters who attended Lark Hill House Convent in the 1940s, recalled:

> You know, one or two of the girls, because they didn't like the brown velours, they'd put a big crease in the back so the hat would tilt back. Well if any girl was caught with a crease in her hat, dear me! Some would take them off on the bus. Well, if that got back to school! And ladies didn't cross their legs or whistle or anything like this, you know. 'It makes Our Lady cry to hear a lady whistle'.[43]

The leverage used to command obedience at the non-Catholic schools did not contain this religious dimension, and the stress on ladylike behaviour was possibly greater at the convents than at other girls' secondary schools. It was certainly believed to be so. 'We always said the girls at the Catholic school were better behaved than we were', recalled Joyce Westall, at BHS in the 1930s.[44] Convent girls had to curtsey to the nuns and their uniforms were more obviously feminine than those of BHS and the Park School. The convents clung to dresses into the 1950s, long after the non-Catholic schools had gone over to gym slips and blouses for everyday wear, a transition which happened at the Park and BHS in the 1920s.

The arts' sixth form at the Park School, Preston in 1920. The girls are with their form mistress, Miss Muncaster, and are wearing the school uniform: a navy blue gym slip with a velvet yoke over a white square-necked blouse and black stockings.

Likewise, there were certain school girl crimes that have only been mentioned by convent girls, such as riding a bicycle to school or carrying parcels, both of which were deemed unladylike at Lark Hill in the 1940s.[45] But the convents were at one extreme of a continuum of views about the kind of appearance and behaviour to be expected from middle-class girls. At all the schools there were, apart from tunics, dresses or skirts, regulation blazers, coats, hats, blouses, stockings, pants, sportswear, indoor shoes, outdoor shoes and especially gloves, which had most emphatically to be worn at the appropriate times. Schoolmistresses shared similar views of what constituted a misdemeanour. Thus at all the schools strict checks were maintained on uniform inside the school and out, eating in the classrooms and especially in the streets was forbidden, silence was enforced in cloakrooms, corridors, classrooms, assemblies and even during mealtimes, running up stairs was punishable, and any form of disrespect to a mistress was regarded as a crime, from 'answering back' to failing to open a door for her, or stand aside while she went past, or rise when she came into a room. More surprisingly, girls at both Lark Hill and the Park were told in the 1930s and 1940s not to go into Woolworths, which was referred to as 'a place of temptation',[46] and was presumably seen as 'cheap and nasty' and therefore socially unsuitable for 'nice' girls.

All these transgressions were met with punishments which varied from school to school but which were essentially equivalents, on a scale of severity from the reprimand of a mistress or a prefect to 'order marks', loss of merit, detention, lines, a seat outside the headmistress's room, or, worst of all, being carpeted in her study itself. In contrast to the punishments regularly meted out to both sexes at elementary schools and to boys at grammar and public schools, physical assault was never involved. In class and gender terms it would have been inappropriate. Girls nevertheless felt that the system was a relentless one. For example, Jane Miller at the Park School in the 1920s said, 'You got order marks for, well, looking crooked sometimes.'[47]

The biggest misdemeanour of all involved having any contact with the opposite sex, and the non-Catholic schools were no more relaxed in this respect than the Catholic ones. At the Park and BHS there was to be no contact whatsoever with boys from the neighbouring schools. Park School girls from the 1910s to the 1950s were not allowed to walk along 'Park Avenue' with any Preston Grammar School boy, even a younger brother,[48] and Anne Gordon who was at BHS in the fifties remembers: 'We were told all the time that you're young ladies and we don't talk to boys, and – the boys' grammar school at Blackburn was on the other side of the road and the girls walked at one side and the b– . . . you weren't supposed to even *look* across!'[49]

Girls plying their daily passage on public transport were bound to come into contact with boys, but respondents remember that the schools' attempts to segregate the sexes extended even to public transport: girls downstairs on buses, boys up. Evasion of such rules required great discretion, as Catherine Tipping, at the Park School from 1915 to 1920, recounts:

> Of course we weren't allowed to talk to the boys at all. If we were seen talking to them we were really in hot water. And of course some of them had to come from Preston . . . Well of course we used to meet these grammar school boys, you know, and we got to know them, waiting for trams, and we used to chat them up and so forth, you know, but we had to be very careful we weren't seen, or else we were in hot water.[50]

If casual contact with boys was unacceptable it goes without saying that boyfriends were taboo. As Muriel Cowperthwaite said in answer to the question 'Did Park School girls have boyfriends?' in the 1930s, 'they were naughty girls if they did'.[51] Mildred Howarth remembers the opprobrium which descended on a friend who 'got friendly with a bank clerk' in the 1910s:

> She was still at school and he used to meet her out of school. And you know, we were in the Park School at the park, and at some point they were sitting closely together on a seat before she went home you see, because she lived out a way, and this Headmistress of ours passed them walking home. She lived at Fulwood. Eventually the girl was expelled![52]

Girls who associated with the opposite sex or who went dancing or to parties outside the jurisdiction of their parents and their parish were seen in the schools as 'rough'.[53] They were flouting all the social norms of the girls' school community: academic, since boyfriends and homework were seen as incompatible; in terms of class, since secondary school girls were supposed to be pursuing a different course from working girls in their teens, who were already participants not only in the labour market but also in the marriage market; and in terms of sexuality. Part of the preparation for middle-class status in which the secondary schools specialised involved the perpetuation of sexual innocence for as long as possible.

How should this grooming in middle-class manners and segrega-

tion from the opposite sex be understood? It may, as Madeleine
Arnot has suggested, have 'provided the conditions for the mainten-
ance of female adolescent virginity and the preservation of the
concept of bourgeois marriage.'[54] But though virginity was as far as
we know maintained, few girls from both Catholic and non-Catholic
schools felt they were really being prepared for marriage. Many felt
that they had been so completely sheltered from the opposite sex that
they barely 'knew what a lad was' when they left school. Furthermore, particularly at the non-Catholic schools, old girls appear to
have learnt from their unmarried mistresses that marriage was not
everything. As Joyce Westall, at Blackburn High School in the
1930s, remembers 'their outlook was that you didn't have to get
married, that you could make a good life without it.'[55] Particularly
before the Second World War many old girls were evidently far more
interested in their school and college work, their careers and their
networks of women friends, than in attaching themselves to any
particular man, and at least one deliberately postponed marriage
until she was in her fifties: 'I seemed to be having such a good time,
you know . . . he wanted to get married long before I said I
would.'[56] Between the wars, of course, entry to most careers was
hard enough for a single woman and virtually impossible for married
women, especially in the context of the formal and informal marriage
bars which operated in those professions which educated single
women were entering in large numbers, like teaching, nursing and
clerical work. And the demographic imbalance of 1.5 million more
women than men in 1931 meant that marriage was simply not in
prospect for many women.

The shaping of femininity could, in the light of these considerations, be seen as preparation not for bourgeois marriage but for
'professional spinsterhood'. Such an interpretation puts quite a
different slant on the foregoing evidence. First, the ladylike
behaviour and decorum taught within the schools by female
authority figures could serve independent women taking their places
within a new female professional class as well as, if not better than,
those destined for a dependent married status. Secondly, the ban on
contact with boys could be seen not primarily as a way of supplying
virgins to the middle-class marriage bed, but as protection against
the distraction from academic work presented by boyfriends and the
dilution of ambition effected by adolescent marital aspirations.
Stories of 'underachievement' told by those who maintained secret
relationships with boys from the 1920s to the 1950s testify to such
impediments.[57]

Conclusion

In conclusion, what are the answers to the initial questions posed in this chapter? Did the girls' secondary schools aim to produce middle-class women? Was the occupational goal marriage, and if it was not, what were girls being prepared for?

All the schools investigated here were designed to groom girls for membership of the middle class. They did so through the pursuit of academic success, the preparation of girls for a few carefully chosen post-school destinations, and the lessons in femininity which they taught them. But in no case was the objective as uncomplicated as Madeleine Arnot depicts it:

> while the dominant form of transmission of the sexual division of labour amongst the bourgeoisie – single-sex schools – allowed for the reproduction of class cultural unity, it also provided for the reproduction of intra-class gender differentiation which maintained the notion of the bourgeois family form of salary-earning husband, and a dependent housekeeping wife who would provide the only legitimate heirs to the economic and cultural wealth of that social class.[59]

Within each area of school life investigated here there lurked challenges to 'gender differentiation which maintained the notion of the bourgeois family form'. Thus academic scholarship as defined for the schools by the Board of Education, the examining boards and ultimately the universities, was the education of a gentleman. In a 'lady's' hands however it could be applied to the purpose of giving her the same kind of economic independence which gentlemen enjoyed. This was of course not always what happened, and was contradicted by the perception that class identity depended to some extent on stressing the advantages of such an education for girls both in itself and for the cultural regeneration which women who had experienced it would be able to undertake in the home and in public life, as a form of unpaid service. Blackburn High School, like most of the Girls' Public Day School Trust schools, had been founded upon such an ethos, and its first headmistresses did their best to sustain it. There were other aspects of the non-Catholic schools' pursuit of class status which played down the schools' 'instrumental' provision of routes by which girls could become salary earners. Examples are their attempts to maximize recruitment of girls from the fee-paying sector and minimize the 'scholarship' element (a feature which has not been explored here for reasons of space), and their lack of encouragement to girls who wanted clerical careers. However, the non-Catholic schools' endeavour to cultivate as many girls as possible for university and the 'higher' professions, especially secondary school teaching, and their willingness to channel other girls into elementary teaching, (gradually becoming accepted as a suitable career for a middle class girl, if regarded as 'second best' by the schools right through to the 1950s), did enlarge the possibilities for feminine independence.

Even though the convent schools were prepared to regard marriage, and its converse, becoming a nun, as legitimate goals for girls, and even though they did not fix their sights on sending girls to university in the way that the non-Catholic girls' secondary schools did, their dedication to increasing the supply of teachers to the Catholic elementary schools meant that the convent schools also contributed to the ranks of 'breadwinning' women. Convents and high schools shared a view of domestic science as essentially incompatible with a 'liberal education' and responded to the requirement that they should include it in the curriculum by giving it an obviously marginal role, emphasizing their orientation to middle-class professional, rather than matrimonial, destinations.

Femininity as taught in the convents had special religious connotations, embedded in a highly patriarchal interpretation of Christianity. But even in the Catholic schools and especially in the others, the lessons contained ambiguities. The numerous rules concerning decorum and segregation from the opposite sex can be seen as preparation for the status of 'dependent housekeeping wife' within the middle class. On the other hand, these rules can be interpreted as inculcating the mode of behaviour expected of and by professional middle-class women, especially in view of the context in which they were taught. It was, after all, not men whom school girls were being taught to respect (male governors were shadowy figures who played an insignificant part in schoolgirls' lives), but the discipline and authority of women, who were required to be spinsters until after the Second World War. The strong ethos of competitive outdoor games, a development in all the schools, including the convents, which has not been examined here, was part of the redefinition of femininity in which the schools were engaged. The contradictions are encapsulated in a vignette of lunchtime hockey practices contributed by a Winckley Square girl of the 1920s: 'The dear nun who ran along with us on lunch time jaunts had on her long flowing habit. With hindsight one realises how athletic she must have been.'[59]

The ambiguity of the mission to create a new breed of middle-class woman was probably not resolved within the minds of those running the girls' secondary schools themselves. Tensions were mounting by the 1960s, particularly over the issues of authority and femininity. The schools attempted to remain in their successful pre-war pattern, conditioned by demographic imbalance, the mutual exclusion of marriage and careers, and the acceptance within the schools of their mission to mould girls for the middle class. The 1944 Act both enlarged the social mix, and by its removal of the marriage bar for teachers, contributed to the increased possibility for a woman of combining marriage and a career, which altered the orientations of both mistresses and girls, especially in a context of mounting expectations of 'sexual freedom'.

This exploration of the cultural reproduction in which girls' secondary schools were engaged between 1900 and 1950 should help to explain why the two principal educational changes since 1944 represented such a threat to them, and were opposed in such apparently 'reactionary' ways. Co-education, which both the Park School and Winckley Square convent successfully resisted as an immediate consequence of the 1944 Act, represented a challenge to their gender orientation. But it eventually arrived as part of the second major change, the policy of 'comprehensivization'. All the secondary schools studied here were forced to surrender between 1965 and 1980, bewailing piteously as they did so the loss of both the class identity and feminine culture so carefully nurtured over the preceding century.

Acknowledgements

I should like to give warm thanks both to all those who have contributed their memories, and to my project workers for the great care they have taken over interviews and transcripts. I am also indebted to Janet Finch for her critical and constructive comments, and to the North-West Oral History Society and the Lancaster University Women's Research Group for their lively discussions of earlier versions of this chapter.

Bibliographical Note

The analysis in this chapter took off from sociological work on gender, class and education, in particular that of Rosemary Deem and Madeleine Arnot (formerly MacDonald) referred to in notes 1 and 5. This work has been most useful for its theoretical insights into the possible purposes of particular types of schooling for the two sexes. My understanding of the late nineteenth- and early twentieth-century development of education for girls has been informed by the work of Shelia Fletcher, Joan Burstyn and Carol Dyhouse referred to in the notes and has been enriched by many discussions in the archives and elsewhere with Felicity Hunt. But the main sources on which this paper draws are the Board of Education files on the establishment and inspection of the girls' secondary schools of Preston and Blackburn in the period 1900–50 found in the Public Record Office, and the growing collection of interview transcripts and ephemera being amassed by my project on the Oral History of Girlhood in Lancashire. This project (which is Manpower Services Commission funded) is on-going and aims to interview secondary and elementary school girls in five Lancashire towns. The target sample of those who attended secondary schools consists of one respondent per 100 pupils in average annual attendance, per decade of each school's existence. Confidentiality has been preserved by the use of pseudonyms where requested, but otherwise the name by which the respondent is currently known has been used.

9

Pioneer Women Students at Cambridge, 1869–81

Perry Williams

Higher education for women was created and established in England over a remarkably short period. It was in 1869 that Emily Davies opened her College for Women with five students in a rented house in Hitchin, Henry Sidgwick started his Association for the Promotion of the Higher Education of Women in Cambridge, and the campaigning of Anne Jemima Clough resulted in the University of Cambridge instituting a new public Higher Local Examination to act as a qualification for schoolteachers. Before that date, there had been no institution in England through which a woman could get a university education or receive a public qualification beyond secondary school level.[1] By 1881, at Cambridge the schemes started by Davies and Sidgwick had developed into fully-fledged women's colleges, housed in newly-built halls in the villages of Girton and Newnham respectively, and their students were taking the University's degree examinations and receiving official certification. The provision of higher education for women had multiplied elsewhere too, with the foundation of two women's colleges at Oxford and many local associations to provide university-level lectures, and most importantly the full admission of women to the University of London and the new Victoria University (founded in 1880 out of the Midlands civic colleges).

The provision of higher education has always been assumed to have been a critical factor in the changing social position of women, not least by the feminists and educationalists behind those first institutions. This provision has been associated with the end of the traditional middle-class feminine ideal of 'the angel in the house', with opening possibilities of paid employment for middle-class women in the professions, especially teaching, and the alteration of the marital relationship from dependency towards companionship.[2] Rather than try to assess the extent of any of these social changes directly, this chapter will concentrate on the change which higher education made at a personal level, attempting to see how it was experienced by the women who underwent it. In particular, we shall look at those for whom the change was most dramatic, because most new and unexpected: the early students at the first permanent institutions, the Cambridge women's colleges. Many of them became well-known in later life and left sufficient personal records to enable us to reconstruct their experience of higher education and to see how and in what ways it changed their lives, and what it meant to them.

That higher education meant something special for them is shown by the fact that they went to college at all – something for which there was no precedent, no established pattern, and against which there was a good deal of prejudice and hostility. All of them were very strongly motivated, and many of them showed the same kind of enthusiasm as Constance Louisa Maynard, who later recalled that she 'used to wake every morning in my first term or two with a sort of sting of delight, and think "Here is a whole day more at College!" '[3]

In Maynard's case, the enthusiasm becomes more comprehensible when we consider her upbringing. Her parents were strong evangelicals, believing in the Fall and rigidly separating the things of the World from the things of God, and they had carefully protected Constance and her five brothers and sisters from such 'worldly' things as parties, novels, and (with a few exceptions) other children. The first time she was allowed to travel alone, apparently, was when she went to Scotland to spend her twenty-third birthday with her aunt. It was while she was there that she was told about Emily Davies's College for Women, then located in Hitchin in order to obtain lecturers from Cambridge, Oxford and London. 'It was a new world to me', she recalled. 'A quiet suggestion arose in my heart, as clear as a whisper from without, "There, *that* is what you have been waiting for." Aloud I said, "How interesting! How I would like to go!" adding mentally in response to the voice "Yes, yes, I won't disobey my parents in the least thing, but Oh! I'll move heaven and earth to get there." '

Despite the scorn for her abilities continually expressed by her sisters and brothers, she was in fact an intelligent woman, only waiting for the room to use her intelligence free from the confines of a family atmosphere. Her parents, however, remained to be persuaded, and her businessman father at first refused to take her seriously: 'There was a frowning and a smiling and "I say, Conse, this is something new," and then a pinch on the cheek or the ear and "But where's the *use*? What's it for?" and a murmur or two about staying at home and being like my sisters, and he offered to get me a new pony if I would give it up.' But he made no real opposition. Her mother, who suspected that the college would be very 'worldly', was more difficult to persuade, but under continuous pressure, she relented, by degrees.[4]

Louisa Lumsden too remembered feeling that the college was just what she had been waiting for as soon as she heard of it through a prospective article in *Macmillan's Magazine*;[5] 'my ambition was at once fired with the thought of possibly belonging to such a community of studious women.' Her school education had been entirely traditional. She herself had wanted to go to Cheltenham Ladies' College when the family moved nearby after the death of her father, but her mother sent her instead to a poor Flemish school near Brussels, and then to a small boarding school in Harley Street, where she found the teaching to be just as bad as at the Flemish school: 'Accomplishments made the whole curriculum – history, geography, arithmetic had no place . . . Something to look forward to, something to prepare for, some aim which would make it worth while to study, this was lacking in the old-fashioned school.' The ten years after leaving school she spent doing the rounds of Scottish polite society, the life for which her education was supposed to have prepared her. Loyalty would not allow her to call them other than 'happy years', but if she was not unhappy she was certainly not content; her sister said that living with her was like living beside a suppressed volcano. In 1868, aged 28, she found her release through the lectures for women given in Edinburgh by University professors under a scheme organized by Anne Dundas. And it was thus that she was offered the chance to go to the College for Women at Hitchin, for Anne Dundas gave her name to Emily Davies as a possible student.[6]

The first students at what was to become Newnham College were similarly drawn in through the lecture scheme at Cambridge. When in 1871 Henry Sidgwick and Millicent Garrett Fawcett opened the first of a succession of houses and halls in the charge of Anne Jemima Clough to provide student accommodation, one of the first occupants was Mary Kennedy, who had already been attending the lectures and preparing for the Higher Local Examination for a year.[7] Another was Mary Paley, who had recently studied for and taken the Higher Local Exam 'for want of something to do'. Like many others, she came to college to escape from the idle boredom of a young woman's life in a middle-class family, in her case the family of an evangelical clergyman in a country parish.

> It was after . . . the governess stage was past and we had no regular occupation that we began to feel bored, especially in winter. The roads were muddy and had deep ruts, . . . and visiting the poor, practising the singing for the church services and teaching in the Sunday school were hardly adequate occupation. In fact an illness in the village was hailed with satisfaction as it gave one something to do.

The traditional activities of a clergyman's daughter seemed duller than ever after her sister married. Having wondered for a time about getting married herself, she became engaged to an army officer, but it soon became clear that they had little in common so it was broken off. Her father proved willing to coach her for the Higher Local Exam, but at first strongly opposed her going to Cambridge to take up the scholarship she had been offered. Only a personal admiration for Miss Clough in the end overcame his objections.[8]

The opposition of friends and relatives could be no less devastating than the opposition of parents, as Anna Lloyd discovered. She wrote in a letter, soon after she had decided to go to the College at Hitchin:

> My sisters and friends look on astonished – it is such a new sensation. They say I must go my own way, they cannot judge for me; but I see they think it would be much better if I was going to be married. Perhaps it would, but that state does not fall to the lot of all, and I think that some thorough occupation, some defined business is good for un-married ladies. The difficulties I get into are the necessity I am under to refuse invitations. I see that the married world considers single young ladies its perquisites. I am breaking away from it, but not without difficulty and some burnings of heart – and what, as I often say to myself in fear and trembling, what if I lose the friendship and love of all these dinner eating people whom I love so well? What shall I do then? It is a serious consideration.

She was the youngest child in a Quaker family of nine children, and while she grew up her sisters married one after another, so that by the time she was 22 she was the only daughter left at home, looking after three unmarried brothers and two parents in failing health. After the death of her parents, the family broke up, the large family house was taken over by an elder brother who was getting married, and Anna, at 30 cast out of the only home she had known, began her travels by visiting Switzerland, Italy and Paris. Homeless and aimless, the College for Women had strong appeal for her when she heard of it through meeting Emily Davies in 1868. A strong sense of inner duty carried her through the preparation for the entrance exam and the whole of her first year, despite the opposition of her sisters. They persuaded her, however, to spend most of the long vacation in visits to them, which she disliked since it was impossible to get time to herself for study and she felt totally incompetent with their children. But if her sisters failed to convince Anna Lloyd of the joys of marriage and domesticity, they did succeed in persuading her to withdraw from the college after her fourth term by accusing her of self-indulgence. Since none of them offered her a home, she went off on her travels again, until her youngest brother took pity on her and suggested that she come and live with him.[9]

Even when parents and relatives were willing, they might still lay on a woman a burden of responsibility which would prevent her from going to college. Emily Gibson, for instance, was nearly removed from Hitchin by her strong sense of family duty, stronger even than her strong sense of self-determination. When she was 17 she had been looking forward to keeping a school some day ('it is a good thing for me to have a future to build Castles about'), and as soon as she heard about the College for Women through the *Macmillan's Magazine* article, she wanted to be a student there, writing in her diary:

> I have announced my determination to take teaching as the occupation of my life, secondly to be a student at the College, and thirdly to set about preparing myself for it without delay . . . At all events I hope I may keep the one decision I have made. It will serve to avoid a life of long, listless idleness, than which almost anything would be better . . . I am far from clever or able, but I have a certain life and energy in me which is a direct warning from God to shun idleness.

This was all right at first, because her sister was caring for their sick mother, but when the illness worsened during her first term she nearly gave up the College, feeling she ought to be at home. The only reason that she returned for the Lent Term was that her mother had recovered during the vacation.[10]

What emerges most clearly from the students' accounts of how they came to college are the obstacles which they had to overcome, and their own very strong motivation and determination. The first hurdle which they all faced (Anna Lloyd excepted) was parental consent, and the parents had to be prepared to pay fees of between £50 and £100 a year.[11] The next hurdle was the entrance exams, in preparation for which, because of their poor previous education, most of them had to spend much time and effort. Home duties could force the abandonment of their plans at any time, and their preparations were made in the face of the disapproval of friends and relatives. When they arrived at college, they had to put up with living conditions that were, for women accustomed to comfortable middle-class homes, cramped and spartan; it was not until the end of the 1870s, when the two colleges had raised enough money to move into custom-built halls in the villages of Girton and Newnham, that students could enjoy a more comfortable (still by no means luxurious) existence. Repeatedly we find that they were driven by a need for something which would relieve the tedium of their cossetted middle-class idleness. They saw in higher education the promise of something which would give their lives purpose and point. Even for the first students, therefore, the practical hardships were more than compensated for by what they gained intellectually and socially. Thus we find Emily Gibson writing in her diary in the course of her first term: 'College life is to the full as delightful as I expected. Work, above all, geometry, is most delightful. My companions are, on the whole, the pleasantest I have ever lived with; indeed, one of the things here that has pleased me is to find that I can enjoy the society of women as much as the society of men'.[12] Emily Davies must have been pleased when she questioned them about their experience at the end of the first year. As she reported in a letter to a colleague,

> The thing Miss Lloyd feels to have gained is some appreciation of the scholarly, as distinguished from the man-of-business way of looking at things. Miss Lumsden said that before she came, she used to feel fearfully solitary. She was always having said to her, 'Oh, but you're so exceptional.' Now, she feels herself belonging to a body, and has lost the sense of loneliness. [Emily Davies then asked whether it would be worthwhile for a student to come for one year only.] Miss Gibson replied briefly that one year was much better than nothing. Miss Cook said she would rather not come at all than that, and being asked why, explained that it was because she would be so sorry to go away. Miss Gibson said she should feel that just as much at the end of the three years, to which there was a chorus of assent. Miss Woodhead answered my question with an emphatic 'Oh, I should think it *quite*

worth while.' I asked what was the good of it and she replied with a still more emphatic *Oh!* – which remains unexplained, as my train would not wait. You will understand that we were not talking about the amount of *learning* to be gained.[13]

What they received from higher education, then, came partly from their academic studies, but more especially from their corporate life in a community of women. We will now look at both of these in more detail, to see how they were experienced by the first ten years or so of women students, for whom these things were wholly new.

In the early years, the courses of study pursued were very diverse. At Girton, the situation was relatively straightforward; Emily Davies wanted her students to reach standards that were indisputably equal to those achieved by Cambridge men students, so they aimed at identical exams under identical conditions: they had just three years to pass first the preliminary 'Previous Examination' or 'Little-Go', and then a Tripos or final exam, preferably in mathematics or classics (for Emily Davies's educational ideas were fairly traditional). At Newnham, on the other hand, whose founders were liberals and educationalists rather than feminists, students were allowed to study for as short or as long a period as they wished, and take just such exams – or no exam at all – as seemed worthwhile. This difference was a source of friction between the two colleges, since Emily Davies roundly condemned what she saw as a special soft-option for women, while the liberals lamented her insistence on the Little-Go, which included compulsory Greek – something which they were trying to abolish in the University anyway. By the end of the 1870s, however, over half the students at Newnham were taking a Tripos, and over half of those had taken the Little-Go first.

The exam papers were released and the scripts marked by the University's official examiners, under private arrangements individually negotiated each year. In 1881 the University undertook this responsibility on a regular basis, and awarded the candidates offical 'Tripos Certificates'. By that date too, women students had begun to attend regular undergraduate lectures. Though they still received most of their teaching inside their own college, either from an old student who was staying on as a tutor or from a sympathetic University professor or college don, it had not taken long for lecturers, who were effectively giving the same courses twice over, to decide that it would be easier to give them once to a combined audience of undergraduates and women students. These mixed lectures were uncomfortable for everyone at first, with the women sitting apart, in a gallery or in separate chairs at the front, being regarded by the undergraduates with an embarrassing curiosity.[14]

More significant for the women students' feelings about their work was the fact that they could now pursue their chosen studies continuously, without the constant interruption of family duties or social affairs. Hertha Marks (later the experimental physicist Hertha Ayrton) was exultant, almost ecstatic about it in a letter to Barbara Bodichon, one of the Girton founders, who was sponsoring her through college.

> Work doesn't seem work, but rather some delightful form of amusement. I can't tell you how happy I am this term. All my imaginings of what it was going to be like to have nothing but mathematics to work at were small compared with the real thing. I do a little other work besides – my half-hour of Odyssey after dinner; and every day except Thursdays and Sundays I work at my embroidery for the two hours immediately after lunch.[15]

Like many others, she had been poorly taught before she came up, and had to spend much time on basics. She made up for it with enthusiasm, dedication and originality, as did Margaret Merrifield, later the classicist and psychical researcher Margaret Verrall, who related in a letter home:

> I have succeeded in 'humbugging' Mr Archer Hind, so that he does not dream of dismissing me to the other class, on the contrary he treats me with great respect, always asks my opinion of a difficult passage, etc. The other day I was bold enough to strike out a new idea. [She explains her re-interpretation of a passage of Aeschylus, which turns on the ambiguity of the word *chouris*.] He was very much interested when he heard my idea was original, and said it was a very good one. At first he seemed disposed to adopt it, but finally he said that the ordinary interpretation was perhaps more in accordance with Aeschylean ideas, tho' one might bear mine in mind. Wasn't that a triumph. After learning Greek about two months, to strike out a new interpretation of the *Agamemnon* and be told that it was a good one! Shan't I get conceited?[16]

These little triumphs were important for the students. To produce original ideas of one's own and have them validated by an authority was a quite novel experience for most of them, one which built up their confidence enormously. They could feel that their work at college was *real* work – not just dilettantism or passing the time, but definite and serious academic study with clear standards to achieve – and most of them found it exhilarating. It was possible to react the other way, however. Emily Gibson, for instance, in the course of her three years at Hitchin, was deeply impressed by the aesthetic mysticism of her fellow student and close friend Isabel Townshend. The idea of devoting oneself to the enjoyment of the beauties of nature and art came as a revelation to Emily Gibson; a whole world of experience and feeling opened up for her, and college studies began to seem increasingly irrelevant. In her last term at college, she wrote a poem, beginning:

I sit removed and look and wonder as you work at your books –
What is the meaning of these Mathematics and this dull grind at Greek?
Does the Student live more because he has studied?
Do you love better for knowing Sanskrit? . . .
  Lay hold, O man, on these dry bones if thou canst make them live!
  If not, let them be buried . . .

She had already drifted from maths to classics to moral sciences, and eventually left without taking a Tripos.[17]

Yet however they experienced their academic work, it was only part of the women students' life at college. Their day typically began at 7 a.m. with the arrival of a servant to wake them, sweep the room and lay the fire. There were prayers at 8.00; these were not compulsory, but most attended, having been used to family prayers at home. Breakfast would be on the table from 8.15 till 9.00, and after that the students would settle down to a morning of study in their own rooms or the library, or at lectures in the college or in town. After lunch there might be more study or lectures, but most students would devote an hour or so to exercise of some kind; lawn tennis and fives were popular, as was walking, and both colleges had a gymnasium for wet weather use. Dinner at 6.00 or 6.30 was a formal meal, but even so it would not last more than half an hour. Afterwards, when all the college was conveniently assembled, there might be a meeting of some club or society, or a discussion and vote on what newspapers and magazines they would get that term. By 7.30 or 8.00 p.m., the students would be back in their rooms for a couple of hours more work before the time for visiting each other and drinking cocoa.[18]

These evening gatherings are mentioned very frequently in the students' reminiscences and contemporary accounts, and they must have been extremely significant to them. Although they rapidly became virtual institutions at both colleges, there was no set pattern. There might be an ostensible purpose to the party, such as needlework (usually mending) or reading a play, but the main thing that happened was that the students met and talked. Most of us are familiar with the sense of awakening, of self-discovery, through early adult friendships, as it was familiar to university men at the time, but for the early women students it was not only more unexpected but more powerful, because the transition from home to college was more dramatic. 'At home', one of them remarked, when arguing for the benefits of college life, 'a woman is the squire's daughter, or the clergyman's, or the doctor's'; that is to say, her identity was borrowed and her social role strongly confined to that of the not-yet-married woman. 'At college [on the other hand], her position is of no consequence; her disposition, as manifested to others, of the greatest . . . Nowhere else perhaps are people valued so entirely for what they are.'[19]

Again, the fact that college life gave them opportunities to develop self-confidence – for organizing, for action, for developing and expressing opinions of their own – was especially significant for women who had had little such opportunity before. They attached great importance to their societies, especially their Debating Societies, for which the motions were no flippant affairs but serious questions, usually of literature or politics.[20] Speaking in a debate was at first quite a challenge for the students, as a letter home from Margaret Merrifield shows.

> We had a very interesting debate last Tuesday . . . The subject was Theatres as a means of Education. When I went into the room I had no intention of speaking, but I had to do so after all . . . Evelyn began, very well indeed, but she was so nervous that she broke down in the middle, leaving her sentence unfinished. Miss Green came next. She stood up and spoke as if she had been accustomed all her life to Public Speaking. She said nothing worth hearing, however, uttering about two platitudes, wh. had no bearing on the subject, in an exceedingly forcible manner. Then Conny Brodhurst, and little Miss Hunt spoke, for a very few minutes, and then there was no one else. So I had to get up . . . I really was intensely interested in my subject, and I did so want some of them to agree with me, and the result was that I spoke for some minutes without the slightest hesitation or difficulty, and, a thing I have never done before, spoke of my own feelings on the subject – I mean, what I really feel, not what I feel when I am asked my opinion.[21]

That last sentence shows the importance of what the debating societies encouraged the students to do.

Cocoa parties and debating were two often-mentioned institutions of college life through which it seems the early women students experienced a strengthening sense of identity and individuality. Another, equally stressed in their accounts of their college, was the 'room of one's own' (in the case of Girton, two rooms) enjoyed by every student. One's college room can assume a great importance for a student even today; for most of the early women students, it represented a privacy and a freedom of expression never before encountered. Their rooms came provided with a sofa-bed, bureau, table, bookcase, chintz-covered box and armchair, and the rest was up to them. Those of a Pre-Raphaelite disposition, such as the classicist Jane Harrison, might put up William Morris papers and Burne-Jones photographs (she and Mary Paley also embroidered their tennis dresses with pomegranate and Virginia creepers respectively); others still might wish for no more than plain white and buff. The details of their furnishings were related in their letters home at extraordinary length; Margaret Merrifield gave as much space to the details of her picture-hanging and the placing of her vases, china jars and flower basket as she did to her reinterpretation of Aeschylus. Even if their room was only 14 by 12 feet (the smallest at Newnham) it was entirely *theirs*, and even the Principal would not enter without first knocking. More crucial still was the convention quickly established at both colleges that if one wished to work without interruption one could put a card with the word 'Engaged' on the door, and one would not be disturbed. 'The inestimable advantage of being free from distraction', as she called it, was something that Emily Davies had from the first striven to provide; 'this great boon', she wrote later, '– the power of being alone – is perhaps the most distinctive feature of college life.'[22]

For middle-class women to be able to shut the world out, when they were usually perpetually on call; for them to develop the confidence to say what they thought, when they were usually expected to remain silent or acquiesce in the opinions of others; for them to refer themselves to a peer group of other women, when they were usually expected to refer to men, particularly fathers and husbands; – all of these features of college life were potentially extremely radical. Did the students see them as such? Did they, like the founders, connect the issue of women's higher education with other issues of women's rights?

The recollections of Constance Maynard suggest that there was vague support for the women's movement from some students, but little unanimity except, unsurprisingly, on the issue of higher education.

> The Parliamentary Suffrage was not much talked of in those days, but
> 'woman's rights' were greatly discussed, and a reliable instinct guided
> us to the belief that the one 'right' to be laboured for was the right to
> education, and that all else might follow as it would . . . Since the
> whole movement was young, we naturally had but indefinite aims,
> and yet what was lost in clearness of vision was made up in
> enthusiasm.[23]

If Maynard thought that their vision had been 'unclear', it shows
that they did not support the women's movement to the extent
expected from the vantage point of 1909. Hertha Ayrton too recalled
that few, by later standards, had been suffragists in her time at
Girton (1876–80) – perhaps half a dozen (including herself) out of 30
to 50 students.[24] The remainder most probably held no definite
opinion on the subject, though there were those such as Anna Lloyd,
who declared in a letter to a friend that she was 'not in favour of
women's rights' (which was like saying today 'I am not a feminist').
She did, however, subscribe to some of the movement's values,
while repudiating its name, for though she did not approve of
professions for women 'except in a limited sense' she believed that
women should go on the School Boards, and told her friend angrily
how an electors' meeting had received the proposal of Elizabeth
Garrett's name with laughter; she herself was later to act as a Poor
Law Guardian.[25]

Clearly there was *some* conscious radicalism among the students –
by contemporary standards, even six suffragists represented a very
large proportion among middle-class women – but it was minimized,
or (as Maynard hints) channelled into the more neutral area of
education. This was a strategy the founders themselves had judged it
necessary to adopt while the higher education of women was still
new and vulnerable, and campaigners for women's rights were
supposed to be stereotypically spinsterish, ugly and aggressive (the
antithesis of the feminine ideal). To avoid jeopardizing their
educational projects, they felt it necessary to sever or avoid
connections with other aspects of the women's movement (especially
the campaign for repeal of the Contagious Diseases Acts). They
encouraged the same attitude in the students, so that when Eliza
Minturn, an American student, came to write a pamphlet about
Girton, she deliberately presented a thoroughly down-to-earth and
conventional picture of student life.

> One feels it difficult to convey an idea of their vigorous tone without
> arousing in the imagination of American readers a suspicion of the
> 'strong-minded' type, which has become so justly odious. Perhaps one

may best indicate how false such an idea of Girton students would be by dwelling on their great unconsciousness of any representative character. They never seem to regard themselves as the exponents of a cause; there is rarely any reference made among them to their conspicuous position before the eyes of the public. They are simple-hearted English girls and women, doing work for its own sake, spontaneously and with pleasure . . . If one student threatens some eccentricity, there is a general outcry by the others. 'Do not let us make too many experiments at once,' they often say.[26]

It is difficult to say how far this attitude was genuine and how far assumed to present an acceptable public face.

One attitude which was very substantially assumed was the extreme caution which they inculcated in each other to dress tidily and behave demurely when in public, for the safety of the college. Constance Maynard recalled that,

One student . . . was mentally condemned because (save the mark!) she wore an *ulster*, which at that time was a rare and sporting garment and confined to the sex which in grammars is designated as 'the more worthy'; and the very least deviation, whether in dress or manner, from the ordinary rules of society was laid down in unwritten laws to be avoided. The main idea in all these matters was to escape observation, and we were delighted with the verdict of a Cambridge lady who, in some fear and trembling, had asked one of us to dine with her, and who then explained as an excuse to a friend, 'My dear, she was a nice girl, with nice rosy cheeks, nice manners, and nicely dressed, and you wouldn't have thought she knew anything.'[27]

For the same reason, the demands of propriety surrounding young women were rigidly observed. This placed a heavy burden on Anne Clough, Emily Davies and the staff of their colleges, for the students had to be chaperoned to most of their lectures and whenever they were alone in the presence of a man who was not an immediate relative.

Yet however cautious she might be, and however conventional her views on women's roles, no student could fail to be aware that what she had done, simply by coming to college, was to many people highly unconventional and shocking.

It was [recalled Jane Dove] an unheard-of event in the lives of all our neighbours and friends, and I was at once set apart by them as an eccentric and somewhat awesome person, and in vacations found myself avoided by all young persons, and was obliged to take refuge in the society of those who had known me from childhood. My contemporaries, I think, suffered from sheer fright lest they should be humiliated by being addressed in either Greek or Latin – poor things, if they had only known![28]

Louisa Lumsden found, soon after she applied, that old family friends were trying to persuade her mother to refuse her sanction, believing that to go to college would mean social extinction for her. Anna Lloyd too found that her plans to go to Hitchin were thought by friends and relatives to be worldly, shocking, and even unchristian. She had an unpleasant shock in the London train one day when she heard a clergyman say: 'Ha! This is Hitchin, and that I believe is the house, where the College for Women is – that *infidel* place.'[29]

The cardinal objection, variously conceived as a violation of the laws of God, the laws of health or the laws of social conduct, was that the accepted role of a middle-class woman was being repudiated.[30] Higher education, in the early years, was seen to have no utility for a woman's supposed destiny of marriage and raising a family. Jane Harrison's aunt put the matter succinctly: 'I do not see how Greek grammar is to help little Jane to keep house when she has a home of her own.'[31] Many saw higher education as not merely irrelevant but positively hostile to the role of wife and mother; would not a learned woman hold in scorn all men less learned than herself, and what man would marry such a woman?

In 1881 these objections were by no means dead and the hostility by no means dissipated (hence at Oxford and Cambridge women were not admitted to formal membership of the University till 1919 and 1948 respectively).[32] Yet most of those who had formerly opposed the higher education of women had come to accept it – not because there was any weakening of their view that women should be wives and mothers, but because this role was expanded to accommodate the new educational ideas. Many, it seems, took their cue from Tennyson's poem 'The Princess'.

This story-within-a-story about the college for women founded by Princess Ida was a convenient source of illustrations and literary allusions for the occasional journalists who visited Girton and Newnham. Some of them saw Tennyson as having made a prophecy and the women's colleges as being its fulfilment, and almost all of them made quotations from the poem, in particular the line about 'sweet girl-graduates in their golden hair'.[33] But they were remembering Ida's college very selectively. In the poem, it was a radical feminist institution, strictly women-only with male intruders facing a death penalty and new students receiving a cross-cultural survey of the oppression of women including classic instances:

Islam, Chinese foot-binding, Indian suttee. Ida had left her home to found her women-only college in order to free women from their social conditioning and change their position in society, and while accepting that some of her students would marry, hopefully on a more equitable basis than formerly, she herself had on principle opted for celibacy. Now when journalists compared Girton and Newnham to Ida's college, all of this was forgotten; the comparison was only supposed to extend to the general picture of beautifully-dressed women gliding smoothly around lovely gardens and majestic architecture, and poring over their books with a silent intensity.

A reason for this selective recall, perhaps, is the eventual fate of the college in the poem. The hero of the story is a prince betrothed to Ida in childhood. Disguised as women, he and two friends infiltrate the college to persuade her to honour the agreement, and they declare the Prince's love for her. Their identity is discovered, but the Prince, more determined than ever to succeed, declares his love for her openly. Meanwhile, the prince's father and Ida's father raise an army and come to rescue him, and fight a battle with the army of Ida's brother. The college becomes a hospital, the students become nurses and fall in love with the wounded soldiers, and Ida falls in love with the nearly-but-not-quite mortally wounded prince whom she has been tending herself. He declares himself a supporter of her educational cause, but insists that she is wrong to deny love and marriage for it, wrong to make it independent of men. The higher education of women meets with his (and Tennyson's) approval, but only when it is in the service of marriage.

'The Princess' was published in 1847. By 1881, public opinion had caught up with Tennyson. There was general agreement that girls' education should have more intellectual content than the old training in accomplishments and that women should have access to higher education. But acceptance of the higher education of women did not necessarily mean acceptance of women being educated for an independent life. For many people, the principle of educating women to be ornamental wives, accomplished, ignorant and idle, was replaced by the principle of educating women to be intellectually capable wives, interesting companions for their husbands and better able to bring up their children. Women were still seen only as future wives and mothers; it was simply that the feminine ideal changed, or diversified.

An example of how this happened is provided by the *Saturday Review*, which through the late nineteenth century was a consistent and virulent opponent of the women's movement, yet as early as

ST. VALENTINE'S DAY AT GIRTON.

First Young Lady (opens Valentine, and reads):—

" 'Ερως ἀνίκατε μάχαν,
'Ερως, ὃς ἐν κτήμασι πίπτεις,' . . . &c., &c.

CHARMING, ISN'T IT? GUSSIE MUST HAVE SENT IT FROM OXFORD?"

Second Young Lady (overlooking). "YES, IT'S OUT OF THE *ANTIGONE*-THE LOVE CHORUS, YOU KNOW. HOW MUCH JOLLIER THAN THOSE SILLY ENGLISH VERSES FELLOWS USED TO SEND!"

Punch (26 February 1876) satirizes the new generation of female undergraduates. Notice how the joke turns on the fear that an educated woman will be too much for an ordinary man. Notice also that the woman on the left is smoking a cigarette – part of the stereotype of the 'advanced woman'.

1871 gave its approval to Girton College. Reporting the speech of the Bishop of Peterborough at a big London meeting to raise funds for the first building at Girton, the *Saturday Review* endorsed his appeal 'that women should have the highest possible education, no matter for what objects collaterally and exceptionally, yet for this object in the main, that they may the better succeed in the "profession of a matron".' Raising children, managing a home and supporting a husband, it was argued, needed 'higher and fuller preparation' than was currently provided. According to the *Saturday Review*, the solution to the controversy over the higher education of women lay 'in a blending of all aims into the family principle as the main guiding channel.'[34]

That higher education was a good preparation for 'the profession of matron' had often been argued by women educationalists, but only while they argued that it was a good preparation for *any* future occupation. With broadened interests and greater intellectual competence, a woman would make a better teacher, a better politician – or, if she so chose, a better wife and mother. Some gave the argument an emphasis which suggested that domesticity should be a woman's first choice, but they were all well aware that not every woman would marry (as a simple matter of demography and arithmetic, there were not enough men), and the focus of their defence of higher education was its suitability for the fulfilment of a woman's own needs and ambitions. The focus of the *Saturday Review*'s defence was its suitability as a preparation for the role of wife and mother.

If these were the terms on which the higher education of women became accepted, there are extraordinarily close parallels between what happens to Ida in 'The Princess', what happened to the poem itself, and what happened to Girton and Newnham in the minds of many people. Ida was made to give up her radical feminism and become a wife and (presumably) a mother. The poem, like her, was tamed, domesticated; the subversive aspects of the college were forgotten and left unquoted so that just the romantic imagery remained. Girton and Newnham were seen as educating women for 'the profession of matron'.

All this raises an important question. Despite what the *Saturday Review* said, higher education provided the early women students with the possibility of a career, most obviously in the expanding teaching industry, which could offer them economic independence and personal fulfilment through work rather than through a family; it also gave them a deepened sense of identity and showed them the possibility of living to satisfy their own needs, desires and aspirations, rather than, as in the traditional marital relationship, subordinating themselves to the demands of others. Yet the general societal expectation that their destiny lay in marriage and mother-hood was unchanged. How did they face this expectation? Did the experience of higher education, which had changed the early women students so much, lead to a change in the sorts of relationships they could have with men – or with women?

A few examples will indicate the range of possibilities. The first thing to be clear about is that higher education did not necessarily imply any change in the traditional marital relationship at all. Mary Paley, for instance, married Alfred Marshall, her lecturer in Moral Sciences. She had been attracted to him from the first for his intellectual brilliance and power, although he was socially gauche and without conversational skill.[35] In their married life, he was completely emotionally dependent on her, and used to declare that without her he could not live a day; she for her part, while within the house, entertained his guests and acted dumb. Their friend John Maynard Keynes could not recall her ever talking economics when visitors were around; 'for the serious discussion she would leave the dining-room to the men[,] or the visitor would go upstairs to the study, and the most ignorant Miss could not have pretended less than she to academic attainment.'[86] And yet outside the home she lectured on economics wherever her husband's job took them – Bristol, Oxford and Cambridge. She only lectured, however, to audiences of women, that is to say in a way which did not compete with him. It seems Marshall never managed to resolve the idea of educating women and the idea of having an educated wife, for after his marriage he came to despise women's intellectual ability, and he was one of the strongest opponents of the formal admission of women to the university. He ended up as a domestic autocrat like his father, who had once written a strongly-worded tract on *Man's Rights and Women's Duties*.[37]

But there were other women who found or created more equal marital relationships. One such was Hertha Marks, who married Will Ayrton, an electrical scientist who had helped her get into the London technical college where he was a professor and so to embark on her career of scientific research. Unlike Alfred Marshall, he continued to respect and support his wife's work – she became an acknowledged authority on the electric arc and the physics of fluid motion – and when in 1906 she gave her allegiance to the militant suffrage campaign, he supported her in that too. We should note, however, the condition that made this relationship possible. In the first six years of her marriage, Hertha Ayrton did little in the way of research, for her energies were taken up in domestic and social matters, such as the entertainment of guests; the turning point in her return to active research was the death of her patron Barbara Bodichon, who left her a large legacy which gave her the independent means not only to support her aged mother herself but more importantly to engage a full-time housekeeper to take over the domestic routine. Her husband gave her his goodwill and was glad to see her succeed in a career of her own, but he evidently had not been prepared to do anything to relieve her of the workload of the traditional wife's role.[38]

The women students also had the option of non-marriage – a much more attractive option than formerly. While spinsterhood still carried a certain stigma, there were now roles which could allow one to remain unmarried with dignity and not appear to be a failure. As a classical lecturer at Newnham, Jane Harrison could remain single and content, delighting in strong intellectual friendships with her male colleagues; the stimulus of mutual inspiration and continual 'falling in love' kept her young in spirit. Schoolteachers too, in the new wave of girls' high schools, could remain unmarried and turn to each other for emotional support, as did Louisa Lumsden, Constance Maynard, Jane Dove and others in the new St Leonard's School and Westfield College; their intense 'homoerotic friendships' formed a complex pattern, which has recently been reconstructed by Martha Vicinus. Even these relationships, however, sometimes followed a traditional pattern of dominant 'husband' and submissive 'wife', most notably between the male-identifying Louisa Lumsden and the compulsively self-denying Constance Maynard.[39]

What these examples indicate is that while higher education gave the women who underwent it more personal resources and the possibility of a career in the professions or in public service, the feminine ideal was modified rather than replaced, and the basic power relationship of a traditional marriage remained substantially unaltered. As a result, those women who did make use of their career opportunities came to occupy mainly low-status positions, often voluntary and unpaid, in areas concerned with children or philanthropy – an extension of the domestic, caring female role. This should be no surprise, for the transformation of personal relationships between women and men was not one of the aims of the founders of the colleges. The higher education of women was the product of a liberal individualism, in which politics was a matter of removing legal and customary barriers to individual development and expression, and personal relationships, like contracts, were a private matter for negotiation between individuals. Such social transformation as was desirable would follow naturally from the promotion of free individual development and expression, for which education was the key. If this seems conservative by the standards of later politics, we should remember that in the 1870s its implication for the first women to receive higher education were tremendous. Individuality was precisely what they lacked, and what they found at college. Louisa Lumsden, revisiting Hitchin many years after she had been a student there, summed it up for them all:

> 'Twas here I worked, 'twas here I read,
> Here learned the worth of friendship, here
> Felt the world wider round, saw clear
> Horizons stretch, and overhead
> A bluer heaven. For here I came
> Sick to the soul, you know, my friend,
> Of balls and croquet without end
> An empty life and ne'er an aim
> Worth spending strength on, can I tell
> My gain? . . . [40]

Acknowledgements

My thanks to Troy Cooper and Felicity Hunt; many of the ideas in this chapter originated from conversations with them. I am also indebted to Andrew Cunningham and Adrian Wilson for their lessons in how to do history.

Bibliographical Note

The early years of the Cambridge women's colleges are best described in the founders' biographies: Barbara Stephen, *Emily Davies and Girton College* (Constable, 1927); A. S[idgwick] and E. S[idwick], *Henry Sidgwick: A Memoir* (Macmillan, 1906); Blanche Athena Clough, *A Memoir of Anne Jemima Clough* (Edward Arnold, 1897). These include much contemporary material, as does also Ann Phillips (ed.) *A Newnham Anthology* (Cambridge University Press, Cambridge, 1979). The subjects of female friendship and female communities are discussed more fully in Martha Vicinus, ' "One life to stand beside me": emotional conflicts in first-generation college women in England', *Feminist Studies*, 8 (1982), pp. 602–28; also her *Independent*

Women: Work and Community for Single Women, 1850–1920 (Virago, 1985), especially ch. 5. The basic history of women's relationship with the University of Cambridge is Rita McWilliams-Tullberg. *Women at Cambridge: A Men's University – Though of a Mixed Type* (Victor Gollancz, 1975); see also her more analytical 'Women and degrees at Cambridge University 1862–1897', in Martha Vicinus (ed.) *A Widening Sphere* (Methuen, 1980). The corresponding events at Oxford are covered in M. A. H. Rogers, *Degrees by Degrees* (Oxford University Press, Oxford, 1938). The opposition to women's higher education is covered in Joan N. Burstyn, *Victorian Education and the Ideal of Womanhood* (Croom Helm, 1980). Finally, no reader of this chapter should omit to read Virginia Woolf, *A Room of One's Own* (1929; Granada Publishing, St Albans, 1977), which on this subject, as on so many others, is concise and penetrating.

Notes

Place of publication throughout is London unless otherwise stated.

Introduction

1 Ivy Pinchbeck, *Women Workers and the Industrial Revolution 1750–1850* (1930; Virago edn, 1981). At a meeting of the Historical Association in January 1986 Professor Sir Geoffrey Elton criticized 'this non-existent history of ethnic minorities and women', *Guardian*, 14 January 1986.

2 See for example Patricia Hilden, 'Women's History: the Second Wave', *The Historical Journal*, 25, 2 (1982), Elizabeth Sarah, 'Towards a reassessment of feminist history', *Women's Studies International Forum*, 5, 6 (1982) (where she puts forward an alternative definition of 'feminist history' as 'the history of feminism') and the introduction to *The Sexual Dynamics of History* by the London Feminist History Group (Pluto Press, 1983).

3 Sheila Rowbotham, *Hidden from History: 300 Years of Women's Oppression and the Fight Against It* (Pluto Press, 1973).

4 See for example V. Beechey, 'On patriarchy', *Feminist Review*, 3 (1979), the articles by Eisenstein in Z. R. Eisenstein (ed.), *Capitalist Patriarchy and the Case for Socialist Feminism* (Monthly Review Press, New York, 1979) and, for an example of the critical use of theories of patriarchy, Penny Summerfield, *Women Workers in the Second World War* (Croom Helm, 1984).

5 Joan Kelly-Gadol, 'The social relation of the sexes: methodological implications of women's history', *Signs*, 1, 4 (1976).

6 Leonore Davidoff, unpublished paper, 1986, and for a critical assessment see Joan W. Scott, 'Gender: a useful category of historical analysis', *American Historical Review*, 91 (1986).

7 Angela V. John (ed.), *Unequal Opportunities: Women's Employment in England 1800–1918* (Basil Blackwell, 1986), p. 5; Jane Lewis (ed.),

Labour and Love: Women's Experience of Home and Family 1850–1940 (Basil Blackwell, 1986), p. 20.

8 There is a telling comment to this effect in *The Headmistress Speaks* (Kegan Paul, 1937), a collection of essays by members of the Association of Head Mistresses (M. G. Clarke, 'Feminine Challenge in Education', p. 57).

9 For example (inter alia) Alice Zimmern, *The Renaissance of Girls' Education: a Record of Fifty Years' Progress*, (A. D. Innes, 1898), Margaret J. Tuke, *A History of Bedford College for Women 1849–1937* (Oxford University Press, Oxford, 1939), G. A. N. Lowndes, *The Silent Social Revolution: an Account of the Expansion of Public Education in England and Wales 1895–1965* (Oxford University Press, Oxford, 1969).

10 For example, Josephine Kamm, *Hope Deferred: Girls' Education in English History* (Methuen, 1965).

11 Sara Delamont, 'The Domestic Ideology and Women's Education' in Sara Delamont and Lorna Duffin (eds) *The Nineteenth Century Woman: Her Cultural and Physical World* (Croom Helm, 1978), but see also the opening comments by Penny Summerfield in chapter 8 in this volume.

12 Joan N. Burstyn, *Victorian Education and the Ideal of Womanhood* (Croom Helm, 1980).

13 See, in particular, Carol Dyhouse, *Girls Growing Up in Late Victorian and Edwardian England* (Routledge & Kegan Paul, 1981).

14 See notes 11, 12 and 13.

15 Gillian Sutherland, *Elementary Education in the Nineteenth Century* (The Historical Association, 1971), pp. 10–11.

16 Thomas W. Laqueur, 'Working-class demand and the growth of English elementary education 1750–1850', in Lawrence Stone (ed.), *Schooling and Society: Studies in the History of Education* (Johns Hopkins University Press, Baltimore, 1976).

17 Sutherland, *Elementary Education*, pp. 15–16, 24–6.

18 Gillian Sutherland, *Policy-Making in Elementary Education 1870–1895* (Oxford University Press, Oxford, 1973) pp. 212–14.

19 Ibid., p. 5.

20 Ibid., pp. 5–7.

21 J. R. de S. Honey, *Tom Brown's Universe: the Development of the Victorian Public School* (Millington Books, 1977) pp. 32, 37; David Newsome, *A History of Wellington College 1859–1959* (John Murray, 1959).

22 Joyce Senders Pedersen, 'The reform of women's secondary and higher education: institutional change and social values in mid and late Victorian England', *History of Education Quarterly*, Spring 1979.

23 *Schools Inquiry Commission Report*, Parliamentary Papers (henceforth PP) 1867–68, I.

24 For an account which focuses on boys' schools see F. E. Balls, 'The Endowed Schools Act, 1869 and the Development of English Grammar Schools in the Nineteenth Century', *Durham Research Review*, 20

(1968). For an analysis of the effects of both Report and Act on girls' schools see Sheila Fletcher, *Feminists and Bureaucrats: a Study in the Development of Girls' Education in the Nineteenth Century* (Cambridge University Press, Cambridge, 1980).

25 Such a description was employed first by Matthew Arnold in 'A French Eton or middle-class education and the state' (first published in *Macmillan's Magazine* 1863–4), in Gillian Sutherland (ed.) *Arnold on Education* (Penguin, Harmondsworth, 1973), p. 117.

26 *Royal Commission on Secondary Education*, PP 1895, XLIII–XLIX.

27 Lowndes, *The Silent Social Revolution*, p. 64. County or county borough councils, borough councils with a population over 10,000 and urban districts with a population over 20,000 were empowered to become LEAs, but the latter two authorities had powers only over elementary education in their area.

28 E. J. R. Eaglesham, *The Foundations of Twentieth Century Education in England* (Routledge & Kegan Paul, 1967), p. 27.

29 Brian Simon, *Education and the Labour Movement 1870–1920* (Lawrence & Wishart, 1965), p. 246.

30 Contemporary research showed that levels of ability fell below the selected quotient in nearly 50 per cent of fee paying pupils. Conversely among children of high ability there was room in secondary schools for only one free place pupil to every seven fee payers. J. L. Grey and Pearl Moshinsky, 'Ability and Opportunity in English Education', in L. T. Hogben (ed.), *Political Arithmetic: a Symposium of Population Studies* (George Allen & Unwin, 1938), p. 375.

31 Gillian Sutherland, *Ability, Merit and Measurement: Mental Testing and English Education 1880–1940* (Clarendon Press, Oxford, 1984), pp. 284–6.

32 R. G. Wallace, 'The origins and authorship of the 1944 Education Act', *History of Education*, 10, 4 (1981) and Olive Banks, *Parity and Prestige in English Secondary Education: a Study in Educational Sociology* (Routledge & Kegan Paul, 1955) p. 130.

33 Banks, *Parity and Prestige*, pp. 8 and 248.

34 Miriam E. David, *The State, The Family and Education* (Routledge & Kegan Paul, 1980), pp. 167, 188.

Chapter 1   Divided Aims: the Educational Implications of Opposing Ideologies in Girls' Secondary Schooling, 1850–1950

1 *Report of the Consultative Committee on Differentiation of the Curriculum for Boys and Girls Respectively in Secondary Schools* (HMSO, 1923) p. 30.

2 *Journal of Education*, 60 (May 1928), p. 306.

3 *Journal of Education*, 64 (August 1932), pp. 560–1.

4 I. Tod, 'On the education of girls of the middle-classes', (1874), pp. 9–10, Fawcett Library, *Women's Education Pamphlets*, Vol. II.

5 Maria Grey, *On the special requirements for improving the education of girls: paper read at the Social Science Congress, October 1871* (William Ridgeway, 1871), pp. 4, 5.

6 PP 1867–8 XXVIII (SIC Vols I–XVII), Vol. I, pp. 16-22.

7 J. R. de S. Honey, *Tom Brown's Universe: the Development of the Public School in the 19th Century* (Millington Books, 1977), p. 238 et seq.

8 For example, Dorothea Beale's evidence, SIC, Vol. V, p. 734 and Frances Buss's evidence, Vol. V, Pt II, p. 254.

9 Emily Davies, 'Special systems of education for women' (1868), in *Thoughts on Some Questions Relating to Women* (Cambridge University Press, Cambridge, 1910), p. 123.

10 Many schools followed the models of Cheltenham Ladies' College and the North London Collegiate School. For a detailed description of the former see Dorothea Beale, *On the organisation of girls' day schools. A paper read at the Social Science Congress, October 1873* (Longman, 1873), p. 9.

11 The introduction of the university local examinations in the 1850s helped provide part of the framework of the evolving curriculum. However it was not until the 1920s that head teachers began to make serious complaints about the constraints of the examination system.

12 Of the 17 headmistresses present at the Association of Head Mistresses (AHM) Annual Conference in 1878 only three allowed instrumental music to be taught during school hours; three others did not provide any musical teaching at all ('AHM Annual Conference Report', March 1878, Minute Book I 1874–1882 (MB I)).

13 AHM Meeting, February 1876, MB I.

14 Frances Buss to Annie Ridley, 1871. Quoted by Ridley in *Frances Buss and Her Work for Education*. (Longman 1895), p. 93.

15 Quoted in Grace Toplis (ed.), *Leaves from the Notebook of Frances M. Buss* (Macmillan, 1896), pp. 46, 124.

16 Beale, 'The Ladies College at Cheltenham', *Transactions of the NAPSS* (1866), p. 286.

17 AHM Annual Conference Report, March 1879, MB I. Curiously enough it was Frances Buss who pursued experiments in teaching domestic subjects and tried (but failed) to get the support of the AHM for doing so.

18 *Reports Issued by the Schools Inquiry Commission on the Education of Girls. With Extracts from the Evidence and a Preface by D. Beale*, (David Nott, n.d. [1869]), p. v.

19 Janet Howarth, 'Public schools, safety nets and educational ladders: the classification of girls' secondary schools, 1880–1914', *Oxford Review of Education*, 11 (1985), pp. 59–69 and Felicity Hunt, 'Social class and the grading of schools: realities in girls' secondary education 1880–1940', in June Purvis (ed.) *The Education of Girls and Women* (History of Education Society, Leicester, 1985).

20 *Royal Commission on Secondary Education*, PP 1895, XLIII–XLIX (Bryce Commission Vols I–IX), Vol. I, pp. 136, 175.

21 AHM Report of a Special Conference at NLCS, 6 December 1890, Minute Book II 1884–1895 (MB II). This was held to discuss the implications of the Technical Instruction Act of 1899.

22 For the medical opposition see Joan Burstyn, *Victorian Education and the Ideal of Womanhood* (Croom Helm, 1980), ch. 5.

23 Carol Dyhouse, *Girls Growing Up*, pp. 158–9.

24 Sheila Fletcher, *Women First: the Female Tradition in English Physical Education 1880–1980* (Athlone Press, 1984), pp. 32–34, 48, 49.

25 See Carol Dyhouse's chapter in this volume, especially note 13.

26 David Barker, 'How to curb the fertility of the unfit: the feeble-minded in Victorian Britain', *Oxford Review of Education*, 9, (1983), p. 200.

27 Karl Pearson, 'Woman and labour', *Fortnightly Review*, (1894), p. 577.

28 Elizabeth Sloan Chesser, *Woman, Marriage and Motherhood* (Cassell & Co, 1914), p. 2.

29 Pearson, 'Woman and labour', p. 562.

30 The Report advised compulsory teaching in cookery, hygiene and domestic economy for 'elder girls at school' (PP 1904, XXXII, p. 96).

31 Newman was later to become the first Chief Medical Officer to the Board of Education, *Board of Education Annual Report 1906–7*, PP 1908 XXVI, p. 9.

32 Dyhouse, 'Social Darwinistic ideas and the development of women's education in England, 1880–1920', *History of Education*, 5 (1976), pp. 49–50.

33 G. R. Searle, 'Eugenics and class', in C. Webster (ed.) *Biology, Medicine and Society 1840–1940* (Cambridge University Press, Cambridge, 1981), pp. 224–5.

34 Dyhouse, *Girls Growing Up*, p. 97.

35 Searle, 'Eugenics and class', pp. 224–5.

36 Dyhouse, *Girls Growing Up*, p. 98.

37 Ibid., ch. 3, and see Annmarie Turnbull's chapter in this volume.

38 On the orders of Robert Morant, Permanent Secretary at the Board of Education, Dr Janet Campbell, a medical officer at the Board who sympathised with eugenic ideals, prepared Circular 758, *Memorandum on the Teaching of Infant Care and Management in Public Elementary Schools* (HMSO, 1911) which strongly advocated the teaching of domestic subjects and mothercraft.

39 Morant's views were expressed in the Prefatory Memorandum of the *Regulations for Secondary Schools* 1904–5 (RSS), PP 1904 LXXV, p. 536 et seq.

40 Ibid., pp. 545–6.

41 Along with schools set up by local education authorities, any school which sought grant aid or wished to be recognized as efficient by the Board had to conform to the Regulations.

42 E. W. Jenkins, 'Science education and the Secondary School Regula-

tions, 1902–1909', *Journal of Educational Administration and History*, X, (1978), p. 31. For Morant's influence see E. J. R. Eaglesham, 'Implementing the Education Act of 1902', *British Journal of Educational Studies*, X, (1962), passim.

43 *Regulations for Secondary Schools (RSS) 1905–6*, PP 1905, LIX, p. 180.

44 In 'The curriculum of a girls' school' Sophie Bryant (Frances Buss's recent successor at NLCS) suggested that domestic science subjects were suited to 'the girls with rather less than average ability' (*Special Reports on Educational Subjects*, Vol. II, (HMSO, 1898), p. 101).

45 Educational Pamphlet No. 20, *Report on the Teaching of Latin at the Perse School, Cambridge* (Educational Experiments in Secondary Schools No. ii) (HMSO, 1910).

46 Public Record Office (henceforth PRO) ED 12/48 HMI Mr Headlam to CI Mr Fletcher, n.d. [October 1908].

47 PRO ED 12/65 'Music in Secondary Schools', 1906.

48 PRO ED 12/52 A. Cardew to W. N. Bruce, 14 October 1904.

49 PRO ED 12/52 CI Mr Fletcher to J. W. Mackail, 27 June 1906; R. Morant to W. N. Bruce, 24 October 1906.

50 'Report by the Chief Inspector of Secondary Schools [W. C. Fletcher] on the Teaching of Mathematics in Secondary Schools', *Board of Education Annual Report 1910–11*, PP 1912–13 XXI, pp. 307–8.

51 *RSS* 1907–8, PP 1907 LXII, p. 617.

52 *RSS* 1909–10, PP 1909 LXVII, p. 486.

53 PP 1908 XXVI, p. 75.

54 See for example Sara Burstall, *English High Schools for Girls: their Aims, Organisation and Management*, (Longman 1907), pp. 195–6.

55 'Memorandum to the Board of Education on the Regulations for Secondary Schools 1904'; 'AHM Annual Conference Report', June 1908, *AHM Annual Report 1909*; Burstall, *English High Schools for Girls*, pp. 198–201; Sara Burstall and E. M. Douglas, *Public Schools for Girls* (Longman, 1911), pp. 145, 159, 166–8.

56 AHM Memorandum of Domestic Science, March 1907 (*AHM Reports 1907–1911*).

57 *School World*, 14 (December 1912), pp. 452–65.

58 See for example the *Interim Memorandum on the Teaching of Housecraft in Girls' Secondary Schools*, (HMSO, 1911), passim, and Penny Summerfield's chapter in this volume.

59 PRO ED 12/43 AHM Annual Conference Resolutions, June 1911.

60 PRO ED 12/41 J. W. Mackail to the Hon Maude Lawrence, 30 August 1908.

61 PP 1913 XX.

62 Quoted by Burstall, *English High Schools for Girls*, pp. 14–15.

63 Circular 1112, *Memorandum on Advanced Courses*, (HMSO, 1919), para. 7.

64 Dyhouse, 'Towards a "feminine" curriculum for English schoolgirls', p. 306.

65 *Differentiation of the Curriculum Report*, pp. 85–6, 90, 93.
66 Ibid., pp. 94–5.
67 Ibid., p. xiii.
68 Ibid., p. 32.
69 Ibid., p. xii.
70 Ibid., p. 126.
71 Ibid., p. xv.
72 Ibid., p. xi.
73 Ray Strachey, *The Cause: A Short History of the Women's Movement in Great Britain* (1928, Virago edn, 1978) pp. 370–1.
74 Patterns of women's participation in the workforce are complex. See Jane Lewis, *Women in England 1870–1950* (Wheatsheaf, Brighton, 1984), pp. 147–55.
75 *Differentiation of the Curriculum Report*, p. 130.
76 Ibid., p. xiv.
77 Ibid., p. 62.
78 *Journal of Education*, 55 (March 1923), p. 137.
79 For example, Professor Nunn to the National Council for Domestic Studies, *Journal of Education*, 55 (December 1923), p. 81 and K. E. Jenkinson, 'A commercial bias in higher education', *Journal of Education*, 64 (May, 1932), p. 286.
80 *Board of Education Annual Report 1929*, PP 1929–30, XIII, p. 37.
81 Circular 1463, 1938, *Board of Education Annual Report 1938*, PP 1938–39, X, p. 694.
82 *Journal of Education*, 705 (April, 1928), p. 233.
83 For example, 'The first school examination', *Journal of Education*, 705 (April, 1929), p. 233.

Chapter 2 Miss Buss and Miss Beale: Gender and Authority in the History of Education

1 R. R. Dale, *Mixed or Single Sex School?* Vol. I, *A Research Study in Pupil–Teacher Relationships* (Routledge & Kegan Paul, 1969), p. 237.
2 Ibid., p. 114.
3 See, *inter alia*, J. Shaw, 'Education and the individual: schooling for girls, or mixed schooling – a mixed blessing?', in R. Deem (ed.), *Schooling for Women's Work* (Routledge & Kegan Paul, 1980); E. Sarah, M. Scott and D. Spender, 'The education of feminists: the case for single-sex schools', in D. Spender and E. Sarah (eds) *Learning to Lose: Sexism and Education* (The Women's Press, 1980); R. Deem (ed.), *Co-Education Reconsidered (Open University Press, 1984); and P. Mahony, Schools for the Boys? Co-Education Reassessed* (Hutchinson, 1985).
4 Florence Nightingale, *Cassandra*, published as an appendix to *The Cause: a Short History of the Women's Movement in Great Britain* (G. Bell & Sons, 1928; reprinted by Cedric Chivers, 1974). The same point about

popular biographies of Nightingale failing to deal with her ambitiousness and ruthlessness has been made by Martha Vicinus in her study *Independent Women: Work and Community for Single Women 1850–1920* (Virago, 1985, p. 21).

5 J. Gathorne-Hardy, *The Public School Phenomenon* (Penguin, 1977).

6 Ibid., p. 271.

7 There is much relevant to this theme in Vicinus, *Independent Women* (see note 4).

8 J. Kamm, *How Different From Us: a Biography of Miss Buss and Miss Beale* (Bodley Head, 1958), pp. 237–8.

9 See, for instance L. Davidoff, and C. Hall, 'The architecture of public and private life: English middle-class society in a provincial town 1780–1850', in D. Fraser and A. Sutcliffe (eds) *The Pursuit of Urban History* (Edward Arnold, 1983). The essay is part of a larger research project being carried out by the authors at the University of Essex, exploring the relationship between the development of domesticity and the growth of the middle class in late eighteenth- and early nineteenth-century England.

10 The nature and impact of these changes in legislation is very fully discussed in Lee Holcombe, *Wives and Property: Reform of the Married Women's Property Law in Nineteenth Century England* (Oxford, Martin Robertson, 1983).

11 M. Todd, *The Life of Sophia Jex-Blake* (Macmillan, 1918), pp. 70–1.

12 J. B. S. Pedersen, 'The reform of women's secondary and higher education in nineteenth-century England: a study in elite groups' (University of California (Berkeley) D.Phil thesis, 1974). See also the same author's 'The reform of women's secondary and higher education: institutional change and social values in mid and late Victorian England', in *History of Education Quarterly*, 19 (1979).

13 J. B. S. Pedersen, 'Schoolmistresses and headmistresses: elites and education in nineteenth century England', in *Journal of British Studies*, XV (1975), and the same author's 'Some Victorian headmistresses: a conservative tradition of social reform', in *Victorian Studies*, 24 (1981).

14 Report of the Schools Inquiry Commission, 1868, Vol. VIII, p. 478, quoted by Pedersen in 'The reform of women's secondary and higher education', p. 241.

15 E. Raikes, *Dorothea Beale of Cheltenham* (Constable, 1908) and A. E. Ridley, *Frances Mary Buss and Her Work for Education* (Longmans, Green, 1896).

16 Kamm, *How Different From Us.*

17 Ibid., pp. 120–1.

18 Ibid., pp. 75–6.

19 Ibid., p. 158.

20 Ibid., p. 34.

21 Ridley, *Frances Mary Buss*, p. v.

22 Kamm records that only once in her life did Miss Beale appeal for funds

– for her teacher training college – and on that occasion she knew that she could rely on the goodwill of staff and old girls (Kamm, *How Different From Us*, pp. 107–8).

23 Kamm, p. 108.

24 Ibid., p. 104.

25 There was more at stake in this kind of fund raising than the ladylike reputations of the fundraisers. The idea of *public* provision for middle-class girls' education trespassed upon notions of paternal provision and pride. Pedersen illustrates this by citing a letter from one father to Miss Buss complaining about attempts to secure endowment. He insisted that many parents would receive the impression 'that the institution is a charitable one, and therefore unsuited for those members of the middle class who stand in no need of pecuniary assistance in the education of their families'. Letter dated 19 November 1971 in North London Collegiate Archives, quoted by Pedersen in 'The Reform of Women's Secondary and Higher Education', p. 67.

26 Report of Schools' Inquiry Commission, Vol. XXVIII, p. 251. For further discussion of the problems faced by women on the governing bodies of educational institutions at the time see C. Dyhouse, *Girls Growing Up in Late Victorian and Edwardian England* (Routledge & Kegan Paul, 1981), pp. 60–5.

27 E. Kaye, *A History of Queen's College, London, 1848–1972* (Chatto & Windus, 1972), p. 737. See also Raikes, *Dorothea Beale*, pp. 33–5.

28 Kamm, *How Different From Us*, pp. 124–5.

29 Ibid., p. 102.

30 Ridley, *Frances Mary Buss*, pp. 235–7.

31 See (for instance) Ridley, *Frances Mary Buss*, pp. 241–2.

32 Kamm, *How Different From Us*, p. 185.

33 A. Price and N. Glenday, *Reluctant Revolutionaries: a Century of Headmistresses, 1874–1974* (Pitman, 1974).

34 M. Littlewood, 'Makers of Men', in *Trouble and Strife*, 5 (1985), and see Alison Oram's chapter in this volume.

35 *New Schoolmaster* (May 1936), quoted by Littlewood, ibid. p. 27.

36 Ibid., p. 27.

37 A. Oram, 'Serving two masters? the introduction of a marriage bar in teaching in the 1920s', in The London Feminist History Group's *The Sexual Dynamics of History* (Pluto Press, 1983). See also G. Partington, *Women Teachers in the Twentieth Century in England and Wales* (Windsor, NFER Publishing, 1976), p. 28 ff.

38 See The Association of Head Mistresses' Memorandum entitled *Mixed Secondary Schools Under the Headship of a Man*, 1912 (Association of Secondary Heads, 129 Gordon Square, London WC1, or in Modern Records Centre, University of Warwick).

39 See Association of Head Mistresses, *Report of Conference Held at the Clothworkers' Hall, Mincing Lane, on October 25 1905*, pp. 6–9, among papers and reports lodged with Secondary Heads' Association, as above.

Chapter 3   The Ideology of Femininity and Reading for Girls, 1850–1914

1 See description of *The Family Magazine; or, A Repository of Religious Instruction, and Rational Amusement*, in the file card catalogue, Osborne Collection of Early Children's Books, Toronto.

2 For the RTS, see J. S. Bratton, *The Impact of Victorian Children's Fiction*, (Croom Helm, 1981), pp. 32–46.

3 For 'penny dreadfuls' see Michael Anglo, *Penny Dreadfuls and Other Victorian Horrors*, (Jupiter, 1977) and *Penny Dreadfuls and Comics: English Periodicals for Children from Victorian Times to the Present Day. A Loan Exhibition from the Library of Oldenburg University, West Germany at the Bethnal Green Museum of Childhood 2 June–2 October, 1983* (Victoria & Albert Museum, 1982).

4 I discuss this question more fully in chapter 3 of my book, *The Victorian Girl and the Feminine Ideal* (Croom Helm, 1982).

5 For a discussion of some of the other writers of domestic fiction for girls, see Bratton, *Impact*, ch. 5 and for a late-Victorian discussion, see Edward G. Salmon, 'What girls read,' *The Nineteenth Century*, 20 (October, 1886), pp. 515–29.

6 *The Daisy Chain: or Aspirations – A Family Chronicle* (John W. Parker & Son, 1856)

7 Ibid., p. 11

8 Ibid., p. 641.

9 Ibid., p. 660.

10 Ibid., p. 661–2.

11 On changing employment opportunities for middle-class women, see Lee Holcombe, *Victorian Ladies at Work: Middle-Class Working Women in England and Wales, 1850–1914* (David & Charles, Newton Abbot, 1973) and Martha Vicinus, *Independent Women: Work and Community for Single Women 1850–1920* (Chicago, University of Chicago Press, 1985).

12 For the history of *The Girl's Own Paper* and *The Boy's Own Paper*, see Patrick Dunae, 'Boy's Own Paper: origins and editorial policies', *The Private Library*: Second Series, 9: 4, (Winter, 1976); Wendy Forrester, *Great-Grandmama's Weekly: a Celebration of The Girl's Own Paper, 1880–1901* (Guildford and London: Lutterworth, 1980); Jack Cox, *Take a Cold Tub, Sir!: the Story of The Boy's Own Paper* (Guildford, Lutterworth, 1982).

13 Claim quoted by Edward Salmon, 'What girls read', p. 520.

14 Earlier publications had existed, for example a publication edited by Clara Hall, *The Young Lady's Annual*, whose contributors included the well-known evangelical writer for children Mrs Sherwood (author of *The Fairchild Family*) existed for a brief period in the 1830s (the Osborne Collection of Early Children's Books, Toronto, Canada holds one volume, c. 1835). Charlotte Yonge was closely associated for 30 years

with a much longer lived periodical, *The Monthly Packet of Evening Readings for Younger Members of the English Church*, published by Joan and Charles Mozley between 1859 and 1899, and designed for an audience of 'young girls or maidens or young ladies' of the upper middle class. A comparison between *The Monthly Packet* and *The Girl's Own Paper* clearly illustrates the contrast between the old and the new style of improving literature: *The Monthly Packet* consisted exclusively of 'serious' fiction and articles. There was none of the variety of content that was found in the *Girl's Own*, no articles on fashion, hobbies or home decorating. In the 30-year period in which the *The Girl's Own Paper* flourished it had many competitors. The most successful of these rivals was *Every Girl's Magazine*, published by Routledge, which had begun publication a year before *The Girl's Own Paper*. It was similar to the *Girl's Own* but appealed more exclusively to a middle- and upper middle-class audience.

15 Until 1908 the editor was Charles Peters. See Patrick Dunae, 'Boy's Own' and Mary Cadogan and Patricia Craig, *You're a Brick, Angela! A New Look at Girls' Fiction from 1839 to 1975* (Victor Gollancz, 1976) pp. 75–80.

16 'Three years of a girl's life', chapter XIV, *The Girl's Own Paper*, 4 September 1880, p. 563.

17 'Three years of a girl's life', chapter XV, *The Girl's Own Paper*, 11 September 1880, p. 578.

18 Examples include Sara Doudney's 'When we were girls together: a story of school-girl life', serialized in August and September, 1885, a school-girl tale that takes place mostly during school vacation, and S. M. Crawley's 'Ella's visit to fire country', a story about young children, which appeared in the 7 September 1895 issue. In the same issues, the feature stories follow the standard romantic pattern.

19 The article on 'The working girls of London' is in the issue of 4 September 1880; 'The standing evil: a plea for shop girls,' 25 September 1880; 'Servants and service', 5 September 1885; 'The girl's outlook: or what is there to talk about?', which includes a discussion of a report of Clara Collet's on women's employment, 31 August 1895.

20 The comment was included in the 'Varieties' column, 4 September 1880, p. 575.

21 The phrase was made popular by an article written by W. R. Greg, 'Why are women redundant?', *National Review*, 15 (1862), pp. 434–60.

22 *The Girl's Own Paper*, 4 September 1880, p. 564.

23 It should be explained that the queries themselves were not published, but only the editor's answers. The answers do in most cases reveal the nature of the questions.

24 *The Girl's Own Paper*, 4 September 1880, p. 576.

25 For a discussion of fiction in two Victorian penny weeklies published for adults, see Sally Mitchell, 'The Forgotten Women of the Period: Penny Weekly Family Magazines of the 1840s and 1850s', in Martha Vicinus

(ed.) *A Widening Sphere: Changing Roles of Victorian Women* (Indiana University Press, Bloomington, 1977).

26 After Charles Peters' death, Flora Klickmann became editor in 1908, and introduced a number of changes. See Cadogan and Craig, *You're a Brick*, p. 80. For developments in periodical publishing for girls after this period, see Penny Tinkler's chapter in this volume.

27 On Meade and her prolific career, see Bratton, *Image*, pp. 201–3.

28 L. T. Meade, *A World of Girls: the Story of a School* (Cassell & Co., 1886), p. 8.

29 Ibid., p. 123.

30 Ibid., p. 66. This girl is caught reading a forbidden book, Charlotte Brontë's *Jane Eyre*, and is reminded that 'this special book is not allowed to be read at any time in Lavender House'. p. 70.

31 L. T. Meade, *A Sweet Girl Graduate* (Cassell & Co, 1891).

32 Ibid., p. 51.

33 See Perry Williams's chapter in this volume.

34 See Sheila Fletcher's interesting comments on Brazil and her fictional schools in her *Women First: the Female Tradition in English Physical Education 1880–1980* (The Athlone Press, 1984), pp. 78–9.

35 Angela Brazil, *The Nicest Girl in the School: a Story of School Life* (Blackie & Son, 1910).

36 Angela Brazil, *The Girls of St Cyprian's: a Tale of School Life* (Blackie & Son), 1914.

37 As Sybil Oldfield puts it in *Spinsters of this Parish: the Life and Times of F. M. Mayor and Mary Sheepshanks* (Virago, 1984), p. 21: 'What [Sheepshanks and Mayor] were responding to as they sat . . . engrossed in *Jane Eyre* or *The Mill on the Floss*, was nothing less than the articulation of their own secret dreams of rebellion and of heroism.'

Chapter 4 Learning through Leisure: Feminine Ideology in Girls' Magazines 1920–50

1 P. Jephcott, *Girls Growing Up* (Faber & Faber, 1942), p. 98.

2 S. Brownmiller, *Femininity* (Paladin, 1986), p. 59.

3 J. M. Brew, 'Young people and reading', *Journal Of Education* 76 (1944), p. 110.

4 Jephcott, *Girls Growing Up*, p. 110.

5 Ibid., p. 108.

6 A. J. Jenkinson, *What Do Boys And Girls Read?* (Methuen, 1940), p. 211.

7 Ibid., pp. 214–15. Leaving school represented a significant break for working-class girls. See for example, Dolly in P. Jephcott, *Rising Twenty, Notes on Some Ordinary Girls* (Faber & Faber, 1948), p. 10.

8 See Deborah Gorham's chapter in this volume.

9 Interview with Pat Lamburn.

10 *Silver Star*, 13 November 1937, p. 31.

11 'Readership of women's weekly periodicals by social class for females, 14–24 years', *Survey Of Press Readership*, Vol. 1, Table 5 (Institute of Incorporated Practitioners in Advertising, 1939), p. 45. Jenkinson, *What Do Boys And Girls Read?*, p. 218.

12 Jephcott, *Girls Growing Up*, p. 101.

13 *Pam's Paper*, 7 May 1927, p. 5.

14 *Woman*, 5 June 1937, p. 20.

15 *Girls' Favourite*, 12 March 1927, p. 122.

16 Ibid.

17 For contemporary comment on the spinster see P. Jephcott, *Rising Twenty*, p. 101; J. Newsom, *The Education Of Girls* (Faber & Faber, 1948), pp. 141, 146–7. A good example of a fictional characterization can be found in J. B. Priestley, *Daylight On Saturday* (Heinemann, 1943), p. 30. For a feminist historical analysis of the spinster see, S. Jeffreys, *The Spinster And Her Enemies, Feminism and Sexuality 1880–1930* (Pandora, 1985), ch. 5.

18 *Lucky Star*, 9 January 1950, p. 19.

19 Mary Cadogan and Patricia Graig, *You're a Brick, Angela!: The Girls' Story 1839–1985* (Gollancz Paperbacks, 1986), p. 316.

20 E. Mercer, 'Some occupational attitudes of girls', *Occupational Psychology*, XIV, (January 1940), p. 20.

21 *Girls' Own Paper*, February 1940, pp. 238–40.

22 Ibid., p. 240.

23 J. Burnett Knowlton (ed.), *Girl's Own Annual*, L11 (1931), p. 369.

24 *Girls' Favourite*, 4 February 1922, p. 12.

25 *The Schoolgirl*, 6 January 1940, p. 13.

26 *Woman*, 24 February 1945, p. 18.

27 *Poppy's Paper*, 2 February 1924, p. 1.

28 *Lucky Star*, 6 January 1940, p. 18.

29 *Girls' Weekly*, 3 January 1920, p. 2.

30 *Girls' Favourite*, 2 April 1927, p. 199.

31 *Miss Modern*, October 1930, pp. 42, 22.

32 Cadogan and Craig, *You're A Brick*, p. 246.

33 *Red Star Weekly*, 16 September 1950, p. 31.

34 Ibid.

35 *Poppy's Paper*, 25 January 1930.

36 J. Hemming, *Problems Of Adolescent Girls* (Heinemann, 1960), p. 34.

37 Ibid., pp. 128–31.

38 Ibid., pp. 70–1.

39 Cadogan and Craig, *You're A Brick*, p. 244.

40 Interview with Pat Lamburn.

41 Interview with James Hemming.

42 Hemming, *Problems Of Adolescent Girls*, p. 70.

43 A. Rodaway, *A London Childhood* (Virago, 1985), p. 77.

44 J. McCrindle and S. Rowbotham (eds), *Dutiful Daughters: Women Talk About Their Lives* (Allen Lane, 1977), p. 219.

45 *Woman's Own*, 15 October 1932, p. 35.

46 *Peg's Paper*, 8 June 1940, p. 26.

47 H. Powell, 'The Problem of the Adolescent Girl', in M Scharleib (ed.) *Sexual Problems Of Today* (William & Norgate, 1925), p. 112.

48 In 1938, 40 per cent of brides under 20 years of age were pregnant according to D. Mace, *Marriage Crisis* (Delisle, 1948), p. 70.

49 R. Kent, *Aunt Agony Advises: Problem Pages Through the Ages* (Allen Lane, 1979), p. 247.

50 *Peg's Paper*, 10 August 1940, p. 27.

51 *Lucky Star*, 6 January 1940, p. 11.

52 Hemming, *Problems Of Adolescent Girls*, ch. 6.

53 *Girls' Weekly*, 3 January 1920, p. 2.

54 *Poppy's Paper*, 2 November 1929, p. 7.

55 Ibid., 2 February 1924, p. 7.

56 R. Roberts, *The Classic Slum* (Penguin, Harmondsworth, 1980), pp. 160–1.

57 Jephcott, *Girls Growing Up*, p. 110. See also D. Wall, *The Adolescent Child* (Methuen, 1948), p. 113. Also, G. Jordan and E. Fisher, *Self Portrait Of Youth* (Heinemann, 1955), pp. 107, 108.

Chapter 5 Learning Her Womanly Work: the Elementary School Curriculum, 1870–1914

1 J. Hurt, *Elementary Schooling and the Working Classes* (Routledge & Kegan Paul, 1979), pp. 27–8.

2 See the regulations and suggestions on needlework teaching introduced by the Committee of Council on Education in the *Instructions to Inspectors, Minutes and Reports* (1839–99) (DES Library).

3 A. Digby and P. Searby, *Children, School and Society in Nineteenth Century England* (Macmillan, 1981), p. 31.

4 For London see D. Rubinstein, *School Attendance in London: a Social History* (University of Hull, 1969) and J. Lewis 'Parents, children, school fees and the London School Board 1870–1890', *History of Education*, Vol. II, No. 4 (1982). Hurt, *Elementary Schooling*, Part 3 considers the national picture.

5 A. Davin, ' "A centre of humanising influence": the schooling of working-class girls under the London School Board, 1870–1902', (unpublished paper, 1978), pp. 4–5.

6 'Co-education: some comparisons between boys and girls', *Educational Review*, Vol. I, No. 3, (1899), p. 174.

7 A. Davin, ' "Mind that you do as you are told": reading books for Board school girls', *Feminist Review*, 3 (1979), pp. 91–2.

8 Jarrold, *New Code Reading Books II*, (1871), quoted in ibid. p. 95.

9 This was fanned by fears of the effects of competition resulting from the growth of European industry.

10 Second Report of the *Royal Commission on Technical Instruction*, quoted in G. Sutton, *Artisan or Artist? A History of the Teaching of Art and Craft in English Schools* (Pergamon Press, Oxford, 1967), p. 179.

11 *Report of the Royal Commission to Inquire into the Working of the Elementary Education Acts* (1888), quoted in Sutton, ibid. p. 182.

12 Board of Education, *Annual Report 1912–1913*, pp. 88–9.

13 P. Magnus, *Educational Aims and Efforts, 1880–1910* (Longmans, 1910), p. 181. The introduction of childcare, the fourth 'C' of women's domestic work, into the curriculum is examined in A. Davin, 'Imperialism and Motherhood', *History Workshop Journal*, 5 (1978).

14 Rev. J. G. C. Fussel, Report in *Minutes of the Committee of Council on Education, 1857* quoted in Sutton, *Artisan or Artist?*, pp. 75–6. See also E. A. Pennington, *The Education of a Village Girl* (Hatchards, 1888), p. 8.

15 R. Robinson, *The Aims and Methods of Teaching Needlework* (Edward Arnold, 1912), Introduction.

16 By the 1890s Singer and other firms were loaning machines to schools, but expansion was slow.

17 Board of Education, *Circular 719, The Teaching of Needlework in Secondary Schools* (1909).

18 Robinson, *Aims and Methods*, p. 4.

19 Quoted in C. E. Grant, *Farthing Bundles* (published by the author, 1930), p. 48. Grant, a London head teacher, was appalled by the Board's requirements.

20 Board of Education, *Annual Report, 1900–1901*, p. 50.

21 The ideas of Froebel (1782–1852) contributed to child-centred and interest-based curriculum developments. He believed children learned not by being taught specific knowledge but via activity and play. See for example C. I. Dodd, 'Needlework as Manual Training', *Journal of Education*, 1895.

22 Quoted in Grant, *Farthing Bundles*, p. 48.

23 That their work heralded a new direction for needlework teaching can be seen in M. Swanson and A. Macbeth, *Educational Needlecraft* (Longmans, 1913), and A. Macbeth, 'The craft of the needle', *The Parent's Review*, Vol. XXV, No. 8 (1914), pp. 614–26.

24 E. M. Sneyd-Kynnersley, *HMI* (Macmillan, 1908), p. 314.

25 *Report of the Committee of Council on Education, 1882*. In his reports for 1889–90 Reverend Byrne went so far as to suggest: 'Home is the proper place for skilled instruction in labour of the hands . . . I should be glad to think that needlework holds its position in the elementary school only temporarily and on sufferance, with a view to its so rapidly improving itself as that it should improve itself away altogether.'

26 See reminiscences of this aspect of schooling by Charles Cooper in J. Burnett, *Destinies Obscure: Autobiographies of Childhood, Education and*

the Family from the 1820s to the 1920s (Allen Lane, 1982), p. 195 and of Joseph Ashby quoted in C. Adams, *Ordinary Lives, A Hundred Years Ago* (Virago, 1982), p. 43.

27 See R. Colborne's report on needlework teaching, Education Department, *Annual Report, 1894–1895*, pp. 196–206.

28 Miss Blackmore, Head of Roan School, Greenwich, *Bryce Commission*, Vol. II (1895), quoted in Sutton, *Artisan or Artist?*, p. 191.

29 Board of Education, *Annual Report, 1900–1901*, p. 50.

30 Board of Education, *Report by the Chief Woman Inspector on the Teaching of Needlework in Public Elementary Schools* (1910), p. 10.

31 This method had been used in German schools since the 1860s.

32 See T. A. Spalding, *The Work of the London School Board* (P. S. King and Son, 1900), p. 236 and H. K. Brietzche and E. F. Rooper, *A Manual of Collective Lessons in Plain Needlework*, (Swan Sonnenschein, 1885).

33 Board of Education, *Annual Report, 1898–1899*, p. 668. *School Hygiene*, the official organ of the school medical officers, carried a number of articles deprecating needlework's effect on girls' eyesight between 1911 and 1913.

34 Kate Taylor in Burnett, *Destinies Obscure*, p. 292.

35 Sneyd-Kynnersley, *HMI*, pp. 314–15. See also Adams, *Ordinary Lives*, p. 43. An even more economical method of dealing with needlework was its introduction into school prize systems. While boys received books as prizes, girls were instead permitted to take home their sewing without first paying for it.

36 Board of Education, *Report of Chief Woman Inspector*, p. 8.

37 *The Board Teacher*, 1 September, 1893, p. 183 and F. Thompson, *Lark Rise to Candleford* (Penguin, Harmondsworth, 1973), p. 32.

38 A. Webster, *A Housewife's Opinions* (Macmillan, 1879), p. 280–1.

39 F. K. Prochaska, *Women and Philanthropy in 19th Century England*, (Oxford University Press, Oxford, 1979), p. 7.

40 *The Epicure*, March 1884, p. 82.

41 Quoted in D. Stone, *The National. The Story of the National Training College of Domestic Subjects* (Brighton Polytechnic Press, Brighton, 1973), p. 26.

42 M. E. Scott, *A History of F. L. Calder College of Domestic Science, 1875–1965*, (F.L. Calder College, Liverpool, 1967), p. 17.

43 *Report of the Royal Commission to Inquire into the Working of the Elementary Education Acts*, pp. 36–40. The exception here was HMI Mathew Arnold, who believed cookery should form no part of elementary schooling.

44 Education Department, *Special Reports on Educational Subjects, Vol. 1, Mrs Pillow, Domestic Economy Teaching in England, 1896–1897*, p. 9.

45 See Davin, 'Imperialism and motherhood', C. Dyhouse, 'Social Darwinistic ideas and the development of women's education in England, 1880–1920', *History of Education*, 5 (1976), pp. 41–58 and J. Lewis, *The*

Politics of Motherhood: Child and Maternal Welfare in England 1900–1939 (Croom Helm, 1980).

46 *Report of the Inter-Departmental Committee on Physical Deterioration* (3 vols, 1904), Vol. 1, pp. 62–3.

47 Board of Education, *Circular 758, Memorandum on the Teaching of Infant Care and Management in Public Elementary Schools*, (1910).

48 For Liverpool see J. G. Legge, *The Thinking Hand or Practical Education in the Elementary School* (1914), for London *Final Report of the London School Board* (1904) and R. D. Bramwell, 'Elementary school work 1875–1925', PhD thesis, University of Durham, 1961, Vol. 1, p. 121 for Northumberland.

49 *The Board Teacher*, 2 July 1883, p. 5.

50 Ibid., 1 February 1884, p. 74, and 1 May 1886, p. 122.

51 Greater London Record Office (GLRO), SBL/715. See for example the evidence of one head, Mrs E. W. Macaulay, p. 6.

52 See for example GLRO, SBL/709 *Minutes of Sub-Committee on Domestic Subjects* (July 1899), p. 398 and Board of Education, *Annual Report 1907–8*, p. 35.

53 GLRO SBL/709, p. 103.

54 Board of Education, *Annual Report 1899–1900*, p. 330.

55 *Education*, November 1912.

56 I am grateful to Anna Davin for showing me this unpublished autobiography.

57 Oral testimony quoted in A. Turnbull, 'Home economics – the disintegration of a curriculum', MSc dissertation, Southbank Polytechnic, 1977, p. 36. See also Board of Education, *Report of the Education (Provision of School Meals) Act, 1906* (1909).

58 Education Department, *Annual Report 1894–1895*, pp. 117–18.

59 In Leeds board school girls had lessons on cleaning mincing machines and dinner services; C. Buckton, *Food and Home Cookery: a Course of Instruction in Practical Cookery and Cleaning for Children in Elementary Schools, as Followed in the Schools of the Leeds School Board* (Longmans Green, 1879) p. 15, while in Edinburgh, cheese graters, fish slices and flour dredgers were essential utensils; C. E. Guthrie-Wright, *The School Cookery Book* (Macmillan 1899), p. 153.

60 PRO ED 11/60, 'Special subject syllabuses', July 1905.

61 Ibid., Lawrence to Morant, 16 October 1905.

62 See Felicity Hunt's chapter, 'Divided aims', in this volume.

63 Board of Education, *Special Report on the Teaching of Cookery to Public Elementary School Children in England and Wales by the Chief Woman Inspector of the Board* (1907) prefatory memorandum, p. xiv.

Chapter 6 Inequalities in the Teaching Profession: the Effect on Teachers and Pupils, 1910–39

1 Secretary of Oldham branch NAS, *Manchester Guardian*, 25 February 1930.

2 Presidential address, NUWT conference, *Daily Herald*, 3 January 1935.

3 Presidential address, NAS conference, *Times Educational Supplement* (*TES*), 19 May 1921, p. 227.

4 Presidential address, NAS conference, *TES*, 18 April 1925, p. 159.

5 *Manchester Guardian*, 22 April 1930.

6 Vera Brittain, *Lady into Woman* (Andrew Dakers, 1953), p. 93.

7 Resolution passed at NUWT conference, *Manchester Guardian*, 4 January 1935.

8 *TES*, 10 January 1925, p. 18.

9 *TES*, 5 January 1924, p. 6. For a parallel contemporary feminist discussion of the importance of role models for girls' expectations and recent research which has found that in mixed classes girls receive less teacher attention than boys see Dale Spender, *Invisible Women: the Schooling Scandal* (1982), p. 54–61.

10 Presidential address, NUWT conference, *Manchester Guardian*, 31 December 1930.

11 See Alison Oram, 'Serving two masters? The introduction of a marriage bar in teaching in the 1920s', in London Feminist History Group, *The Sexual Dynamics of History* (1983), and Alison Oram, ' "Sex antagonism" in the teaching profession: the equal pay issue 1914–1929', *History of Education Review* (Australia & New Zealand), Vol. 14, No. 2 (1985), pp. 36–48

12 NAS conference, *TES*, 6 April 1929, p. 160.

13 NUWT conference, *Manchester Guardian*, 7 January 1933.

14 NUWT archive, Box 93. Memorandum on reorganization and headships of schools, May 1928, p. 3.

15 Speaker at NUWT conference, *Manchester Guardian*, 7 January 1933.

16 Report to LEAs by NAS, *News Chronicle*, 25 January 1934.

17 NUWT conference, *The Times*, 2 January 1930.

18 *Daily Telegraph*, 31 December 1931.

19 *TES*, 6 Jan 1934, p. 6.

20 Speech to NAS conference, *Manchester Guardian*, 22 April 1930.

21 NUWT conference, *The Times*, 2 January 1930.

22 *TES*, 7 January 1928, p. 6.

23 Article in *TES*, 6 October 1914, p. 161.

24 PRO ED 24/1820, letter to Board of Education, 16 November 1929.

25 Resolution at NAS conference, *Daily Herald*, 11 April 1939.

26 Presidential address, NAS conference, *TES*, 18 April 1925, p. 159.

27 *Evening Standard*, 13 July 1932; 22 April 1933.

28 J. D. Browne, *Teachers of Teachers: a History of the Association of Teachers in Colleges and Departments of Education* (1979) p. 18. B. Simon, *The Politics of Educational Reform 1920–1940* (Lawrence & Wishart, 1974), p. 225–45.

29 *The Times*, 2 January 1930.

30 Letter to *Manchester Guardian*, 8 June 1933.

31 A. M. Pierotti, *The Story of the National Union of Women Teachers* (1963) p. 27.

32 Speaker at NUWT conference, *Manchester Guardian*, 4 January 1935.
33 NUT archive. Executive Committee minutes, October 1924.
34 TES, 13 April 1929, p. 170. The union also argued that this would be to the educational benefit of the children.
35 NUT, *Group Home Rule – A Reply to the NAS*, Leaflet No. 42 (1924).
36 NUT, *The NAS states the Union is not in favour of men teachers for boys! That is not true*. Leaflet No. 88 (1926).
37 NUT, *A Heart to Heart Talk*, Leaflet No. 128 (1934).
38 *TES*, 12 February 1927, p. 81.
39 *Woman Teacher*, 27 March 1931.
40 *Woman Teacher*, 13 July 1933.
41 NUT Ladies Committee minutes, November 1930.
42 *Schoolmaster*, 21 April 1933, p. 674.
43 PRO ED 60/158. London staffing, note for meeting, 30 January 1923.
44 PRO ED 24/1820, Letter of 29 April 1930, referring to House of Commons answer on 12 December 1929.
45 PRO ED 24/1820. Letter from H. Ramsbotham to Capt. W. F. Strickland MP, 19 March 1934.
46 PRO ED 60/158. Questionnaire and minute to LEAs, 14 February 1927.
47 Secretary of the Assistant Masters Association in the *News Chronicle*, 22 March 1934.
48 PRO ED 60/158, Letter to LCC from Board of Education, 13 January 1923.
49 *Schoolmaster*, 9 May 1924, p. 791.
50 P. Ballard, *The Changing School* (1925), p. 314.
51 *Manchester Guardian*, 22 November 1938 and 19 December 1938.
52 *TES*, 3 March 1934, p. 70.
53 A. E. Ikin, *Organisation and Administration of the Education Department* (1926) p. 64.
54 See Annmarie Turnbull's chapter in this volume.
55 See Felicity Hunt's chapter in this volume.
56 NAS conference, *News Chronicle*, 18 April 1931.
57 *Daily News*, 8 April 1930.
58 Speaker at NAS conference, *TES*, 15 April 1939, p. 142.
59 Presidential address to NUWT conference, *Manchester Guardian*, 31 December 1930.
60 All these figures are calculated from tables in Board of Education, *Annual Reports and Statistics of Public Education* 1910–1938.
61 At the same time it did allow men teachers to encroach on the traditional territory of women teachers by taking more than their previous share of the *headships* of the new junior mixed schools.

Chapter 7 Better a Teacher than a Hairdresser?
'A Mad Passion for Equality' or Keeping Molly and Betty Down

1 Liz Heron (ed.), *Truth, Dare or Promise: Girls Growing Up in the Fifties* (Virago, 1985), p. 75.
2 Ibid., p. 32.
3 Centre for Contemporary Cultural Studies, *Unpopular Education* (Hutchinson, 1981), p. 303.
4 D. Riley, *War in the Nursery* (Virago, 1983); D. Thom and J. Austoker (eds), *Eugenics, Population Decline and Social Policy in Europe* (Cambridge University Press, Cambridge, forthcoming).
5 J. Lewis, *The Politics of Motherhood* (Croom Helm, 1980); J. Macnicol, *The Movement for Family Allowances* (Heinemann, 1980).
6 D. Gittins, *Fair Sex* (Hutchinson, 1982); Report of the Royal Commission on Population, Cmnd 7695, PP 1949.
7 M. Spring-Rice, *Working-Class Wives* (Penguin, 1939).
8 M. Freeden, 'Eugenics and progressive thought', *Historical Journal*, 22, 1979; 'Eugenics and ideology', *Historical Journal*, 26, 1983.
9 D. Thom, 'The 1944 Education Act – the "art of the possible"?' in H. Smith (ed.), *War and Social Change* (Manchester University Press, 1986).
10 H. Smith, 'The effect of the war on the social status of women', in Smith (ed.), *War and Social Change*.
11 *Times Educational Supplement*, 15 May 1943, p. 233.
12 G. Sutherland, *Ability, Merit and Measurement* (Clarendon Press, Oxford, 1984) for an excellent account of the development of separation at 11 and the 'special places' exam.
13 Board of Education, *Handbook of Suggestions for Teachers* (HMSO, 1937), pp. 128–9; Beverley Shaw, 'The education of girls reconsidered', in F. Coffield and R. Goodings (eds), *Sacred Cows in Education* (Edinburgh University Press for Durham University, 1983), p. 143.
14 As Geoffrey Thomas's reports for the wartime Social Survey showed; see Riley, *War in the Nursery*, pp. 122–3; see also P. Summerfield, *Women Workers in the Second World War* (Croom Helm, 1984).
15 *Times Educational Supplement*, 22 May 1943, p. 241.
16 Ibid., p. 247.
17 R. and K. Titmuss, *Parents Revolt* (Secker & Warburg, 1942); R. H. Tawney (ed.), *Equality* (Allen & Unwin, 1931), *Secondary Education for All* (Allen & Unwin, 1922); K. Leybourne and G. White, *Education and the Birthrate* (Cape, 1940).
18 J. Newsom, *The Education of Girls* (Faber & Faber, 1948), p. 111 for quote.
19 On Curriculum and Examinations in Secondary Schools (The Norwood Report) (HMSO, 1943), pp. 2–3.
20 Cyril Burt, 'The education of the young adolescent: the psychological

implications of the Norwood Report', *British Journal of Educational Psychology*, 13, 1943.

21 London and Wiltshire.

22 Norwood Report, pp. 127–8.

23 Report of the Central Advisory Council for Education (CACE), *15 to 18* (The Crowther Report), 1959, p. 35.

24 Crowther Report, p. 34, para. 51–2.

25 *Times Educational Supplement*, letter from J. L. Brereton, 14 December, 1951, p. 968.

26 J. J. B. Dempster, *Selection for Secondary Education* (Methuen, 1954), pp. 24–5.

27 CACE, *Early Leaving* (HMSO, 1954).

28 See Penny Summerfield's chapter in this volume.

29 Centre for Contemporary Cultural Studies, 1981, p. 165.

30 A. H. Halsey, A. F. Heath and J. M. Ridge, *Origins and Destinations* (Clarendon Press, Oxford, 1980); J. W. B. Douglas, *The Home and the School* (Panther, 1967).

31 W. G. Emmett, *British Journal of Psychology (BJP)*, Statistical Section, 2 (1949), pp. 3–16; A. B. Fitt and C. A. Rogers, *BJP*, 41 (1950), pp. 186–92.

32 Board of Education, Report of the Consultative Committee, 1938 (The Spens Report), p. 323.

33 Douglas, *The Home and the School*, p. 99.

34 Ibid., p. 102.

35 A. H. Halsey, *Trends in British Society since 1900* (Macmillan, 1979), p. 181.

36 Sutherland, *Ability, Merit and Measurement*, ch. 6.

37 C. Burt, 'The mental differences between the sexes', *Journal of Experimental Pedology*, 1912; see L. Hearnshaw, *Cyril Burt Psychologist* (Hodder & Stoughton, 1979), p. 28.

38 C. Burt, *Mental and Scholastic Tests* (King & Son, 1921), p. 193; 4th edn (Staples, 1964), p. 242.

39 P. B. Ballard, *Mental Tests*, July 1920, reprinted 14 times (University of London Press, 1946), p. 140.

40 W. McClelland, *Selection for Secondary Education* (University of London Press, 1942), pp. 28, 187, 198.

41 Scottish Council for Research in Education, *The Trend of Scottish Intelligence* (SCRE, 1949), pp. 86–9.

42 P. Vernon, *Intelligence and Attainment Tests* (University of London Press, 1960), p. 170n.

43 P. Vernon, ibid., pp. 170–1.

44 P. Vernon (ed.) for the British Psychological Society, *Secondary School Selection* (Methuen, 1957), p. 41.

45 Wiltshire Education Committee, 'Report of the Chief Examiner to the Examination Board', 17 October 1944, p. 2.

46 W. G. Emmett, *Report on Sex Differences*, in Godfrey Thomson archive,

University of Edinburgh Library, with the annual report to the Thomson research fund for 1949.

47 *Education*, 110, 10 October 1957, report of the BPS symposium on the 11+.

48 *Education*, 88, 26 July 1946, p. 166.

49 Isle of Ely Education Committee minutes, 1944–51.

50 *Times Educational Supplement*, 7 March 1952, Questions in the House of Commons; *TES* 1 August 1952, reports from the local authorities, Lincolnshire, Lindsey.

51 *Times Educational Supplement*, 29 January 1954, p. 94.

52 A. H. Halsey, R. Martin and J. Floud, 'Social class, intelligence tests and selection for secondary schools', *British Journal of Sociology*, 8, 1957, pp. 33–9.

53 *Times Educational Supplement*, 5 December 1958, Questions in the House of Commons. The NUT had raised the issue much earlier in looking at the admission of children to grammar schools as 'intending teachers' when more girls passed the exam but there were fewer places for them in grammar schools; NUT H3, Secondary Schools Sub-committee of the Advisory Committee for Higher Education, correspondence, 20–27 October, 1944.

Chapter 8 Cultural Reproduction in the Education of Girls: a Study of Girls' Secondary Schooling in Two Lancashire Towns, 1900–50

1 See for example: P. Bourdieu, 'Cultural reproduction and social reproduction', in R. Brown (ed.) *Knowledge, Education and Cultural Change* (Tavistock, 1973); M. MacDonald, 'Schooling and the reproduction of class and gender relations', in L. Barton, R. Meighan and S. Walker (eds) *Schooling, Ideology and the Curriculum* (The Falmer Press, Lewes, Sussex, 1980); R. Deem, 'Gender, patriarchy and class in the popular education of women', in S. Walker and L. Barton (eds) *Gender Class and Education* (IPS, The Falmer Press, New York, 1983).

2 J. Shaw, 'Education and the individual. Schooling for girls, or mixed schooling – a mixed blessing', in R. Deem (ed.) *Schooling for Women's Work* (Routledge & Kegan Paul, 1980); D. Spender and E. Sarah, *Learning to Lose. Sexism and Education* (The Women's Press, 1980); P. Mahony, *Schools for the Boys? Co-education Re-assessed* (Hutchinson, 1985).

3 S. Fletcher, *Feminists and Bureaucrats. A study in the development of girls' education in the nineteenth century* (Cambridge University Press, Cambridge, 1980); J. Burstyn, *Victorian Education and the Ideal of Womanhood* (Croom Helm, 1980); C. Dyhouse, *Girls Growing Up in Late Victorian and Edwardian Britain* (Routledge & Kegan Paul, 1981).

4 See in particular F. Hunt, 'Social class and the grading of schools, realities in girls' secondary education 1880–1940', in *The Education of Girls and Women*, J. Purvis (ed.) (History of Education Society, 1985).

5 M. Arnot, 'A cloud over co-education: an analysis of the forms of transmission of class and gender relations', in Walker and Barton (eds) *Gender Class and Education*.

6 Lark Hill House was exclusively a boarding school until it introduced day scholars in 1920 in order to obtain Board of Education grants.

7 PRO ED 35/1225 1897–1920, Blackburn, Convent of Notre Dame Secondary School, Memorandum, January 1908; PRO ED 12/192, Area Record, Preston 1913.

8 M. A. G. óTuathaigh, 'The Irish in nineteenth-century Britain: problems of integration', *Transactions of the Royal Historical Society, 1981*, especially pp. 154–7 (thanks to Dr J. K. Walton for this useful reference); P. Joyce, *Work, Society and Politics* (Methuen, 1980), pp. 251–3.

9 *Northern Daily Telegraph*, 28 November 1912.

10 Board of Education, *Secondary Schools in England Recognised as Efficient* (List 60), 1908/09 and 1938/39.; PRO ED 35/1393, Preston, Park Secondary School 1904–1921, 17 February 1905 and 17 July 1918.

11 PRO ED 12/192, Area Record, Preston 1913; C. G. Green, 'Fulwood: the social development of a Victorian suburb', unpublished MA dissertation, University of Lancaster, 1976, ch. 4; G. Trodd, 'Political Change and the Working Class in Blackburn and Burnley 1880–1914', unpublished PhD thesis, University of Lancaster, 1978, ch. 1.

12 See Burstyn, *Victorian Education*, and Dyhouse, *Girls Growing Up*.

13 Oral History of Girlhood Project, University of Lancaster, 1986, Transcripts (henceforth OH Transcripts) of: M. Adams, p. 31; J. Gibson, p. 29; M. Mundy, p. 7; O. Hamby, p. 14; R. Seed, p. 25; E. Smithies, p. 18.

14 M. O'Leary, *Education with a Tradition, An Account of the Educational Work of the Society of the Sacred Heart* (University of London, 1936), pp. 231, 237.

15 PRO ED 12/192, Area Record, Preston, 1913.

16 Ibid., and A. M. Stoneman, *A Short History of the Park School 1907–1930* (Preston, no date).

17 Medora Whewell, 'Work in the Girls' Friendly Society', *Newsletter of the Blackburn High School Old Girls' Association* (Henceforth *BHS Newsletter*), 1891; Miss M. Green, 'Letter to all', *BHS Newsletter*, 1893; Miss F. Tate, 'From Miss Tate', *BHS Newsletter*, 1902; Kathleen Eckersley, 'Our Civic Guild of Help', *BHS Newsletter*, 1907. See also B. Harrison, 'For Church, Queen and Family: the Girls' Friendly Society 1874–1920', *Past and Present*, November 1973.

18 OH Transcripts of E. Spencer, p. 10; B. Grey, p. 25; M. Robinson, p. 19.

19 C. Dyhouse, 'Towards a "feminine" curriculum for English schoolgirls:

the demands of ideology 1870–1960', *Women's Studies International Quarterly*, 1978.

20 C. Manthorpe, 'Science or domestic science? The struggle to define an appropriate science education for girls in early twentieth-century England', *History of Education*, Vol. 15, No. 3, September 1986, especially pp. 207–9.

21 PRO ED 109/2653, Full Inspection Report (FIR), Blackburn High School for Girls, 1921.

22 OH Transcript of B. Tomlinson, p. 15.

23 PRO ED 35/1394, Preston, Winckley Square Convent School, 1896–1921, correspondence, 28 August 1907.

24 PRO ED 109/3155, First Inspection, Park Secondary School for Girls, Preston, 1909; ED 109/3158, FIR Park SS 1933.

25 OH Transcript of K. M. Reynolds and M. M. Bailes, p. 12.

26 OH Transcript of E. Berry, p. 14.

27 PRO ED 109/3161, FIR Winckley Square 1926.

28 OH Transcripts of M. Adams, p. 29; E. Smithies, 1, p. 18.

29 Miss M. Green, 'A Letter to All', *BHS Newsletter*, 1890.

30 OH Transcript of C. Tipping, p. 24.

31 'School News', *BHS Newsletter*, 1905.

32 OH Transcript of P. Porritt, p. 11.

33 PRO ED 109/3158, FIR Park SS 1933; ED 35/4802, BHS 1938–1941, Form 363S.

34 OH Transcripts of J. Gibson, pp. 39–40; M. Cowperthwaite, pp. 22–3; E. Berry, p. 27.

35 OH Transcript of O. Hamby, pp. 15–16.

36 OH Transcript of K. Hartley and B. Cairns, p. 55.

37 OH Transcript of D. Watkinson, p. 25.

38 OH Transcript of K. Hartley and B. Cairns, p. 40; M. Robinson, p. 15.

39 N. A. Ferguson, 'Women's work: employment opportunities and economic roles 1918–1939', *Albion*, 1963, especially pp. 61–2; Royal Commission on Equal Pay, *Report* (HMSO, 1946), especially pp. 22, 43, 28, 41.

40 *Northern Daily Telegraph*, 28 November 1912; OH Transcript of D. Watkinson, p. 26.

41 PRO ED 109/2665, FIR Roman Catholic (Girls) Pupil Teacher Centre (Convent of Notre Dame) Blackburn, 1906.

42 OH Transcript, C. Hartley and M. Slater, p. 9.

43 OH Transcript, K. Hartley and B. Cairns, p. 28.

44 OH Transcript, J. Westall, p. 8.

45 OH Transcript, K. Hartley and B. Cairns, pp. 20 and 26.

46 OH Transcript, E. Berry, pp. 13–14.

47 OH Transcript, J. Miller, 1, p. 7.

48 OH Transcripts, E. Howarth, p. 20; E. Smithies, 1, p. 10.

49 OH Transcript, A. Gordon, p. 9.

50 OH Transcript, C. Tipping, p. 20.

51 OH Transcript, M. Cowperthwaite, p. 32.
52 OH Transcript, M. Howarth, p. 20.
53 K. Hartley and B. Cairns, pp. 52–3.
54 M. Arnot, 'A Cloud over Co-education' (see note 5), p. 73.
55 OH Transcript, J. Westall, p. 16.
56 OH Transcript, C. Tipping, p. 30.
57 See for example, OH Transcripts of M. Howarth who attended the Park School 1911–16, and T. Williamson who attended Winckley Square Convent 1952–57.
58 M. Arnot, 'A cloud over co-education', p. 73.
59 OH Transcript of C. Rawcliffe (correspondence), p. 4.

Chapter 9   Pioneer Women Students at Cambridge, 1869–81

1 University-level lectures for women were already being provided in Edinburgh. See Louisa Innes Lumsden, *Yellow Leaves: Memories of a Long Life* (Blackwood, Edinburgh and London, 1933), pp. 41–2.
2 Ray Strachey, *The Cause: a Short History of the Women's Movement in Great Britain* (1928; Virago, 1978), ch. 8; Olive Banks, *Faces of Feminism: a Study of Feminism as a Social Movement* (Martin Robertson, Oxford, 1981), pp. 40–2; Jane Lewis, *Women in England 1870–1950* (Harvester Press, Brighton, 1984), pp. 75–9.
3 C. L. Maynard, *Between College Terms*, (James Nisbet, 1910), pp. 181–2.
4 C. B. Firth, *Constance Louisa Maynard* (Allen & Unwin, 1969), pp. 93, 102.
5 J. Llewelyn Davies [Emily Davies's brother], 'A new college for women', *Macmillan's Magazine*, 18 (1868), pp. 168–75.
6 Lumsden, *Yellow Leaves*, p. 23.
7 Ann Phillips (ed.), *A Newnham Anthology* (Cambridge University Press, Cambridge, 1979), pp. 2–3.
8 Mary Paley Marshall, *What I Remember* (Cambridge University Press, Cambridge, 1947), pp. 8–10.
9 Edyth M. Lloyd, *Anna Lloyd 1837–1925: a Memoir* (Cayne Press, 1928), pp. 50–1.
10 [Anon.] *Emily Townshend* (privately published, 1926; copy in Cambridge University Library), p. 29.
11 Newnham was slightly cheaper and had concessionary rates for those intending to go into teaching.
12 [Anon.] *Emily Townshend*, p. 44.
13 Stephen, *Emily Davies*, pp. 235–6.
14 Ibid., pp. 250, 287.
15 Evelyn Sharp, *Hertha Ayrton 1854–1923: a Memoir* (Edwin Arnold, 1926), p. 67.
16 Phillips (ed.), *Newnham Anthology*, p. 8.

17 [Anon.] *Emily Townshend*, p. 65. (A few years after leaving college, Emily Gibson married Isabel Townshend's brother.)

18 E[liza] T[heodora] M[inturn], 'An interior view of Girton College Cambridge' (1876; copy in bound volume 'Miss Emily Davies and Girton', Girton Archives). M. A. Bennett, 'Life at Girton College', *Social Notes*, 5 (1880), pp. 203–6. Eva Knatchbull-Hugessen, 'Newnham College from within', *Nineteenth Century*, 21 (1887), pp. 843–56.

19 Knatchbull-Hugessen, 'Newnham College from within', p. 854.

20 Ibid., pp. 849–50.

21 Phillips (ed.), *Newnham Anthology*, p. 6.

22 Knatchbull-Hugessen, 'Newnham College from within', pp. 847–8; Bennett, 'Life at Girton College', p. 203; Jessie Stewart, *Jane Ellen Harrison: a Portrait from Letters* (Merlin Press, 1959), pp. 5, 8. Davies, quoted in Muriel Bradbook, *'That Infidel Place': a Short History of Girton College 1869–1969* (Chatto and Windus, 1969), p. 40.

23 Maynard, *Between College Terms*, p. 183.

24 Sharp, *Hertha Ayrton*, p. 191.

25 Lloyd, *Anna Lloyd*, p. 70.

26 Minturn, 'Interior View of Girton College', pp. 7, 12.

27 Maynard, *Between College Terms*, pp. 189–90.

28 Stephen, *Emily Davies*, pp. 225–6.

29 Lloyd, *Anna Lloyd*, pp. 57–8.

30 Burstyn, *Victorian Education and the Ideal of Womanhood*.

31 Jane Ellen Harrison, *Alpha and Omega* (Sidgwick & Jackson, 1915), p. 117.

32 Rogers, *Degrees by Degrees*; McWilliams-Tullberg, *Women at Cambridge*.

33 *Daily News*, 6 February 1879, p. 5; *Pall Mall Gazette*, 8 June 1874, p. 3, 9 June 1874, p. 3.

34 *Saturday Review*, 20 May 1871, pp. 627–8.

35 Mary Paley Marshall, *What I Remember*, pp. 11, 15–16.

36 *The Economic Journal*, 54 (1944), p. 277.

37 J. M. Keynes, 'Alfred Marshall, 1842–1924', *The Economic Journal*, 34 (1924), pp. 311–83; also in A. C. Pigou (ed.) *Memories of Alfred Marshall* (Macmillan, 1925), pp. 1–65.

38 Sharp, *Hertha Ayrton*, pp. 111–17, 187, 122, 128.

39 Stewart, *Jane Ellen Harrison*, p. xii. Vicinus, ' "One life to stand beside me" '; *Independent Women*, pp. 148–62. 'Homoerotic friendship' is Vicinus's term. It is difficult to know what word to use, since although to us their relationships were clearly sexual, they did not usually experience them as such.

40 E. Welsh's selection of Girton MSS, Girton Archives.

Index

Acts of Parliament
  Board of Education Act 1899 11
  Education Act 1870 xv, xvi, 47, 83;
    1902 xv, xvii, 11; 1944 xix, 131,
    136–7, 169
  Endowed Schools Act 1869 xvi
  Sex Disqualification Removal Act
    1919 154
adolescence 72, 78, 73–6, 164–6
*Aims and Methods of Teaching Needle-
  work, The* (R. Robinson) 87, 88
Amalgamated Press publications 48,
  62–77 *passim*
appearance 68–71
arithmetic 13, 84, 90
Arnot, Madeleine 150, 164, 167
Association of Headmistresses (AHM)
  7, 8–9, 12, 15, 19, 36–7, 38
authority
  femininity and 75–6
  women teachers and xx–xxi, xxiii,
    22–37 *passim*, 104, 115–16, 168
Ayrton, Herta (née Marks) 178, 182,
  188–9
Ayrton, Will 188–9

Ballard, P. B. 138
Beale, Dorothea xx–xxi, 3, 6, 7, 22–37
  passim
Blackburn (Lancs) 151–69 *passim*
Blackburn High School 151–69 *passim*
Board of Education (Education Depart-
  ment)
  Consultative Committees 16–19, 115,
    116, 128, 136

domestic curricula 92–9 *passim*, 155
equal opportunities for teachers
  113–17
gender differentiation in curriculum
  11–12, 15, 20, 84, 85–6
Handbook for Suggestion for Teachers 128
history xvii, 11
needlework teaching 87–8 *passim*
Board Teacher, The 96
Bodichon, Barbara 178, 189
Bondfield, Margaret 67
boys
  curriculum 5–20 *passim*, 83, 86, 90
  male teachers 101–23 *passim*
  reading 41, 77
  truancy 84
Boys Own Paper, The 48
Brazil, Angela 53, 55–8
Brownmiller, Susan 61
Bryce Commission 1895 xvii, 8, 90
Burt, Cyril 137–8
Buss, Frances xx–xxi, 3, 6, 7, 22–37
  passim
Byrne, Rev. (HMI) 86, 206 n.25

Cadogan, M. 66–7
Cambridge, University of xxiv–xxv,
  171–90
Camden School, The 33, 35
careers *see* women's work
charity *see* philanthropy
Cheltenham Ladies College 32, 34
  see also Beale, Dorothea
Chesser, Elizabeth Sloan 10
civil service 159, 160

Clarendon Commission 1864 5
class
  Catholics and 151
  cultural reproduction xxv, 150–69
    passim
  education and xv–xvii, 83, 98–9
  gender and xii, xiv, 45–6
  leisure and reading xxi–xxii, 57–8,
    61–79 *passim*
  social mobility 47–8, 124–44 *passim*
classics 5–6, 8
clerical work 160
Clough, Anne Jemima 171, 173, 174,
  183
co-education
  attitudes to xviii–xix, 22, 105
  development of 110, 169
  male headships 37, 118–21
  sexism 103
College for Women, Hitchin 172, 173,
  174, 184
comics 40–1
Committee of Council for Education
  (Privy Council) xiv, 88
cookery 92–9 *passim*, 156
  see also domestic curriculum
Craig, P. 66–7
Cross Commission 1888 86, 95
Crowther Report 1959 133–7
cultural reproduction xii, 149–69
  domestic curriculum 84–99
  role of books and magazines 39–78
curriculum
  'accomplishments' 173
  arithmetic 13, 84, 90
  class xiv, 83, 98–9
  classics 5–6, 8
  gender differentiation xxii, 5–21
    passim, 83–99, 102–3, 116
  girls' single sex education 152–3
  government control xv, 85, 92, 155
  health 9, 90, 207 n.33
  music 13
  Norwood Report 131–3
  science 6, 13
  sport 168
  technical education 86, 95, 128, 132
  see also domestic curriculum; liberal
    education

Daisy Chain, The (Charlotte Yonge)
  43–5, 57
Dale, R. R. 22
Davidoff, L. xi
Davies, Emily xvi, 6, 25, 27, 28, 33,
  171–90 *passim*
Davin, Anna 84, 85
Deane, Hyacinthe (HMI) 97
delinquency 109
Dempster, J. J. 134
Dent, H. C. 129
discipline 85, 109, 162, 164
division of labour by gender xxii, 26,
  101–23 *passim*
domestic curriculum
  class and xxii
  convent schools 168
  Crowther Report 133–4
  development 11–20 *passim*, 83–99
    passim, 155–7
  Norwood Report 131–3
domestic service 87, 95
domesticity
  girls' absence from school 84
  literature 41–3, 45
  school as preparation xxii, xxiv,
    11–20 *passim*, 83–99
Douglas, J. W. B. 136–7
Douglas, Mary Alice 24–5
dress
  femininity 68–71
  school 95, 162–4
  university students 183
Dundas, Anne 172
Dyhouse, Carol xxiii, 155

education
  convent schools 149–69 *passim*
  cultural reproduction 83–99, 149–69
  elementary schools xiv–xix *passim*,
    11, 47–8, 83–99, 101–23, 128
  governors 33, 35
  grammar schools xv, 124–44 *passim*
  higher 4, 54–5, 171–90
  public schools xv–xvi, 5, 24–5
  school buildings 84
  school leaving age xvii–xviii, xix,
    135
  school meals 98

secondary xv–xix, 3–21, 22–37, 124–44, 150–69
selection 124–44
single sex 3–21, 22–36, 118–21, 149–69
technical 86, 95, 128, 132
see also Board of Education; co-education; curriculum; domestic curriculum; examinations; finance; Her Majesty's Inspectorate; liberal education; teachers
Education Department *see* Board of Education
Education of Girls, The (John Newsom) 130–31
elementary schools xiv–xix *passim*
curriculum 116, 128
domestic curriculum 11, 47–8, 83–99
division of labour by gender 101–23 *passim*
eleven plus 124–44 *passim*
Emmett, W. G. 136
equal opportunities
Education Act 1944 xix
selective education 124–44
teaching profession xxii–xxiii, 101–23 *passim*
eugenics
curriculum influenced xxii, 116, 155
motherhood emphasized 9–10, 125–6
role of male teachers 108–9
examinations
civil service 159, 160
curriculum and 195 n.11
eleven plus selection 124–44 *passim*
intelligence testing xviii, 124–44 *passim*
role in school finance xv
School Certificate xix, 16, 19, 152–3
university 152–3, 177

family life and marriage
attitudes to, in books and magazines 41–6, 61, 64–7, 69–70; in girls' secondary schools 157–8, 160, 166, 168
daughters' role 43–5, 50, 84
girls' education and 97, 159, 172–3, 174–6

higher education and xxv, 172, 184–9
marriage bar 104, 110, 113, 166, 168, 169
women's primary role 3–4, 50
women's work and 20, 25
family wage 104
Family Magazine, The 40
Fawcett, Millicent Garret 173
fees, school *see* finance
femininity xii, xix
appearance and dress 68–71, 162–4
attitudes to, in books and magazines xxi–xxii, 39–59, 60–79; in teaching profession 101–23
authority and power 22–37 *passim*
convent schools 162–4
higher education and 171–2, 185–90
liberal education and 3, 20
money and 26–7
mothering 129–30
needlework 88
schools' role in cultural reproduction xx, xxiv, xxv, 6–7, 149–69 *passim*
sexuality 74–6
see also domestic curriculum
feminist movement
'absent feminism' 142
attitudes to, in teaching profession 101–3, 117–18
eugenics 10
single sex education 149–50
university students 181–3
fiction 39–78
finance
Catholic schools 151
education xiv–xv, xvi, 34–5, 85–6, 95, 128, 155, 200 n.25
education cuts 113–14
needlework 91–2
women and 26–7
Fitzmaurice, J. (HMI) 89
Floyer, Louisa Sara 88
Fortunes of Phillipa, The (Angela Brazil) 5
Froud, Ethel 105

Gathorne-Hardy, Jonathan 24–5
gender xi–xii
authority and 22–37 *passim*
class and xii, xiv, 45–6

gender differentiation
  attitudes to, in teaching profession
    97–119; in girls' magazines 41, 67,
    69
  cultural reproduction 145–65
  curriculum xxii, 5–21 *passim*, 79–95,
    98–9, 112
  intelligence and selection 120–40
  see also femininity; masculinity
Gibson, Emily 171, 172, 175
Girl (magazine) 72
Girls' Crystal 62, 64
Girls' Favourite 62, 65
Girls of St Cyprians, The (Angela Brazil)
  56, 57
Girls' Own Paper 48–52, 57–8, 62, 66–7,
  73
Girls' Weekly 62
Girton College 167, 172, 173
Glasgow School of Art 85
Governesses Benevolent Institution 4
grammar schools xv, 120–40 *passim*
Grey, Maria 5, 7

Hadow Reports 1926, 1931, 1933
  105–6, 111, 112, 124
Handbook of Suggestion for Teachers
  (Board of Education) 24
handicrafts 82–3
Harrison, Jane 180, 185
Harrison, Mary (HMI) 93
Headlam, J. W. (HMI) 12
health 9, 10, 73–4, 86, 203 n.33
Her Majesty's Inspectorate (HMI) xv,
  xvii, 11–12, 84–8 *passim*
higher education 4, 54–5, 167–86
Holtby, Winifred 98
Home and the School, The (J. W. B.
  Douglas) 132–3
housewifery 12, 91
  see also domestic curriculum;
    domesticity
hygiene 73, 92
  see also health
Idea of a University, The (J. H.
  Newman) 4
ideology
  changes after World War II 121–2,
    139

  role of schools in transmission of xx,
    79–95 *passim*, 145–65
  see also domesticity; femininity;
    feminist movement; liberal educa-
    tion; masculinity; motherhood;
    public and private
Infant Mortality: A Social Problem (Sir
  George Newman) 10
intelligence xxiii, 120–40 *passim*

Jenkinson, A. J. 62
Jephcott, Pearl 61
Jex Blake, Sophia 27
John, Angela V. xii

Kamm, Josephine 25–35 *passim*
Kennedy, Mary 169–70
Kennedy, Nell 62–4
Kent, Robin 74
Kirby, Dorothy 67

*Labour and Love: Women's Experience of
  Home and Family 1850–1940* Jane
  Lewis (ed.) xii
Lamburn, Pat 62
Lark Hill House School, Preston 147,
  156, 158–60, 164
laundrywork 91, 93
Lawrence, Maude (HMI) 15, 94
Lewis, Jane xii
liberal education xx, xxiv, 3–20 *passim*,
  149, 164
literature 39–75
Lloyd, Anna 170–1, 172, 178, 180
Local Education Authorities (LEAs)
  xvii, 106, 109–13, 128–37 *passim*
Lucky Star 74–5
Lumsden, Louisa 169, 172, 180, 185,
  186

Macbeth, Ann 85
Mackail, J. W. 15
Macmillan's Magazine 169, 171
magazines xxi–xxii, 39–59, 60–75
Marks, Herta 174, 178, 184–5
marriage *see* family life and marriage;
  motherhood
marriage bar 100, 106, 109, 162, 164,
  165

Marshall, Alfred 184
masculinity xii, 37, 41, 76, 97–119
   passim
mathematics 13, 80, 86
Maynard, Constance Louisa 168–9,
   177–8, 179, 185
Meade, L. T. 53–5, 56
menstruation 73
'Mental and Scholastic Tests' (Cyril
   Burt) 133–4
Mercer, Edith 67
Merrifield, Margaret 174, 176, 177
militarism 104, 106
Minturn, Eliza 178–9
Miss Modern 70
Mixed or Single-Sex School? R. R. Dale
   22
Morant, Robert 11–12, 13, 91–2
Moray House 132, 136
motherhood
   maternal qualities for infant teachers
     111
   preparation for, in school curriculum
     91–2, 125–6
   role model for authority 29–30, 36
   women's magazines 61, 73–6
   women's primary role 3–4, 10, 121–2,
     181–3
   women's work and 129
music 13

National Association of Schoolmasters
   (NAS) xxiii, 37, 97–119 *passim*
National Foundation for Educational
   Research (NFER) 136, 138
National Training School of Cookery 90
National Union of Teachers (NUT)
   97–119 *passim*
National Union of Women Teachers
   (NUWT) xxiii, 97–119 *passim*
needlework 80, 82, 83–8, 152–3
Newman, George, Sir 10
Newman, J. H. 4
Newnham College 167, 169, 172, 173
Newshoime, Arthur 10–11
Newsom, John 126–7
Nicest Girl in the School, The (Angela
   Brazil) 55
Nicholls, Edith 90

Nightingale, Florence 23–4
North London Collegiate School 7,
   32–3, 34–5
   see also Buss, Frances
Norwood Report 1943 127–9
Notre Dame School, Blackburn 147–8,
   158

Paley, Mary 170, 184
Pam's Paper 62, 65
parenthood *see* family life and marriage;
   motherhood
Parents Revolt (R. and K. Titmuss)
   125–6
Park School for Girls, Preston 147–65
   passim
Pascal, Julia 120
patriarchy xi, 146, 148
pay
   family wage 100
   teachers' 100, 109–10
   women's 26–7
Pearson, Karl 9–10
Pederson, Joyce Senders 27
Peg's Paper 62, 74
'penny dreadfuls' 40–1
philanthropy 48, 90, 150–1
Pinchbeck, Ivy xi
Poppy's Paper 62, 72
Powell, Helena 74
power *see* authority
pregnancy 74–5
Preston (Lancs) 147–65 *passim*
Preston High School 147–65 *passim*
Price, M. and Glenday, N. 38
Princess, The (Lord Tennyson) 180–1
problem pages 73, 74–5
Prochaska, F. K. 94
psychology 109, 132, 136, 137–9
'public and private' xx–xxi, 26–7, 33,
   35–6, 41, 45, 54, 99
Public School Phenomena, The (J.
   Gathorne Hardy) 24–5
public schools xv–xvi, 5, 24–5

Queen's College, Harley Street 4

Raikes, Elizabeth 27
Ralston, Esther 65

reading xxi–xxii, 39–59, 60–78
Red Star Weekly 64
Religious Tract Society 40, 48
Reports
  Board of Education Consultative
    Committee on the Differentiation of
    the Curriculum for Boys and Girls
    Respectively in Secondary Schools
    1923 16–19, 116
  Board of Education Consultative
    Committee on the Education of the
    Adolescent (Hadow Report) 1926
    109–10, 116, 128
  Board of Education Consultative
    Committee on Infant and Nursery
    Schools (Hadow Report) 1933 115
  Board of Education Consultative
    Committee on Practical Work in
    Secondary Schools 1913 16
  Board of Education Consultative
    Committee on the Primary School
    (Hadow Report) 1931 115
  Board of Education Consultative
    Committee on Secondary Education
    (Spens Report) 1938 136
  Central Advisory Council for Educa-
    tion (Crowther Report) 1959 133–4
  Committee of Council on Education
    1882 206 n.25
  Curriculum and Examinations in
    Secondary Schools (Norwood
    Report) 1943 131–3
  Interdepartmental Committee on
    Physical Deterioration (Fitzroy
    Report) 1904 10, 95
Ridley, Annie 28, 34–5
Rodaway, Angela 73
Rowbotham, Sheila xi
Royal Commissions
  Elementary Education (Cross
    Commission) 1888 86–95
  Population 126
  Public Schools (Clarendon Com-
    mission) 1864 5
  Schools Inquiry Commission
    (Taunton Commission) 1864–8 xvi,
    5–6, 27, 28, 33
  Secondary Education (Bryce Com-
    mission) 1895 xvii, 8, 90

Technical Instruction 1882 95
Technical Instruction 1884 86

Sadler, Michael 16
Saturday Review 185–6
School Certificate xix, 16, 19, 152–3
schools *see* education
School Friend 62, 77
Schoolgirl 62, 68
schoolgirl fiction xxii, 48–58, 61–78
science 6, 13
Scottish Mental Survey (Scottish Council
    for Research in Education) 138
Secondary School Selection (British
    Psychological Society) 139
secondary schools xv–xix, 3–21, 22–37,
    124–44, 150–69
sewing *see* needlework
sewing machine 88, 206 n.16
sex and sexuality
  control of 160–2
  femininity and 74–6
  homoerotic friendship 189
  magazines xxii, 68–9, 71–8
  single women 25–6
Sidgwick, Henry 171, 173
single sex education 3–21, 22–36,
    118–21, 149–69
single women
  attitudes to 3, 37, 65–6, 115, 118,
    174–5
  family role 45
  in professions 122–3, 166, 189
  surplus women 4, 18
  unmarried mothers 74, 75
  see also marriage bar
Sneyd-Kennersley, E. M. (HMI) 90, 92
Social Science Congress 1871 5
social mobility 47–8, 124–44,
social reproduction xii, 39–78, 83–99,
    145–65
Somervell, Arthur 13
Spens Report (Board of Education
    Consultative Committee on
    Secondary Education) 1938 136
spinsters *see* single women
sport 168
Sweet Girl Graduate, A (L. T. Meade)
    54–5, 56

Taunton Commission (Schools Inquiry
  Commission) 1864–7 xvi, 5–6, 27,
  28, 33
Tawney, R. H. 130
teachers
  attitudes to curriculum 5–21 *passim*,
    96–7
  friendships 189
  gender discrimination 37, 101–23
  training 135, 158–60, 171
  unions 101–23 *passim*
  women and authority xx–xxi, xxiii,
    22–37 *passim*, 104, 115–16, 168
technical education 86, 95, 128, 132
Tennyson, Alfred, Lord 184–5
Terman, L. and Merrill, M. 138
textbooks 85, 98
Times Educational Supplement 111, 126,
  129, 130
Titmuss, Richard and Kay 129–30
Tod, Isabella 4
tracts 40, 48
Trimmer, Sarah 40
truancy 84
*Truth, Dare or Promise. Girls Growing Up
  in the Fifties* (Liz Heron, ed.) 124

*Unequal Opportunities: Women's
  Employment in England 1800–1918*
  (Angela V. John, ed.) xii
unions 101–23
university 51, 142, 158–9, 171–90
unmarried mothers 74, 75
Unpopular Education (Centre for
  Contemporary Cultural Studies)
  125, 135–6

Vernon, Philip 138–9
Verrall, Margaret (née Merrifield) 178,
  180, 181
Vicinus, Martha 38, 189

Walkerdine, V. 124
Winckley Square School, Preston 151,
  152
Woman 65
Woman's Magazine 62
*Women Workers and the Industrial
  Revolution* (Ivy Pinchbeck) xi
Women's Group for Public Welfare 126
women's movement *see* feminist
  movement
women's work
  attitudes to, in books and magazines
    50, 64–7, 70; in elementary schools
    85; in secondary schools xx, xxiii,
    129–30, 160–61, 168
  division of labour by gender xxii, 26,
    101–23 *passim*
  higher education 171–2, 189
  marriage and 20, 25
  new opportunities 18, 46–7, 130, 133
  power and authority xx–xxi, xxiii,
    22–27 *passim*, 115–16, 168
Working Class Wives Women's Group
  for Public Welfare 126
World of Girls, A (L. T. Meade) 53–4
World War 1 18, 117
World War 2 125–6, 129, 133, 143

Yonge, Charlotte 43–5, 57

Index by Jenny Rudge